TRUST: A New View of Personal and
Organizational Development

The Guild of Tutors Press

INTERNATIONAL COLLEGE

1019 Gayley Avenue
Los Angeles, California

DESIGN BY PAUL O. PROEHL

JACK R. GIBB

TRUST

A New View of Personal and

Organizational Development

PHOTOGRAPHS BY V. M. ROBERTSON

AN ASTRON SERIES BOOK

FIRST EDITION
THIRD PRINTING

LIBRARY OF CONGRESS CATALOG CARD NUMBER: 77-93139

ISBN: 0-89615-002-X (CASE)   0-89615-006-2 (PAPER)

For Lorraine, Blair, John, and Larry

Life, being an ascent of consciousness, could not continue to advance indefinitely along its line without transforming itself in depth.

Teilhard de Chardin

Contents

Preface

This book is my personal statement of my beliefs and attitudes about trust, which is the primary construct of TORI (Trust Level) theory. It is also a description of the theory, meant for the general reader interested in trust and its singular relevance to today's world. It is addressed to all parents, managers, teachers, therapists, ministers — to any person who is interested in becoming more role-free, which is at the heart of the matter of becoming more trusting and more trusted. Lorraine Gibb and I are creating our lives and TORI theory together, and thus in a very real sense we are co-authoring this book out of our shared years of living, loving, trusting, and many co-authorings. Our interbeing relationship is the primary force in my life and is what gives my life its meaning. I know of no adequate way of expressing my gratitude to, and love for her.

This book is the first in an Astron series of publications being written and created by members of the TORI International Community and describing the continuing evolution of the theory and its application. We will present the more formal theory and its empirical and research foundations in a later book in the series. A number of research and training instruments are being developed and will also be discussed in a later volume. Included in the Appendix in this book are two unstandardized forms of one scale which we have used and which are included here for those readers interested in exploring the theory further.

Though Lorraine and I and our colleagues have refined and tested the structure of the theory through many years of research and pilot studies, the heart of the theory, as the reader will see, is experiential. Lorraine and I are developing our trust and our insights about it through our lives in three learning communities. Without any question our primary community is our family. Blair, John, Lorraine and I are living in a high-trust, rule-less, and role-less world that we create together. They have given me an excused absence during the writing of this book. I have dedicated this book to my family and my gratitude to them is communicated throughout the book.

Our larger community is the 10,000 or so members of the TORI International Community. They are our friends, colleagues, life-partners, co-learners, and co-theorists. So many warm feelings and clear images come to me as I think about our community that to express my gratitude to individuals would mean beginning a list that I could not possibily end. I feel particularly grateful to Dean Meinke, who, with many others, has taken over all of my TORI Associates activities and thus freed me to write this book. The community is truly a caring one. Our lives are being unalterably enriched through our community life together.

Our newest community is the TORI Professional Intern community, with whom Lorraine and I are living in a three-year experiment in trust-building. Starting in the summer of 1977, this community is already transcending anything I have experienced before. It is opening new vision for me. We are into each other's lives in redemptive ways.

I wish to acknowledge a special feeling of debt and gratitude to my mother, Ada Dyer, whose life and faithtrust were the genesis of my lifelong focus on trust and its derivations.

Robbie Robertson's pictures speak for themselves. Robbie is a fellow TORI community member and certainly my most empathic life friend. We know that we understand each other in depth, and we created together the twelve concepts that he has portrayed in his art. I wish that my words expressed the twelve concepts as well as his pictures do.

I had a fear of editors! As always, my fear turned out to be self-created and illusory. My relationship with Paul Proehl has been for me a complete joy. I have appreciated Paul's wise counsel and tender criticism, his many, many hours of hard labor over my help-needing manuscript, and his warm friendship. I have learned a lot from this practice run at writing a book, and my next book, as a result of Paul's help, will be a great improvement over this one.

Paul Lloyd has given me many gifts of friendship and love over the years and his special help during the writing of this book made the book possible. I wish to add a warm note of appreciation to Barbara Hulsing, whose heroic and much-skilled response to my need for typing help has eased my days.

Jack R. Gibb
La Jolla, California
January, 1978

TRUSTING

*Trust opens the doorways
to the spirit.*

Chapter 1

Trusting Me, You, and the Process

A farmer-businessman with scarcely any visible means of political support comes out of the Deep South and tells Americans that he trusts them and asks them to "Trust me," — and is elected President. Of course, the nominating and electoral processes in this country are not that simple; many issues, events, and personalities were involved in deciding the fate of Jimmy Carter and those who contested him. But I know of no national election or, for that matter, any at the state level, where such a call for trust was ever made.

In my view, this call for trust did make a difference in the election. After the trauma of Watergate especially, Carter's appeal to trusting struck a deep and responsive chord in Americans. But we will probably never know what effect it really did have in November, 1976; and it is now obvious that, whatever the reasons, the idea of mutual trust between President and people did not survive long, if at all, into Carter's first term. The tragedy may be that his trust in the "decent American people" was never reciprocated. Perhaps because of the "intervenors" — the Congress, the bureaucrats, the special interest groups, and even foreign leaders — trust never had a chance; for these intervenors and their groups have low trust levels, and they are typically power-, fear- and defense-oriented. They are playing roles; they are managing and manipulating. For them, government is a depersonalized system, which in turn accounts for the dehumanized system the governed experience. Trust, unhappily, is not a part of the American, or global, political way of life. In fact, our present national culture — social, economic, even artistic, as well as political — is inhospitable to trust.

Fortunately, it does exist, even thrive, in sub-groups and subcultures of our country. We find it foremost in families, and in other small groups — wherever people are close and intimate, loving, interdependent, and open to one another; wherever instinct or knowledge give us a sense of being able to be ourselves with others, that provides a basis for trust. We see it also working powerfully among members of ethnic groups, certain social and fraternal groups, and in some religious groups, where there are strongly-held commonalities that displace the fears separating strangers. In such groups, trust functions as a lubricant of individual and social life. Trust makes it unnecessary to examine motives, to look for hidden meanings, to "have it in writing," to have someone — priest, minister, lawyer, therapist, or bureaucrat — intervene between you and me so that we can understand each other or be sure that neither of us is going to hurt the other.

As trust ebbs, we are less open with each other, less interdependent, less interbeing — not into each other in deep and meaningful ways; we look for strategies in dealing with each other; we seek help from others; or we look for protection in rules, norms, contracts, and the law. My defenses are raised by my fear that I do not or cannot trust you. The ebbing of trust and the growth of fear are the beginning of alienation, loneliness, and hostility. In a very real sense, we can say that trust level is the thermometer of individual and group health. With it, we function naturally and directly. Without it, we need constraints, supports, leaders, managers, teachers, intervenors, and we surrender ourselves and our lives to them for guidance, management, and manipulation.

Trust is more than confidence. One dictionary tells us that trust (derived from the German word *Trost,* meaning "comfort") implies instinctive, unquestioning belief in and reliance upon something. Confidence implies conscious trust *because* of good reasons, definite evidence, or past experience. Confidence is more cerebral, more calculated, and based more on expectations than trust is. Trust can be and often is instinctive; it is unstrategized and freely given. It is something very much like love, and its presence or absence can make a powerful difference in our lives.

Now, let us put dictionary aside and ask ourselves: What is trust? How will I know, when it touches me? There is no other, or better, way than to tell you how it touches me!

Trust creates the flow and gentles the mindbodyspirit. When I trust myself I am able to enter fully into the process of discovering and creating who I am. When I trust my own inner processes I am able to become what I am meant to become. When I trust you I am able to allow you in. And when I trust the processes of living I am able to join others in the life journey.

Fear stops the flow and arouses the defenses. I direct my energies not into discovering and creating, but toward protecting myself from seen, expected, or fantasied dangers. I am not sure of who I am, cover up and put on protective masks, become concerned about how I *ought* to meet the expectations of others, and find it difficult to be *with* others.

Trust enriches my experience; fear robs it. The child in the picture at the beginning of the chapter seems to be reaching out to a friendly world she knows will be loving and accepting. To me she is transparent, open, ready for experience. She will trust me in her world. In my very best moments, I feel inside the way she seems to be feeling.

Trust is a Catalytic Process

Is the world dangerous? Can people be trusted? Should we try to maintain our childlike trust and to help our children to do so? Or should we develop caution, be "appropriately" wary, be realistically prepared for danger? I remember an experience in an elevator in Washington, D.C. Feeling good, I said "Hi!" to a girl, about five, who was wearing a swimming suit and carrying a towel on her way to the hotel swimming pool. She was so haughty and chilling that a friendly elevator operator, the only other person present, said to me: "I'm sure her mother has told her not to speak to strangers." I understood that, too, and appreciated the man's concern and empathy. But I couldn't help feeling that multitudes of tiny experiences like this escalate into the loneliness, alienation, and unconnectedness of modern life, and I felt sad that the learning of distrust should start so early in life.

Dangers *do* exist. Children and adults are ignored, rebuffed, punished, kidnaped, or raped. Just three weeks ago the papers reported the discovery in Los Angeles of the murdered bodies of two little girls, and as I write, the Hillside Strangler remains at large in Los Angeles. Some city streets *are* dangerous, especially at night. Teachers and students *do* get beaten up in the schoolroom. Offices and factories *are* filled with dangerous, life-draining tension. We *may* be cheated by a dishonest car repair shop, or even by a bank. Watergate *did* happen. Hitler and his minions *did* murder millions of Jewish people. How do we prepare ourselves, or our children or students, to live wholly and fulfillingly in such a world in which they confront so many dangerous possibilities? Do we take our children to school or hire guards to take them? Put extra locks on our doors? Increase the number of policemen? Make tougher laws? Tighten the security at the airports? Increase the number of crimes that get the dealth penalty? How much to trust and distrust, and how to handle our fears and distrusts are dilemmas that face consumers, voters, managers, parents, teachers — all of us.

Trust begets trust; fear escalates fear. Trust catalyzes all other processes, is contagious, softens our perceptions, breeds trust in others, *makes us less dangerous,* and is self-fulfilling. Fear and distrust overperceive the danger, trigger defensive behavior in others, escalate the tension, and are self-fulfilling — that is, *fear creates the danger.*

I have a friend, Pat, who at seventeen hitchhiked alone through Africa for about a year. Listening to her tell of her experiences, and fantasying dangers for a beautiful young woman hitchhiking in Africa in the early sixties, we asked if she were ever molested, cheated, robbed, or raped. She said that things like that just don't happen to her. She is trusting, gives out non-defensive signals, and *creates her own environment.*

Trust and fear are keys to understanding persons and social systems. They are primary and catalytic factors in all human living.

When trust is high, relative to fear, people and people systems function well. When fear is high, relative to trust, they break down.

Trust enhances the flow of mindbodyspirit processes. Energy is created and mobilized. All the creative processes of the person or the system are heightened. Feeling and thinking are both more focused and energized. People act in more direct and effective ways. Consciousness is awakened. When trust is high enough, persons and social systems transcend apparent limits — discovering new and awesome abilities of which they were previously unaware.

When fear levels are high, relative to trust, individual and social processes are impaired. The life forces are mobilized defensively, rather than creatively. Consciousness is restricted. Perceptivity is reduced. Perspectives are narrowed. Feelings and emotions become disruptive and disabling. Thinking, problem solving, and action become unfocused, displaced, or dysfunctional. The processes of the mindbody become segmented and discordant. When fear levels are high enough individuals and the social systems become immobilized, psychotic, or destructive.

Trust is an integrating and wholizing force. It is a property of the whole mindbodyspirit. The child in our picture does not use word language to communicate trust. Her body shows it. And her spirit. She may not even be aware that she is trusting. Words, thoughts, or even consciousness may dilute the trust, mitigate its effects on her and on us. O.J. Simpson, a once-in-a-century athlete, talks of "letting my body take over" and allowing it to find a hole in the defensive line and backfield, and letting it take him on his incredibly successful runs. He clearly describes his searching/creating as a total organic process and not a cognitive-dominant process at all. In fact, he finds that thinking during the run gets in the way of his flow and effectiveness. It is in this sense that we can speak of Simpson as a high-trust runner. His trust is integrating. Trust brings integrity.

Fear constrains and blocks. Fearing, I become congested, inhibited, and restricted. I retard all of my processes: my feeling, my imagination, my play and sense of adventure and fun, my courage, my vision, the flow of energy in my mindbody, my intuition, my awareness — all of my processes. An optometrist told me once that he could tell from seeing persons in the waiting room whether or not they would be able to relax enough to wear contact lenses. The people who tried to control their bodies while sitting in the chair and who tried to control their children while waiting would be too "frightened" to wear such lenses. Golfers use the same expression: the person doesn't have *courage* enough to make the putt!

Trust is a releasing process. It frees my creativity, allows me to focus my energy on creating and discovering rather than on defending. It releases my courage. It *is* my courage. It opens my processes, so that I can play, feel, enjoy, get angry, experience my pain, be who I am. The full life is a spontaneous, unconstrained, flowing, trusting life. Some holistic studies of cancer are relevent here. Researchers discovered that people who could free themselves to *image* their cells as actively and flowingly resisting toxic substances were able to retard the carcinogenic processes. I have discovered a similar phenomenon after about an hour of jogging. When I get into my flow, all of my processes are heightened: my energy and breathing, creativity and imagery, awareness of sights and sounds and smells, courage. I become available to me and to others.

Trust gives me my freedom and my fear takes it away. Freedom comes from my own flow. It is not given to me or taken away from me by others. I create my own mindbody trust, which *is* my freedom. I create my own fears and my own bondage, which *is* my fear. *Freedom is not out there.* It is in me.

Trust transcends fear. We have trust in us always. When it is available to us, it works "miracles." We may discover our unlimited and transcendent powers in many ways: hypnosis, dream analysis, drugs, prayer, biofeedback, mystical and altered states of consciousness, out-of-body experiences — all are functions of our level of trust. I have never known a person whose faith (trust) was as strong and whole as that of my mother. She died alone in her home. The coroner said that in his long lifetime of examining bodies immediately after death, he had never before seen a person whose body and face showed serenity and joy in meeting death. I wasn't surprised. My mother *knew* that she was an eternal spirit and that her death would be the commencement of another stage of her continuing life. It comes to me at this moment that she gave me her most precious gift — my experience of her faithtrust and its power.

Trust as a Focus for Theory and Practice

For those of us who use it, the unique quality of TORI (Trust Level) theory comes from its bridging power — the use of a single set of constructs, minimal in number, to apply to all professional tasks and human institutions. The same theory is applied to the total range of human problems: from the care of the retarded child to the optimal use of space scientists; from diagnosing the counter culture to understanding the board room at General Motors; from the fear of having the incorrect dress length to existential dread; from the learning of the alphabet to acquiring the skills and talents used in firewalking; from child care to international relations; and from the effects of dieting to cosmic adventures during astral trips. However exploratory and postnatal the state of its art and technology, the theory's power lies in its effort to apply a single set of basic constructs to a universal range of phenomena.

The theory is futuristic. It is formulated as an attempt to extrapolate current trends, predict near- and far-future personal, institutional, and cosmic processes, and to deal here and now with the latent forces — both actualizing and destructive — before they become more manifest and less susceptible to our understanding, utilization, or control.

Two seminal cultural developments were predicted in the 1950's by analysis based on trust-level theory. Each has the most profound implications for what will likely happen in the next two decades. They are the loss of confidence in our institutions and their leadership and the escalation of faith which characterizes the transcendence revolution of the human potential movement. Each is a direct function of the manifest trust level. One is an erosion of trust in government and industry, and the other is an escalation of trust in transcendence and healing. Trust-level theory is specifically relevant to both trends.

Trust provides an environment that nourishes personal growth, holistic health, spirituality, and the discovery of the soul. Trust level is a diagnostic cue to the understanding of individuals and groups: to the creation of a fulfilling home environment, an effective classroom, a healing therapy session, a redemptive ministry, a productive workplace, or a nurturing neighborhood. The home has been a place where Lorraine and I have learned most about trust and trusting environments, largely from experiencing our sons, Larry, Blair and John. For instance, I have a vivid memory of a family discussion after both Blair and John had had a thrilling and scary experience cutting down a small jungle in Hawaii with some machetes. Afterwards I asked the boys, who were then six and eleven, what they thought Lorraine and I had been feeling when they were doing this. Blair said that "Jack was concerned that we might cut ourselves, and Lorraine thought we were having a good time." When John didn't respond, I asked him again. His gentle and puzzled "answer" was this: "Do you expect me to be wondering what other people are thinking when I'm doing something?" It was one of the many signs of his trust of his own processes.

Trust level is a key to the understanding of the larger system. As a consultant or as a manager I have an option to focus my "theory" on one or more among many "realities": energy systems, power relationships, role formation, interfaces among sub-units, barriers to productivity, profitability. The possibilities are endless, and there are theories for each. I prefer to start by looking at the trust level. Everything else fans out from there. Social systems can present a bewildering array of symptoms. Recently, a company presented me with massive data gathered from surveys, observations, complaints, interviews, and impressions. One of the most perplexing items for them was the fact that the workers, in a company-wide election, had turned down an obviously beneficent stock-purchase plan. This had previously been available only to members of management, but was now to be open to all employees of the corporation on a voluntary basis. We planned new data collection around trust-theory hypotheses. The employees who were interviewed gave many different responses, but they centered on this theme: "If it looks like those guys are giving you something for nothing, watch out! There'll be a ringer in the small print some place!" A latent and not-easily-visible state of general distrust and fear had been produced by fear-induced management role-taking, covert strategy, persuasion techniques, and efforts to control. Management practices were unintentionally escalating fears and distrusts, which were retarding productivity and creativity.

Trust is the Process of Discovering

To trust with fullness means that *I discover and create my own life.* The trusting life is an inter-flowing and interweaving of the processes of discovery and creation. These processes have four primary and highly-interrelated elements:*

— discovering and creating who I am, tuning into my own uniqueness, being aware of my own essence, *trusting* me — *being who I am.* (T)

— discovering and creating ways of *opening* and revealing myself to myself and to others, disclosing my essence, discovering yours, communing with you — *showing me.* (O)

— discovering and creating my own paths, flows, and rhythms, creating my emerging and organic nature, and becoming, actualizing, or *realizing* this nature — *doing what I want.* (R)

— discovering and creating with you our interbeing, the ways we can live together in *interdepending* community, in freedom and intimacy — *being with you.* (I)

Use of such words as "discovering" and "creating" may suggest to some that I am talking here of largely cognitive and conscious processes. I do not mean to imply this at all. I am referring to organic, holistic, bodymind, total-person processes that have the *quality* of an intuitive or instinctive quest about them. Each process is *both* a discovering *and* a creating — indistinguishable in fusion. I think of the person, the group, and the organization as *total* organisms that

---

*TORI is an acronym for these four processes which are central to all personal, organizational and international growth: *trusting* our being and processes, *opening* our lives, *realizing* or actualizing our intrinsic nature and energy, and *interdepending* or interbeing. The general theory of living is called TORI theory or Trust Level theory. Tables I-IV contain schematic summaries.

TABLE I. THE TORI DISCOVERING PROCESSES

Discovering processes	Orientation of the person	Proactive energy focused on:	Personal wants
TRUSTING- (T) BEING Personing Centering Accepting Warming	*Being me* — discovering who I am How do I create me? What is my uniqueness?	*Accepting self and others* Trusting Expressing warmth Seeing differences	*Love* — giving and receiving love
OPENING- (O) SHOWING Letting in Listening Disclosing Empathizing	*Showing me* — discovering how to reveal myself to others How to let you in and share our space? How to show you how I feel and see?	*Spontaneity* Impulsivity Rapport Tuning in	*Intimacy* — giving and receiving intimacy and communication in depth
REALIZING- (R) ACTUALIZING Asserting Exploring Evolving Wanting	*Doing what I want* — discovering my wants and how to realize them What matters to me? What is my life for?	*Searching* Fulfillment Life enrichment Allowing Achievement	*Fulfillment* — giving and receiving personal fulfillment
INTERDEPENDING- (I) INTERBEING Integrating Joining Sharing Synergizing	*Being with others* - discovering how to live and work with others How do I create my freedom? How do we transcend our own beings?	*Interacting* Participating Cooperating Giving and getting freedom	*Freedom* — giving and receiving freedom

TABLE II. TRUST LEVEL MOBILIZES FORCES IN THE PERSON

Bodymind process	*High trust levels produce these effects:*
1. Motivation	Creates and mobilizes energy, increases strength and focus of motivation.
2. Consciousness	Unblocks energy flow, expands awareness, makes unconscious more available.
3. Perception	Increases acuity of perceptions, improves vision and perspective
4. Emotionality	Feelings and emotions free to energize all processes of the bodymind
5. Cognition	Frees energy for focus on thinking and problem solving
6. Action	Release of person for proactive and spontaneous behavior
7. Synergy	Total person freed for synergistic and holistic integration

develop these processes, especially under climates of high trust. The four processes are:

1. *Being.* My quest for being is a search for and a creation of my identity. It is a continual coming to grips with who I am, in my complexity and in my simplicity. It is a discovery and creation of my center, my meaning, my enduring values. My search is self-determined. I am my own best resource, my own guru and guide. In my attempt to discover who I am, I often find that the object of my search is a moving target. There is no " thing" to find. It is seldom possible to create a still camera shot of my being. The discovering is the significant aspect — not the discovered. The process of discovering is itself the learning and is, *in itself,* who I am. The discovering is me. I am *in* process. I *am* the process. Being is more than simple existence. It is *becoming.*

When I trust myself and when I am trusted by others I am more apt to live quietly with myself and to develop a capacity for accepting and loving myself — to reside comfortably in my being. To allow me to be me. When I know something of who I am and can let me be in my own space, I can then love me, be *in* my uniqueness. Reducing my need to compare myself with others, I create my capacity to accept and love others, to be with them in their uniqueness and selfhood. I allow them their own search. From my own self-caring base I am free to release and share my warmth, my anger, my love, my hurt — my realness.

I find it difficult to communicate what I mean by *being.* It is especially difficult in a culture focused upon the *denial-of-being* processes of role, achievement, persuasion, and reward-punishment. I have discovered that *for me* to be a good father, an effective teacher, a useful consultant, and a trusted therapist it is most effective for me to think and feel my answer to the question "How can I be fully who I am?" or simply "How can I be?" And not to think and feel my answer to the question "How can I be a good father?" or "How can I be an effective therapist?" This seems to make all the difference. This process gets me out of role and into my personing. I project myself — and only myself.

Now that I have learned to focus the issues in these simple terms, I find it easy to communicate when I participate in programs for developing teachers, therapists, or consultants. It is somehow surprisingly meaningful to answer all of the analogues of the question "How can I be an effective therapist?" with the answer "Be," or "Be who you are." It is quite clear that being with someone who is real, and who knows that he or she is real, *is* therapeutic. And, equally, this does provide the optimal environment for learning in the school, lifebuilding in the church, or growing in the family. The inexperienced or poorly-theoried therapist, parent, or teacher starts out by assuming the job to be one of categorizing the patient, the child, or the student, of inferring a deficiency, incapacity, or need based upon the category; and then setting out to learn a technique that will remove the deficiency revealed by the diagnosis. This seductive and much-taught focus and sequence is very pervasive, seems "professional", and is relatively easy to learn from a book or a class. But it is a *denial of the being* of both therapist and client, of parent and child, and of teacher and student. Fulfilled living does not come out of toxic and defensive processes.

Being develops in a climate of trust.

2. *Opening.* My search for my own identity is often aided by seeing myself in the mirror that others provide when our relationship is authentic. My search for a way to connect with you and to create ways of revealing me to you is, in part, my search for my own identity. As I grow in trust, my uncovering of me becomes an intrinsically meaningful quest in its own right. The questing is the being. I show my being to you. Loving me, I can trust you to see me whole, to experience me uncovered, unfiltered. the more fully comfortable I am with my own being, the less risk I experience in showing me to you. And in seeing myself as whole and worthy, I am able to see you as you are, with little defensive distortion. I come to see you not as a threat to me, but as an adventure, an experience in seeing and feeling.

Genuine intimacy is a pervasive human want. It is made possible by our seeing each other as we are, without our masks, filters, or facades. In trust and intimacy I am able to show you my vulnerability. I recognize that *my concept of vulnerability arises out of my defensive and protective fear.* I project into you the capacity to wound me. If I trust you in depth, I know that you will not hurt me and also that I cannot be hurt. Thus, if I am hurt, I hurt myself. I have two sources of inner calm: my trust in myself and my trust in you. Genuine intimacy, achieved only in a state of high trust, is a calming state because risk of hurt is minimized. If risks are present, they loom small relative to the rewards of intimacy.

3. *Realizing.* Free to be, trusted, feeling little or no need to defend, the mindbodyspirit emerges, becomes, flowers, discovers itself, creates itself, emerges in interaction with other organisms, *realizes* itself, fulfills its promise and emerging destiny. There are

apparently no limits to this process. As a person, I create my own internal trust state and an external trust environment, limited only by my own imagination and vision, which I also create.

As I become aware of this emerging process, my increasing awareness expresses itself as a "want". Trusting and trusted, I am able to discover wants that are congruent with the deeper levels of my mindbodyspirit. My total quest for self-determination and self-realization is a process of discovering/creating what I want and how I can satisfy my wants. My wants change as I create new experiences, from day to day, from moment to moment. The significance of this quest is that it makes possible a *want-determined* life, rather than an *ought-determined* one. In a high-trust climate I learn that I am the one who can best determine my wants, who is best able to make choices among them, and who is best able to create an environment in which my wants can be satisfied. I am inner-directed, not ought- or outer-directed, except as I respond to you in our mutual trust and intimacy.

As the final column in Table I indicates, this trust-oriented framework of analysis reveals four major and enduring wants that seem to me to be universal. *I want to give and receive love, intimacy, fulfillment, and freedom.* Under a variety of names, these four human wants are reported again and again by people who are close to their cores of being. The significant thing is not the designation of the wants, or even their classification — neither is of consequence —but the trustogenic opportunity for each person to continue the discovering and creating of the wants that give enrichment and meaning to life *as that person sees it.*

4. *Interdepending.* My quest for a fulfilling way to be *with* others in some depth is a process of learning how to give and receive freedom, how to join together in a way that allows each of us to be ourselves in our fullness, and how to relate in a way that continues to release our love and express it. My search is to learn how to join in creating a relationship that transcends what each of us may be or do alone. The pain, intensity, and prevalence of this want and search are indicated by the multiple alternative institutions that are arising in our culture. The diversity and health of these institutions are both impressive. The pain and difficulty in the quest are indicated by the disturbing number of failures and half-successes. Achieving high levels of trust in an alternative and experimental institution — a church, an extended family, a commune, a business, a school — is difficult in a society in which the environment is distrusting, fearful,

and populated with individuals who have difficulties in learning to trust themselves. It seems that interdependence, withness, and synergy are learned, created, achieved. People who know who they are, show who they are, and do what they want are able to achieve an interdependence that comes without sacrifice, without duty and obligation, and without giving away individual freedoms. *Interbeing* comes from within the persons who are joining. It doesn't come from persuasion, teaching, skill-training, or other outer-inner processes.

In high trust, each person seems to want to seek larger and larger constellations of being, seems to want to be in community with others. In climates of fear, the needs for privacy and aloneness loom large, and the fantasies about loss of freedom and autonomy are heavy. As each person develops a strong and loving base in that person's own being, has discovered that showing the self can be an intimacy-creating and rewarding experience, has discovered that "real" wants can be satisfied in community, then the person is more trusting in reaching out to larger and larger communities of interbeing. The more trusting I am the more able I am to join with others in creating community. It becomes possible to be with more persons in authentic pairings, in intimate small groups, in caring communities, and eventually, perhaps, in a more trusting world. For me, this process of creating a larger world community starts in the high-trust processes of each person's discovering how to create for himself or herself authentic interbeing and intimacy.

I assume that these four discovering processes are self-generating and self-rewarding. They grow best in internal, intrapersonal environments of trust, and in external environments of trust and low fear.

Trust Means That I Don't Need to Defend

When fears are high, the defensive processes are triggered and nourished. When my trust in myself is low and I experience little trust from my larger environment, I feel the need to defend. I discover and create my fears and my defenses. The defense process has four primary and interrelated elements:

1. *Depersoning.* Depersoning is to move away from my person and from being personal to discovering and creating roles for myself. These roles, usually created in response to organizational or other external pressures, have a protective function. Even though I am officially in role — taking on, for instance, a supervisory position — I

TABLE III. THE TORI DEFENDING PROCESSES

Defending processes	Orientation of the person	Defensive energy focused on:	Personal needs
DEPERSONING Coding Role-ing Detaching Appraising Observing	*Finding a role* — discovering and creating a role What is my role? How do I compare with others?	*Punishing self and others* Evaluation Distrust Moralizing	*Punishment* — giving and receiving punishment Need to manage warmth
MASKING Closing up Distancing Filtering Strategizing Covering	*Building a facade* — discovering a strategy How do I protect me? What is my best covert strategy?	*Strategizing* Circumvention Distortion Formality	*Distance* — giving and receiving social distance Need to manage intimacy
OUGHTING Influencing Persuading Parenting Coercing Manipulating	*Finding my needs* — discovering your demands and expectations What should I do? How do I change me or you? How do I get power?	*Persuading* Influence Passivity Resistance	*Influence* — giving and receiving influence Need to manage motives
DEPENDING Controlling Submitting Leading Dominating Rebelling	*Controlling me and you* — discovering rules, boundaries, contracts How do I protect my turf? What is the law?	*Controlling* Dependency Management Rebellion	*Control* — giving and receiving controls Need to manage relationships

TABLE IV. FEAR LEVEL IMPAIRS THE LIFE FORCES
IN THE PERSON

Bodymind process	*High fear levels produce these effects:*
1. Motivation	Unfocused energy often channeled into defense with reduced motivation
2. Consciousness	Fears reduce span of awareness, cut off threatening areas of near-awareness and unconsciousness
3. Perception	Decreases acuity of perceptions, impairs vision and perspective
4. Emotionality	Feelings and emotions are disruptive, often defense-oriented and dysfunctional
5. Cognition	Thinking and problem solving may be unfocused, displaced, defensive, ineffective
6. Action	Behavior is reactive, congested, and inhibited by overconcern for consequences
7. Synergy	Processes and sub-systems out of harmony, not synchronistic, often segmented

still am free to fill the responsibilities of that role by simply attempting to be "personal" and assuming that this process will meet organizational demands. When I am fearful, I am less apt to be personal and more apt to assume the protective coloration and prerogatives of the formal role. The higher the trust, the more apt I am to be personal in fulfilling the role. When I take on a role, I usually take charge and try to institute formal or informal controls. I assume a parental posture, and act as I assume a supervisor would act. This process is intended to protect me from those who have similar expectations of my role-taking, but it is usually an illusory quest. The protection is not effective, and the costs are large. What I gain in respect, deference, and control, I am likely to lose in social distance, induced anxiety, latent hostility, and other counter-productive products of the role-playing. A number of related processes seem to accompany the role posture. I tend to identify people in the roles that they fill relative to my own and to value them in the degree that they perform these roles and meet my expectations. More damaging is the related process in which I evaluate and judge feelings, behavior, and attitudes of others. The more I am into role, where my posture is determined by "oughts" and values external to myself, the more apt I am to evaluate people and to moralize about their behavior. These toxic processes are born in fear and exacerbate or feed the other latent distrusts and fears that we bring to each other.

When I am defending, I am caught up in the polar opposites of the processes which make me "personal". I move away from my person to protect myself. In effect, I move into another being, take on another's clothing, as if to sidetrack or deflect the forces of the perceived or potential enemy, the people who might hurt, derogate, embarrass, ridicule, punish, or damage me in some way. The more fearful I am, the more enemies I see and the more restricted my options for undamaged survival seem to be.

2. *Masking.* As fears build up, I intensify my efforts to discover and create facades to cover up the authentic me and to protect me from the dangers that lurk in intimacy and contact. I filter or distort my messages, take distancing and formal postures, and hide behind my wardrobe of protective coloration.

Accompanying the mask-making is a process that produces even more distrust than the mask-making itself. Mask-makers have a tendency to protect themselves by building an arsenal of covert and latent strategies that are devised to deal with potential hurt and danger. Strategizing becomes a way of life. The strategies may be relatively habitual and unconscious, such as the tendency to be consciously polite to ward off potential retaliation. They may be habitual and conscious. Thinking in terms of strategy is the opposite pole from spontaneity and impulsivity. Because it is associated with deviousness and manipulation, it produces distrust and raises fears. Strategy produces counter-strategy, social distance, circumvention, and an array of counter defenses.

3. *Oughting.* When I am fearful and defensive I focus upon the discovery and creation of ways to meet your expectations and demands and those of the groups and organizations to which I belong. I am likely to use the language and concepts of "need" rather than "want" and to attribute to my needs the same quality of duress that I read into the expectations of others. I am captured on all counts. When I talk about and live in a world of needs and expectations, I am likely to feel that they are demands that cannot be ignored. Wants, on the other hand, seem to imply a choice or option, a conscious control, a greater degree of freedom. When I am oughting, I am defensively and habitually asking myself and others what I should be doing, rather than asking myself what I want to do. With an ought and need focus, I tend to look to power, authority, law, structure, roles, and obligations for help in solving my problems, or I see them as obstacles which prevent my solving them. With a want and choice focus, I tend to look within myself at my own flow, rhythm, and being — and to find the strength and resources with which I can meet the problems I choose to face.

When I see the world in terms of oughts and strategies, I am likely to put energy into attempts to influence, persuade, change, or manipulate others. I put less energy into want-directed and choice-directed action. My power and being is likely to come from outside me. My direction of flow is from outside inward.

4. *Depending.* When fears are high, relative to trust level, I tend to try to control my reactions and yours. My energies are directed toward discovering and creating boundaries, legalities, rules, contracts, protective devices, and various structures that will embody the controls that seem necessary to keep life in order. Sometimes I submit to authority, preferring my world orderly so that I can find protection from and with authority. If authority does not respond to me, I may rebel and fight. Rebellion and dependency have roots in the same authority needs.

Fear predisposes a person to overperceive and overreact to the significance of authority and power figures, and the importance of management and control. In a world perceived as unfriendly or hostile, powerful persons are most dangerous of all. Respect for status, hierarchy, and power is tinged with fear. The presence of people in authority may increase the fearing person's feelings of inadequacy and insignificance, or he or she may derive feelings of adequacy from identification with the authority figures. When in a position of power the fearing person is likely to dominate, protect, manage, or overcontrol. Depending upon his life style, such a person will be benevolent, protective, domineering, or coercive. Feelings of hostility, which develop from fear, underly most dependent or counter-dependent reactions.

These four defending processes are initiated and sustained in climates of fear and distrust. Individuals and institutions develop idiosyncratic patterns of defense that tend to recur as trust reaches low levels.

I create my own life out of the interweaving of these discovering and defending processes. Groups, institutions, and nations — all social systems — emerge from these same interflowing processes. Trust level is the central variable that determines the interaction of the processes and the resulting effectiveness of the systems.

DISCOVERY

Being personal is to be in the process
of discovering each other.

Chapter 2

Discovering
How To Be Personal

Being personal is a *relationship* — made possible as trust grows between us. I invite you to join me in the process of discovering who I am. You invite me to join you in discovering who you are. Together, in this moment, we share in the apprehension, the mystery, and perhaps the ecstasy of creating something together.

And in this discovering process trust grows between us.

What Is It Like to be Personal?

When I am being personal —

1. *I am who I am.* And I make little effort to be what I am not. Being personal starts with *being,* which is always a becoming. I am always unfinished — a process, an event. I am forever discovering myself and re-creating me.

But in my discovering I find an enduring quality. I am the one doing the discovering. I am always more than I think that I am, so there is forever a resident mystery in the process. I assume that this process is also going on in you and I let you be who you are.

2. *I see myself as unique.* And I acknowledge your uniqueness. I am an unreplicated life-process, one event of its kind. I celebrate myself and each of us as persons who form our own constellations of reality and being. Thus, when I relate to you I come from my own private place and respect your private place. When we do this, trust grows, and we are able to create new and unique places that we can inhabit together. Each *relationship* is therefore also unique and special, as much so as each person is unique and special. Just as no

person need intrude on another, no relationship between or among two or more people need intrude on other relationships. This idiosyncratic nature of persons and relationships makes irrelevant and depersonalizing any comparisons or classifications. Acceptance of this uniqueness is a strong base from which to maintain my full personal relationship to others.

This deep awareness of my specialness is one source of my strength. Even with my openness toward others, I am the only one who completely knows me. I am the sole authority for my feelings and inner life. I need not compare myself with anyone else. We need not be competitors, and there is no race.

People who are fully into their own *being and uniqueness* are able to *allow others to be who they are.* Such persons learn to be personal in the sense of allowing others to "have their persons". They nurture uniqueness. Of all the people I have met while consulting, the one who stands out in this capacity is a person who, in spite of multiple corporate norms that pressure him to be otherwise, is very much his own person and allows others to create their own business and personal lives. He also has a talent that I associate with other really authentic people: *He gives credit to others for what they do and what they are.* He has a sign on his desk that reads: "You can do anything you want in this world as long as you are willing to let other people have the credit." He also *lives* this credo to its full extent. To me it is significant, and certainly not accidental, that he is also one of the most productive, creative, widely respected, and sought-after top executives in the business world. He is unique, and, *in all of his relationships allows others their uniqueness.* He respects himself and respects the people he meets or works with in the same honoring way. I've seen him be like this with his son, with other executives, and with workers in the plant. He nurtures their dignity. He is being personal.

3. *I am close to my own internal reality.* Staying with my insideness is especially difficult when there are so many pressures on me to conform to other's views of reality. One road to intimacy is to express to another whatever phenomenal reality is available to me at the moment. To be impersonal is to move toward peripheral areas, and away from my core or center, or away from yours. Intimacy, understanding, and trust come from my inner being touching yours.

4. *I take full responsibility for my feelings, opinions and perceptions* — for my own life. I create what I am and determine what I do. The more trust I have for both of us, the more it is possible for me

to take possession of my own attitudes, accept my own body, make "I statements" about what I see and feel, and "own" what is inside me.

But when I am afraid, I may protect myself from possible controversy, quote an authority to lend credence to my ideas, ride piggy-back on someone else's strong opinion knowing that I have at least one ally, or wait for a more courageous person to take a strong position before I express mine. These behaviors, instigated as safety measures, do not really protect me, are not very satisfying, and keep me from risking depth relationships with others.

5. *I am what I seem to be.* There is face validity to what I do and show. I show my inner feelings to others without distorting or masking the message. To be impersonal is to camouflage my message by deliberate or unconscious-habitual masking, by forced or affected humor, needless formality, complexity, deflection, or other indirections. I do not manipulate myself in dealing with others.

Energy spent in building facades, in trying to seem different from what I am inside, is misdirected into neurotic defense and does not serve me well. It makes authentic relationships very difficult. One day Blair, who was about sixteen, came home from school. Seeing me, he said "Wow! You just got your hair cut. I thought you were letting it grow long." I told him I was leaving the next day to work with a new client organization and was a bit anxious about it. Blair asked, "Isn't it somewhat hypocritical to do that and then go up and tell them about that 'not-meeting-people's-expectations' bit?" And then he added, "But then I suppose you feel you have to do that in order to communicate with people." Blair, who doesn't make such compromises and is *always just what he seems to be,* is also accepting of my fears and the way I handle them. I admire him for his integrity, and I have learned a great deal from him and from his open way of being personal.

6. *I have clear and visible motives.* I spontaneously reveal my motivation in the process of being my message. It feels personal when we, as communicants, have little pretense, know what our motives are, and are aware that we know this. We may be aware, in our communications, that we have large areas of latent or unconscious motivation that are unavailable to either of us. But when we are being personal with each other, we are reducing the disparities between my perceptions and your perceptions of the motives of each of us. To be impersonal is to attempt to hide my motives or to clean them up for presentation to you.

In a discussion the other day, I heard a woman say that she didn't like "people who have motives. They always seem needy and I avoid them." My guess is that she didn't like people who seemed not to be aware of their own motives, whose intentions were manipulative, whose motives were hidden, or who had motives she didn't like. Everyone has motives, and they are likely to be complex. When questioned about our motivations, most of us launder them in showing them to others — and certainly to ourselves. People who come to another person with intent to control, teach, influence, or manipulate, sense the probable resistance; and they consciously or unconsciously attempt to camouflage the motive.

The less trust we have of the other, the more we feel we need to defend, and the more likely we are to pretend to ourselves and to others that our motives are acceptable, simple, pure — uncontaminated with wants that might be seen as unwelcome or negative. Most of the time, and certainly at one time or another, every person is likely to have the full range of human motivations. This is part of the human condition. And each of us, especially at moments of low trust and high defense, will sometimes hide our motivations and seem to be what we aren't. Trust comes with the mutual recognition and acceptance of these realities.

In high trust and low defense, people come to others largely for such motives as desires for companionship, affection, warmth, excitement, listening, or friendship — motives which are not seen as manipulative and do not arouse fear. Being personal means that part of our discovery process is a joint quest for what our motivations are, what we are wanting from life and from each other. Hiding these motivations is likely to decrease trust, which is dependent upon openness in all facets of our lives.

7. *I free myself from my roles.* Duties, expectations, and external demands lead to impersonal role behavior. I am being personal when I respond to my own wants, current feelings, gut impulses, and intuitions, rather than to what you or I see as role demands, responsibilities, or expectations. I cannot be personal when I am consciously or unconsciously being a mother, a teacher, a manager, a helper, or a lover. Even when the institutional or societal structure puts me into a role, pays me for this, and sets up appropriate institutional sanctions and prerogatives, I am still free to respond as a unique person in every situation. To trust — to be personal — is to act on this freedom. Persons who do this are also, in the process, able to

measure up to what others think of as the legitimate demands and responsibilities of the role. They do this without thinking about role requirements or strategy demands. That is, workers, children, students, patients, and subordinates do respond to highly personal supraordinates in ways that would be described by observers as both responsible and responsive. The paradox is that role demands are best met by being non-role. Role fulfillment is not met by manipulating myself or others.

Role-making occurs easily when people are fearing and defensive. I remember becoming suddenly aware of the seductiveness of this process while hurrying to teach a university class. Being quite late and upset at this, I became annoyed at the pedestrians on the crowded campus crossing the roadway and delaying my car. Just seconds later, after hurriedly parking my car, I became even more righteously angry at the inconsiderate drivers who endangered the lives of us pedestrians who were hurrying across the very same driveway. In my frustration and defensiveness at being late, I had reversed roles in a very few seconds, identified strongly with each role, and also scapegoated each role in turn. Depersonalizing, stereotyping, irrational scapegoating, condemning classes of people — all done in a few moments' time by someone who had written often about the unnecessary and harmful effects of role behavior!

8. *I free myself from role perceptions* — from mine and yours. When I categorize myself or others, I start the process of making us nonpersons. It is easy to box people. I build barriers when I label someone as sick, neurotic, or needing treatment; as a child, a worker, or a homosexual. Persons and events flow and emerge into idiosyncratic quality in the process of being. It may sometimes be necessary for technical purposes or in non-personal situations to codify, dichotomize, measure, or miniaturize. Even this "necessity" is being questioned by the "label liberation" movement. What we are objecting to here is such coding in the process of *relating inter-personally*. Parents, managers, and teachers do well to avoid the practice of classification and coding, as enticing as it may seem for administrative and other role functions.

9. *I focus upon the relationship.* The relationship between us is a new reality that transcends either of us. To be personal is to be open to, to be aware of, and to focus upon this relationship, this interbeing, this unique happening — this event that has the potential of nourishing us both; this new organism that emerges, takes life, and can become so

magical. I am being personal when I enter into intimacy and depth.

To venture into being personal is to come to terms with a fundamental aspect of the human condition — our interdependence. There is good cause for the deep ambivalence that persons have about "getting personal". "I don't want to get personal, but..." expresses the push-pull in the impulse to do so, the latent awareness of the excitement and the risk, the potential and the danger of getting close, of getting beyond comfort and safety, of getting out of the low-risk zones. The deadening pervasiveness of meaningless chit-chat and no-risk, impersonal talk is testimony to the constraining and life-dulling effects of our fears, our lack of awareness of how to be satisfyingly personal, and our lack of experience with the deep life-bringing satisfactions of intimacy. I am surprised anew each time I see the eagerness with which people respond to new glimpses of intimacy when coming in contact with authentic, *personal* people in a TORI Community Experience, where the environment nourishes trust and depth.

10. *I come to discover rather than to defend.* When I am fearing, I defend. With emerging trust, I discover that a defensive posture does not really defend me or make me invulnerable. It raises the defenses of others, robs the moment, increases the distance between us, and makes it less likely that we will enter into a co-discovering journey.

One thing to learn about defensive behavior is that I always have a choice. I can choose to continue to defend myself, or I can join you in a discovering process. To learn to trust is to learn that I really do have this choice.

11. *I am spontaneous and natural, and have no plan or strategy.* I am more personal when I am emergent and impulsive, and when I seem to be so. People who are close to life are able to free themselves from role prescriptions and from their own or other's programmings. I depersonalize and create distance when I plan strategy of approach, when I program my messsage in order to influence you, and when I try to anticipate what I will do when we meet. I do not try to manipulate you in dealing with you.

In my consulting I have worked with a number of trusting and spontaneous people. One who is notably personal in this way is the director of organizational development for a corporation widely respected for the quality of its training programs. Having heard of my work, he hired me as the external consultant for a three-day team-development session for top management. During the two-hour drive from the airport to the conference center, he and I — working together for the first time — talked about a multitude of things, but never once did we mention the conference. We walked into the meeting and reacted spontaneously to the situation.

This man obviously trusted me, his top management team, and his own spontaneity and ability. Because I was trusted, I responded well to him, as did those at the conference. One factor that made the two of us so effective as a consulting team is that neither of us had a plan, a strategy, or an "intervention" to impose on the executive team. Fourteen of us started with a fresh slate, immediately became very personal, were very creative and productive, and participated together in a meeting that was rated by the team as one of the best sessions they had ever experienced. Contrary to current management myths, it is quite possible to *be personal* while working effectively even in the most pressure-packed organizational setting. This manager happens to be in industrial relations. I have seen equally spontaneous, natural, role-free, and creative people in manufacturing, research, and other fields of management. Being personal and non-strategic is one way of being an effective manager and a full human being.

12. *I show my feelings.* Feelings are the stuff of personal relationships. To avoid, ignore, or move away from feelings when they are present or are dominant is to depersonalize. Feelings are always present, always a part of the active being. When they become a significant part of awareness — in me or in you — they warrant personal expression. They are ingredients of intimacy. As I write this I am strongly aware of a flood of mixed feelings about this writing. I am excited about the ideas I am focusing on, scared at how they might be received by the reader, bored with the physical typing, impatient with the restrictions I'm placing on myself to be disciplined, afraid that the discipline may not only not be comfortable for me but uncomfortable to the reader as well, and having many start-stop feelings about being so impersonal in talking about being personal. And having some feelings about my many motivations in writing this book. I'm struggling with these feelings, enjoying some of them, and choosing to move on.

13. *I am concrete and specific.* Abstract and generalized speech is associated with depersonalization. When I am personal I talk about specific instances; about concrete feelings, behaviors and ideas that are a specific expression of me and my state of being; or about a concrete and specific perception of you or of our relationship. General speech is

safe speech. The risk is greater when I cite specific instances, talk about specific people, and relate my feelings to concrete events. Persons get lost in abstractions, generalities, and principles.

14. *I am here, now, with you in the moment.* Being in another place, in the past, or in the future is to be impersonal. Living fully in what I am feeling right now about you, responding fully to what you are feeling at this moment, and letting us join in the being and the doing are aspects of being personal.

There are many ways of escaping from the fullness of the moment: talking *about* my feelings rather than being *in* the feelings, analyzing my behavior or your perceptions, observing ourselves doing what we are doing, being into our roles, telling "personal" anecdotes, speculating about what will happen next, asking questions, escaping into humor, "getting down to business" — moving away from what is going on between us in our relationship. Being here, now, with you is to be personal. I am always free to choose whether to do so.

15. *I bring all of me to the moment.* Being personal is to bring all of my person into everything that I do. I am *all* here with you now. To be whole is to integrate my total being into all the moments of my life. To be impersonal is to ration myself in bits and pieces, depending upon the people I'm with and the situations I'm in. It is a matter of presence, wholeness, and integration of one's life. I have a choice as to when and if I want to fragment myself or to bring myself whole to my relationships.

I think of several persons who, even under the frequently depersonalizing pressures of organizational life, are able to maintain a holistic way of life. They can enter with wholeness and integrity into the interpersonal contacts they make during the work day. One person, from whom I have learned a great deal about being personal, is a woman executive who is notably successful as one of the few women executives at her level in a corporation with which I consult. She is feminine, warm, gentle, sexual, personal, and non-defensive, and, at the same time, very competent, creative, job-focused, and excited by her work. She is highly respected by both the men and women who report to her and relate to her laterally. What is so relevant here is that she expresses herself fully as a person in all of her relationships, even in situations in which some women executives feel they must "act masculine" in order to succeed in what has been a "man's world". Whenever I have worked with her or talked with her she is fully available as a total person. She is being personal.

16. *I make available to you my humanness and my vulnerability.* I make no effort to hide my vulnerabilities, darker sides, hidden strengths, unfiltered preferences, or pomposities. I show all of myself in an effort to make all of me available to you.

Intimacy and trust are reduced by consciously trying to put my best foot forward, deliberately doing what is appropriate, seeking to protect you from my reality, or rationing my expressions in the interest of what I think would be good for your peace of mind. Trust and intimacy are not furthered when I use my humanness as a strategy to gain your confidence in my professional skill, or when I try to program our intimacy. Being personal is to be human and to show this, not to use my humanness to influence you.

17. *I somehow incorporate my fears into our meeting.* The fear-trust polarity is the basic dimension of all humanness. Fear is always with me in one or more of its many guises. But it is frightening for me to look at my fears and even more fearful to show you that I am afraid.

I may devote so much energy to the denial of fear that I forget that everyone else is frightened, too. Revealing the form of our fear is a bonding process, a sharing of humanness, a communication that crosses the lines of race, sex, and nationality. Discovery of our oneness allows us to focus, to merge, to tune in — and to recapture energies diluted in the service of pretense.

18. *I include you in my world and in my space.* Being personal involves for most of us a perceptual and attitudinal shift — a shift which includes awareness of both the other person and the relationship between us. It means inviting you into my private world. It means the recognition that each of us is part of every other person. The deep awareness of this allness and having strong feelings about the inclusion are integral parts of being personal.

19. *I enjoy physical, psychological, and spiritual closeness.* It is impossible to be *really* personal without enjoying the process. Genuine intimacy is a *reciprocal* relationship, self-rewarding to each participant. When bodies, minds, or spirits touch, the process is nurturing.

Is there ever a doubt that the newborn infant likes being touched? Or likes touching? Somehow in the process of living many of us learn to fear and to defend, and in this process we "lose touch", our bodies forget the joys of touching, we give our dogs and cats the touching that would nourish our friends and our children, and we inhibit our impulses to touch strangers or friends or even those we love. What keeps us from touching — in mind, body, and spirit — are the fear-bred forces of guilt, anxiety, propriety, expectancy, custom, imitation, and a host of inhibitors of these universal wants. Touching, in wholeness, is an *essential* aspect of being personal.

20. *You are important to me.* Being personal is an authentic invitation to a *full relationship in this moment*. Thus it would not be possible for me to be personal without seeing you as of worth. People who are able to be personal do so because they value persons. My moments are the fabric of my life. Sharing them with you, in this way, is the most caring gift I can bring to you. Because being personal is a joint venture, what I bring must be a gift to both of us — or it is a gift to neither.

Being personal is a self-rewarding process: The more personal I become, the more significant people are to me. There are no limits to the process other than those I create with my fears. Being personal is the genesis of the authentic family, the caring community, and the interdependent world.

Does Being Personal Make a Difference?

"Being personal" is defined above in an obviously more full-bodied way than is often used in popular speech. It is the first of the sequential TORI discovering processes, and it triggers the flow into all of living. Trust starts with trusting myself enough to put myself into everything I do. That is one major theme of this book.

Personal growth starts with being personal. How I integrate my fearing and trusting into my being and becoming determines how personal I am able to be. This synergy determines the flow of my life, my experiences of pain and ecstasy, the paths of my growth, and the effectiveness of my actions.

This book is a presentation of my life-view. It comes from my experience of my trusts and fears. My version of TORI theory is what I have created from these experiences. It is in one sense a description of my personal growth. When one of my psychoanalytic friends interpreted my "preoccupation with trust" as my massive reaction to fearful and distrust-provoking episodes in my life, I readily agreed with him. I assume that this fact goes a long way toward validating the whole theory. Each person who reads, uses, or tests the theory validates it for himself or herself from personal life experiences.

When my fear levels have been high enough, I have been disoriented and immobilized. My first wife left me because of the desperate difficulties I had in trying to be intimate and personal. For a while, I even blamed her for my fears and difficulties. My fears are many and deep. Any interested reader, I would hope, can see them, for they are projected into this book.

At times I have given myself intense pain. Twice I have experienced prolonged, two- or three-month periods of depression during which I contemplated many self-destructive actions, including suicide. About three years ago, I gave myself high blood pressure at a dangerous level. During times of intense pain, I mobilized defenses that didn't defend or protect me. I blamed other people and events for my misfortunes, but more often I punished my own mindbody for hurting me. My depths, at some of these times, have seemed like no other depths.

My "theory" has created my hurts, and it has also helped me integrate my experiences. At the depths of my deepest depression, I decided in mind and body not to commit suicide and I discovered and created me in a way that I had not even fantasied before. I created me and my strength. I know me at a new level. Though I have for many years believed in taking responsibility for myself and my life events, I now find myself taking responsibility in new and more genuine ways. When I was deeply frightened by my self-induced high blood pressure, I took a deeper look at me, what I was showing to me and others, what I really wanted in my life. With much help from people who loved me, I developed a new way of life that reduced my blood pressure to normal in 18 months. From this and other experiences with trust I have given myself a new and deep serenity, a new life.

When my trust levels have been high I have had many beautiful and life-giving experiences. I have loved and been loved in many ways. My life with my family, with Lorraine and Blair and John, feels better than any other life that I can conceive of. More than at any other time in my life, I am doing what I really want to do. I am creating my "theory", and it is making me whole.

I have been consciously creating my theory for as long as I can remember, and unconsciously long before that — certainly since, as a freshman student at Brigham Young University, I became entranced with psychology and had a love affair with William James and his magnificent humanness. Though I have published bits and pieces of my theory in articles and chapters, I have been too fearful until now to put the theory into one visible book and to put myself on the line. Though at times my timidity has astonished me and embarrassed me, at the moment of writing this I look fondly on it as an integral part of my gentleness, which I enjoy and like.

The block that keeps me from being more personal is my fear. The "reasons" that I give myself or others for not being more personal are disguises of my fear. I am able to unblock myself when I recognize that I create my own fears, that I can make them my enemies or my friends, and that being personal is not nearly as dangerous as it appears in my fantasy.

When I trust myself, trust you, and trust the process, my behavior becomes personal, regardless of other factors in the situation. Trust is the catalyst. With it all things are possible. I can be as personal as I wish. It is possible to make small steps, within my fear/trust level, and create satisfying and self-rewarding experiences by being personal. I find that when I am *being authentically personal,* the results are positive and fulfilling. It is when I am playing games and not really being who I am, that I create my problems and dissatisfaction.

I sometimes discover myself making false starts in the direction of being personal. Often these are in the grey areas of consciousness; I am only partly aware of what I am doing when I'm doing it. I tell stories about myself in the hope that listeners will see me as I would like to have them see me. I sometimes stay in "party talk" with a person, wondering why the other person is being so impersonal with me and resenting this, dimly aware that we are both experiencing discomfort and not knowing how (really, being afraid) to be more personal. I am sometimes bored with what another person is saying; not knowing how to express my boredom without hurting the person (really, being afraid to say it), I build up a mild annoyance and search for ways of breaking the connection. And so it goes. Or, rather, so it *did* go. I am learning to be more direct, to be more personal, to reveal what I want. And I'm finding that when I trust enough to be this way, good things happen to me and to people around me. Being personal is a satisfying, even exciting way to be.

TORI theory originates in the user's being personal. Each person who uses the theory creates it as an expression of himself or herself. Only an authentic user (*i.e.,* one who is "being personal") can understand, in the mindbody, the theory itself or can apply it. This "personal" aspect of theory construction is more central than is often apparent. A physicist once told me that he could predict the theories of the major physicists from their personality dynamics and social behavior. This origin-in-the-person aspect is true of all theory building, but it is especially true of Trust Level theory, which is deliberately constructed to optimize this person-centering and idiosyncratic aspect of *both the substance and process* of theory building.

Being personal is the key initial step in creating my environment. Contrary to many messages that we all hear (from our environment!), the environment does not create me; I create my environment. For this statement to be true of me, I must take a proactive attitude toward my life. I have choices — all that I wish to make. I choose to stay in my roles or to move out of them. I see what I want to see and hear what I want to hear. I choose to change my physical or my social environment. I choose to present my authentic self to you, or I choose not to. I create my fear. I choose to be the captive of my fear, or I choose to be free of it. The awesome consequences of such a viewpoint are discussed in the following chapter.

Parents, teachers, therapists, managers, and ministers — everyone, really — are more effective when they are being personal. An unfortunate and persistent myth comes from our common fears. It is the false belief that in order to be effective, people who have positions of responsibility must take appropriate roles in order to meet the legitimate obligations that come with "responsibility". They believe that they must be impersonal at the very times when being fully "personal" is *most needed,* would be most effective, and in fact would be the best or even the only way of meeting the "obligations" that are imputed to the role. In a crisis, a mother needs to be there as Mary, a full-blooded *person,* rather than as a "mother". The minister needs to share the personal grief, not give assurance to the sufferer. The teacher needs to join in the personal search, not teach the student. The manager, as will become so apparent in Chapter X, needs to join the enterprise as a person, rather than to "manage" it. To be effective in a role, we begin by getting out of the role.

Being personal is significantly related to organizational effective-ness and productivity. Research studies and organizational experience are in substantial agreement that high productivity is significantly related to the degree to which there are personal relationships on the job. "Being personal" does not mean, for example, that the manager or supervisor invites the worker home for dinner, tells stories with the gang at the bar after work, asks questions about matters that are "personal" and thus unrelated to the job, or even keeps the office door open. It does mean that the supervisor or manager is an authentic person, expresses honest anger or joy, responds to others as human beings rather than as persons who get the job done, brings his or her wholeness to the moments of interaction on the job or in a meeting, and joins others in discovering how the job can be done rather than telling others how they should do it.

Being personal is the passageway to interbeing, authentic intimacy, depth of community, and to higher states of consciousness. New developments in our theories and experiences with intimacy and depth indicate that all of life can be more personal — *must* be more personal for us to survive as a culture. Starting with being more personal in some of my moments I can carry on the process as far as I wish to take it. Our images of intimacy can be frightening. Last fall, on the first evening of a TORI group, a woman said to us: "I'm afraid that if I get too close to any of you, I will feel bad when I leave on Sunday afternoon: so I'm going to keep things as impersonal as possible." She was unable to stay with her original plan, but her reactions to her own fear fantasies allowed her to keep from getting close to anyone for an impressive number of hours. Whether we express such attitudes, even to ourselves, most (all?) of us at times treat life in the same way. When this woman's trust overcame her fears, she changed her behavior radically and began to be the way she "really" (at some level) wanted to be; she became a warm and outgoing member of the community. It is my assumption that all people want to be intimate and loving, at a level that is very apparent in many of us, and at a depth for some that is almost inaccessible even to themselves. It is from these common wants that a caring community emerges. When trust transcends fear, all things are possible.

All human living is enriched when it is more personal. Thus this chapter is a relevant introduction to the substance of each of the chapters that follow. In the next chapter, let's move from the person to the environment that we, as persons, create.

TRANSCENDENCE

Trust knows no limits —
trusting is an eternal transcendence
of what is.

Chapter 3

Transcending the Environment

I create my own environment. It does not create me. The highest level of trust is to assume that the environment is benign and tractable, that it is susceptible to my creativity, my projections, and my images. To trust is to believe in my unlimited powers to create the world in which I live, and to transcend what is. The eternal paradox is to *be where I am,* and to fully experience what is, in order to free myself to transcend what is and move into ever-changing states of new being and awareness.

The high-trust process is, also, to allow other people to *be where they are,* to join them in an attempt to see together what is, and to collaboratively look at what might be. *Mutual design of a high-quality environment* is a high-trust way to do therapy, teach school, minister a church, govern a country, parent a home, and manage a business.

Describing the High Quality Environment

The following are six ways of describing a quality environment. Each description is an account of the same process. Each description is useful for different purposes. Each calls attention to a significant characteristic of the high-quality environment.

1. *High trust level.* The high-quality environment is one in which trust is high. The higher the trust level, relative to the fear level, the more effective is the environment for enhancing the usual organizational goals: productivity, creativity, organizational vitality, or personal growth. The ten-point environmental-quality scale described below is designed as a degree-of-trust scale.

2. *Low constraint.* The high-quality environment is one that allows freedom, creativity, impulsivity, and growth — that has minimal constraints. The TORI assumption is that all significant barriers to personal and organizational effectiveness are fear-based. Thus, a low constraint environment is a *low fear* environment or a *low threat* environment. Energy directed toward fear- and constraint-removal is more productive than energy directed toward increasing pressures to produce, create, or learn.

3. *Optimization of the four TORI discovering processes.* Efforts directed toward improving the quality of the environment are focused upon creating an environment for *being, showing, wanting, and interbeing.* These four processes mediate the forces that enter into creativity, productivity, and life enrichment.

4. *Self-esteem.* A good environment is one in which persons continue to feel good about themselves. A high attitude about the self makes possible the release of energy and the direction of that energy into productivity, creativity, and other positive personal and organizational outcomes.

5. *Range of enrichment.* A high-quality environment is one in which there is an optimal range of options available. At each new quality level a new avenue of enrichment is functionally available. At each level of quality new energy is released, new experiences are available, and new resources are tapped. A significant criterion in evaluating schools, churches, neighborhoods, or homes is option-enrichment.

6. *Reduced defensiveness.* A low-quality environment is one in which persons feel the need to channel energies into defense of the person or the system against apparent, perceived, or anticipated attack. Energy thus drained is not available for more productive, creative, or enriched living. A high-quality environment reduces defensiveness.

An Environmental-Quality Scale

Practitioners who use TORI theory have found a ten-phase Environmental-Quality Scale useful as a frame of reference to diagnose the system, propose action programs, and improve the quality of life in the family, the workplace, the school, or any other environment.

I will describe each of ten phases briefly and then, following this description, describe the uses and characteristics of the scale.

EQ I — Punitive. Punishment is the dominant and visible process in Environment I. In early and primitive stages of fear and distrust, people attempt to reduce visible or prospective chaos and danger by punishing others. In spite of the overwhelming evidence that punishment accomplishes little or nothing of value, and that it does produce massive negative effects, punishment is amazingly persistent in the modern world. It persists as a regressive form of defense, and even as a deliberate and rationalized form of education, social control, rehabilitation, therapy, parental training, and supervision.

Punishment is sustained by guilt and hostility and can be visited upon any object: upon a child who fails to meet our goals or expectations; upon a subordinate who is a threat; even, animistically, upon a recalcitrant chair.

People who punish justify themselves in a variety of ways: I care enough for you to punish you; you need punishment for your own good; discipline is morally or psychologically necessary; spare the rod and spoil the child.

I look at the person as a social system. The EQ scale can be applied to the development of the internal environment of the person, the intrapersonal system. When fear is high, in relation to trust, the dynamics of blame and guilt are such as to predispose the person to punish self or others, and to see the world with a primitive form of morality in which all actions are viewed moralistically rather than descriptively. Feelings of blame and guilt are associated with a high degree of hostility.

EQ II — Autocratic. Power, order, and structure are the key themes of Environment II. The persistence of this form of environment comes from easily-aroused primitive fears of ambiguity, disorder, and powerlessness. The environment is associated with a morality of obedience to authority and a value-laden view of responsibility.

Autocratic environments foster linear relationships, hierarchy of power and responsibility, span of control, and rational relationships.

The high cost of this fear-sustained environment lies in seemingly inevitable by-products: passivity, dependency, hostility, and conformity. Because autocracy seems so rational and so suited to the fear-based assumptions about an orderly world and its moral superiority, these costly by-products are accepted, overlooked, or not seen as related to autocracy, as such.

At the intrapersonal level, autocracy is represented in tight inner controls, suppression of feeling and impulse, use of rationalization as a mechanism of defense, low tolerance for ambiguity, and an authoritarian character structure.

EQ III — Benevolent. The primary and characteristic theme of Environment III is nurturing and caring. This parental environment is common in the school, the church, and the rehabilitation program. Autocracy is muted, but the concern for order and structure is still present. Because the maternalist does provide security and affection and seems to meet the emotional needs of others, at least in large part, the dependency and resistance produced in such an atmosphere are underperceived and tolerated. Benevolence fits appropriately into the use of rewards and punishments as a control system. The negative effects upon others of rewarding and praising, when these behaviors are used to manipulate and control, are underestimated.

The person caught in the dynamics of benevolency is likely to see the world in terms of punishment and reward, winning and losing, approval and reproof, and acceptance and rejection. Something good is seen as a "win-win" situation, rather than as a natural, intrinsically-rewarded event. The high cost of this parentalism is apathy and emotional dependence.

EQ IV — Advisory. The foci are upon consultative help, data collection, expanding the data base, and enriching communication at all levels. As fear and distrust become less, there is a movement away from the leader group as the primary source of motivation, wisdom, and decision-making. Scientific management uses survey data, rational communication nets, training in decision-making, and external consultants. Management is a rational, scientific process.

As the person develops more trust, the dynamics of dependency and resistance become less crippling, and an internal dialogue begins to happen. The person develops an internal communication system and is able to process data from the outside. This internal data processing is integrated into action and decision-making.

EQ V — Participative. With increasing trust there is a focus upon participation, consensual decision-making, and choice. Groups and communities are involved in all phases of management and group life. Participatory management is seen in most modern management circles as the highest form of management and as the ideal form of social environment.

From the standpoint of this environmental-quality analysis, and trust level diagnoses, participatory life is seen as a key transitional form of life. It is the highest form of leadership and the most effective form of environment within the limitations of leadership as a critical dimension of social life. The crucial limitation is that action and decision-making are only as effective as the leader. The costs of leader-centered living are muted but still present.

At the level of personal development, the internal environment is an integration of the many internalized selves, roles, or aspects of the person. It is as if the many internal parts hold a meeting and make decisions and choices that determine the active life of the person.

EQ VI — Emergent. Environment VI is a quantum jump away from participatory living. The emergent group and community grow a new and leaderless level of reality and interaction. There are vestigial remains of the dynamics of power, control, and influence. Primarily, however, concerns about power, influence, and control are replaced by concerns about interpersonal skills, being, awareness, experimentation, and empathy.

At the governmental level, this environmental form is represented by experiments with socialism, communism, and anarchy. A recognition of the limitations of centralization and leader-centered environments has led to a wide variety of experiments with egalitarianism, community-centering, and spread of control.

TORI theorists have pioneered in the development of leaderless T-groups, consultant-less team training, leaderless communities, teacher-less classrooms, supervisor-less work groups, and therapy groups without therapists. In general the results have been highly successful in terms of learning, productivity, profit, personal growth, and a variety of other outcome measures. There are obvious advantages to such groups, but full development of effective leaderless groups depends upon a cultural revolution in values and beliefs, the acquiring of new skills by a wide variety of people, and more experimentation.

At the personal level this emergence is seen as the growth of the centered person, the ought-free and structure-free individual, and the inner-directed life. The struggle of the person is for freedom from authority and responsibility, from the internalized parents bred in Environments I through V, and from the assumptions born of earlier fear. The search is for an internal security to replace the comforts of structure and controls.

EQ VII — Organic. With evolution of trust and greater familiarity with leaderless freedom and creativity, we begin to see reliance on empathic and intuitive modes of being and communication. We see a move away from dependence upon word interaction. There is a focus upon sensory awareness, physical touching, and nonverbal communication.

With the recognition that defensive life is embodied in verbal communication and the word-related conflicts of the relatively stormy Environments V and VI comes the learning of nonverbal cue systems, the satisfactions of silence, the deep-sensing reality of touch, and new awareness of trust and its significance.

I have seen these environments in children's informal games, small work groups that have been together for long periods, therapy groups, five-day and seven-day TORI communities, hunch-valuing executive groups, alternative communities, and isolated instances in a variety of organizations. It occurs enough for me to know that such groups are possible, that experience with such groups can change lives in significant ways, and that such integrated living is the wave of the future.

At the personal level this form of intrapersonal environment is characterized by new empathic and intuitive awareness, new integration of the sublingual processes into choice and action, greater availability of creativity, and less reliance upon words and concepts as integrative mechanisms.

EQ VIII — Holistic. In the holistic environment there is an integration of the unconscious and archetypical elements of life into all personal and organizational action. There is new creativity and an increasing spread of synergy and integration.

Initial experimentation with this form of environment may be furthered by personal growth experiences with psychosynthesis, hypnosis, dream analysis, holistic healing, prayer, guided fantasy, depth therapy, and a wide variety of other ways of integrating the unconscious and the foreconscious into everyday living. But essentially this EQ level emerges from sustained experiences in deep levels of trust and not from techniques or intrusive intervention.

In the organization we see many instances of the unconscious at work and play: collusive work slowdown, hidden agenda, the following of charismatic persons, bursts of high creativity, the collective punishment of deviants, the Peter principle, displacement of guilt, synergistic team action, leadership martyrdom, sibling rivalry, and a wide variety of quasi-conscious and recurrent processes that reflect the influence of other-than-conscious states.

At the intrapersonal level, new trust brings new retrieval of unconscious life, the expansion of consciousness, the integration of inner urges into conscious life plans, the healing effect of inner serenity, and the more total synergy of life forces.

EQ IX — Transcendent. This is another key transitional environment in which quantum leaps are made into new areas of being. This brings the integration of altered and extra-sensory states into being and consciousness. Environment IX taps new sources of energy.

In talking about this kind of environment I am going beyond the familiar world of organizational reality and management systems into a highly controversial world of mystic events, astral trips, clairvoyance, prayer, visions, out-of-the-body experiences, reincarnation, extra-sensory perception, faith healing, acupuncture, astrology, and a wide variety of events and phenomena which transcend the everyday world of experience. How much effect this new world of experimentation and discovery will have upon the organizational realities of decision-making, productivity, choice, and management is a significant question. My belief is that the next decade or so will see amazing changes, sowing the seeds of a new revolution that will surpass the "industrial revolution" in universal effect.

At the personal level there is clear evidence that many persons are moving into new trust states, have transcended the familiar world of Environments V through VIII, and are pioneering new areas of life enrichment.

EQ X — Cosmic. My speculations about Environment X come from my reading, extrapolation from my studies of the concept of trust, some personal experience with out-of-the-body and cosmic states, and from conversations with persons whose experiences I value and trust.

So far my extrapolations of the fear-trust constructs seem to hold up well in integrating new developments in theoretical physics, holistic medicine, cosmic speculations, and a wide variety of marginal and speculative "scientific" literature. Trust is a unitary concept that differentiates environmental levels. Fear may be a process dependent upon bodily and sensory states, and may disappear in post-cosmic environments.

TABLE V. THE DEVELOPMENT OF ENVIRONMENTAL QUALITY

Phase theme	Definitive nature of phase	Key function best nurtured
I Punitive	Punishment as a form of control and socialization	Reduces frightening chaos and apparent danger
II Autocratic	Power and authority used to maintain control and order	Provides order and structure
III Benevolent	Parental nurturing and caring as a primary theme	Provides security and affection
IV Advisory	Focus on consultative help and data collection	Expands the data base and enriches communication
V Participative	Focus upon participation, consensual decision-making, and choice	Increases involvement, loyalty, and group strength
VI Emergent	Rise of group and community as new and leaderless level of reality, and interaction	Reduces dependency, adds vitality and functional resources
VII Organic	Rise of major role of emphatic and intuitive modes of being and communicating	Taps intuitive and sublingual sources of creativity and being
VII Holistic	Integration of unconscious, archetypical and latent processes into enriched living	Releases wellsprings of energy and creativity
IX Transcendent	Integration of altered and extra-sensory states into being and consciousness	Taps non-sensory sources of being and energy
X Cosmic	Focus on cosmic, universal, and nirvanic states of community and being	Taps into as-yet-little-known universal energy and being

TABLE VI. DYNAMICS OF THE ENVIRONMENTAL-QUALITY STATES

Phase theme	Key limitation of the phase	Primary fear-reducing expanded flow	Focus of the energy
I Punitive	Produces guilt and residual hostility	Fear of rebellion and loss of control	Survival, retribution
II Autocratic	Creates passivity and dependency	Fear of ambiguity, disorder, anarchy	Power, control, obedience
III Benevolent	Fosters multiple emotional disorders and apathy	Fear of emotional weaning	Reward and punishment
IV Advisory	Failure to tap energy and action and to distribute responsibility	Fear of conflict, diversity, and action	Communication, validity of data processing
V Participative	Ambiguity of leader role	Fear of leaderlessness and responsibility	Influence, choosing, resolving conflict
VI Emergent	Overreliance upon rational and verbal processes	Fear of being into non-rational and non-verbal states	Being, freedom, searching
VII Organic	Overreliance upon conscious processes	Fear of mysteries of unconscious and primal	Expression, integration, sensing
VIII Holistic	Overreliance upon sensory data and experience	Fear of loss of conscious and voluntary control	Creativity, spontaneity
IX Transcendent	Overreliance upon mind and body	Fear of leaving security of bodily and sensory base	Transcending sensory and body states
X Cosmic	Little or no data available	Fears may be transcended	Cosmic being

Using the EQ Scale

The environment is a flowing, continuous process. In classifying environments we have done violence to this unitary ebbing and flowing of life experience.

The *environment is what we experience*. Experience is unitary, flowing, global, wholized. The stages or levels are like momentarily freezing the action of a motion picture, so to speak, and are not abrupt or dichotomous.

1. *The scale describes an evolutionary process* — the ontogenetic development of a person, the evolution of an institution, the changes that take place in the history of the race, the evolution of our myths and beliefs, and the development of our attempts to "manage" processes and people.

Some kind of integration takes place at each stage. Each new level of trust brings an emerging set of prepotent needs, a new set of assumptions about people, new functions performed in the system, new capacities and skills that become ascendent, new energy sources being tapped, and new problems and tensions. A new and integrating theme integrates these changes, gives a wholeness to the system, and helps to maintain a perceived rationality and order to the emerging processes.

Values central at one phase seem irrelevant or inappropriate at another. The focus upon obedience and approval-seeking in Environment II and III, say, is seen as dysfunctional and perhaps obscene in Environments VI, VII, and VIII. The focus of research upon the dynamics of power and persuasion is highly appropriate and illuminating in Environments II through IV, but irrelevant and meaningless in Environments VII through IX. In a rapidly changing culture such as we have now, with great diversity in phases juxtaposed in the same city or even neighborhood, the resulting dissonance and incongruence are difficult to bridge. I have found that the perspective provided by this scale is very helpful when working with diverse racial, cultural, and organizational groups.

2. *Trust level is the leverage variable in this evolution.* The scale is essentially a trust level scale. When trust level changes significantly, the disequilibrium and tension in the system provides drives toward new growth, new levels of integration, and new EQ levels.

3. *New needs become ascendent at each level.* A needs- and wants-hierachy is described in Table VII. A new set of dominant needs at each level becomes visible. The group, organization, or culture somehow creates activities that meet these central needs and wants. Needs seem to persist for long periods and attain a kind of functional

autonomy. Thus people who want and get power develop even stronger power needs. Punishment increases the need to punish. Sensory gratification increases the need for more sensuality.

However, as needs become sated, are transcended, or become less relevant to the system state, the environment moves into a new level or phase. New needs and wants begin to replace older ones.

Each environmental level is integrated around a meshing of needs. A punitive climate is maintained by people who need to punish or be punished. These needs encourage the setting up of laws and rules which in turn provide new violators who "need" to be punished, and newly violated persons who "need" to punish. Values and norms arise which sanction and sanctify the rule-violation-punishment sequence which is the sustaining theme of the climate. An autocratic climate is nourished by the power-hungry, the structure-seeking, and the dependent. Those who need to obey and those who need to be obeyed create a dynamic tension that sustains autocracy, provides a visible need for power, and thus sanctions the feeding of power.

The benevolent system flourishes with the inter-meshing of those who need to protect and give counseling with those who need to be protected and counseled. The advisory culture is sustained by information systems and data exchange. There are those who want to give advice, share rumors, tell stories, and give opinions. And those who love to get information, enjoy rumors, and listen. Participatory climates are sustained by group-membership needs to get into the action, influence others, join in decision-making, and create the process.

Emergent flow and leaderlessness are sustained by a number of forces: needs to be counter-dependent, and long-simmering resentments of leader-power figures; the desire for the newly-felt excitement of an emerging community or group; and a variety of long-latent sensitivities awakened and nurtured in the new climate of freedom and emergence. Organic climates are nurtured by newly-sanctioned needs for sensory gratification, the mixed joys of impulsiveness and spontaneity, and new needs to be "real".

Holistic environments are initiated and sustained by newly-awakened needs for wholeness, for voluntary control over bodily functions and unconscious drives, for a re-discovery of the body and the healing processes. The exploding interest in transcendent states, altered consciousness, and ego-less processes is awakening a set of long dormant needs and wants. I suspect that the cosmic environment

TABLE VII. THE WANTS HIERARCHY AND THE ENVIRONMENTAL-QUALITY PHASES

Phase theme	Ascendent want, sustaining the phase	Secondary wants that enrich the basic and ascendent want during the phase state
I Punitive	To survive	To be secure, to punish and be punished, to be moral and to impose morality, to fight, to withdraw
II Autocratic	To give and gain power	To control, to be controlled, to maintain order, to get status, to obey, to rebel, to have authority, to evaluate
III Benevolent	To protect and to be protected	To help, to teach, to parent, to be cared for, to rescue, to be dependent, to give and receive warmth
IV Advisory	To understand and to be understood	To consult, to give and get advice, to be rational, to be aware of order, to gain wisdom
V Participative	To join and to be joined	To collaborate, to encourage involvement, to persuade, to influence, to be a member, to be included, to include others
VI Emergent	To be in community	To be part of a whole, to touch, to be aware, to be self-determining, to be close
VII Organic	To feel and to express feelings	To get sensory gratification, to create self, to get new experience, to be impulsive and spontaneous
VIII Holistic	To be whole	To find my roots, to create a free will, to have voluntary control over all bodily functions, to expand self
IX Transcendent	To transcend	To be egoless, to be need-free, to be born anew, to move into new areas of being and awareness
X Cosmic	To join the universal all	To transcend self, to be want-free, to transcend need for separateness

will transcend needs and wants and move into new and unfamiliar processes.

4. *Each level of integration provides nurturing for a newly-emerging central function.* Column 3 in Table V provides a list of key functions that are best nurtured in each climate. The climate seems to stabilize around activities that provide these functions.

5. *Each level sets up new forces that provide for its own demise and provides energy to transcend the phase and move on to new levels of integration.* Although we see many instances of regression to lower levels of integration (recurrent waves of conservatism in beliefs, attitudes, practices, and theory), these regressions seem to be temporary holding patterns. Growth is a directional process.

Something is worked through at each level, by the person or by the system, that provides resources for new movement in the evolutionary process. Each stage has key limitations, some of which are listed in column 2 of Table VI. Each primary-need system seems to have its day, its time, its season, its period of centrality.

Each level of integration, each environment, sets up forces that overpower the state of being and force new movement. Each stage is a transcendence of a prior dependency. Thus, Environment I produces guilt and hostility that erode the stage; autocracy sets up so much passivity and resistance that it cannot sustain itself; and benevolency produces so much parent-child emotional dependency that energy is displaced and sapped.

The overemphasis upon data and rationality produces an unsatisfying sterility in a consultative system, which fails to tap energy and motor action. Participatory climates focus so much energy on process, procedures, and the structure of living that the energy dies from lack of movement and action. Emergent climates die from a perseverative overreliance upon rational and verbal processes whose sterility becomes apparent with growth.

Organic environments build an overreliance upon conscious processes, and when there is a retrieval of the unconscious it produces dissatisfaction with earlier incomplete experiences. The exclusive focus upon sensory data and experience in the holistic environment creates an anticipation of transcendence, which creates growth tensions. I have not experienced many transcendent group and community states and am not familiar with satiation and "growth through" at this EQ level, but my extrapolative view is that extra-sensory and altered-consciousness states would lead to movement toward out-of-the-body and cosmic-allness states. My conviction is that the cosmic states are passageways into new levels beyond the cosmic. Our limited levels of consciousness prevent us from thinking or talking very clearly about post-cosmic states.

6. *Limits of movement up the scale are determined by fears* that are somehow unintegrated, displaced, unrecognized, or repressed. Table VI, column 3, indicates a listing of the primary fears at each level which reduce the flow through the evolutionary scale. The assumption in TORI theory is that the barrier to all growth is the *way that the person or the social system handles fear.* Table II in Chapter II gives a summary of how fear sets up and sustains the four defending processes which block movement on the environmental scale.

7. *A fear-bred impasse occurs at the interface between levels.* The boundary condition is a state of tension and transition. This point of disequilibrium may be a painful or fearful state, but also a point of optimal learning for the person or the system. It may be at this point where incongruity is most apparent — incongruities in attitude, energy level, wants, assumptions, and behaviors. It is at these impasse points where friends, consultants, ministers, counselors, managers — any empathetic person — may be most helpful.

8. *Dysfunctional perseverance occurs* when concepts and coping modes arise at one level of evolution and then persist beyond useful function into higher levels of environment. Thus it is effective and functional to use power and influence strategies in Environments I, II, and III. It is less functional to use them in Environments IV and V. It is dysfunctional and disruptive to use them in Environment VI and beyond. Punishment as a strategy is probably not effective after Environment I. Leadership concepts and strategies are useful during Environments I through V, and not useful and probably a hindrance in Environment VI and beyond. Assertiveness training is most effective in Environments IV and V, less relevant or perhaps harmful in other environments. Deep sensory awareness is most helpful in Environments V, VI, and VII, and perhaps harmful in other environments. Experiences that strengthen the ego are relevant to Environments I through VIII. To be in Environments IX and X one must be in an ego-less state.

This phenomenon of concept- and theory-lag probably accounts for the very mixed and confusing results of research on power, leadership, sensory awareness, persuasion, and a host of other behavioral science concepts, the relevance and predictive power of which are clearly related to EQ level. The field of research and theory construction needs longitudinal studies *and theories.* Certainly consultants and practitioners need an evolutionary and longitudinal framework to understand the dynamics of environmental quality.

9. *Persons or human systems produce more effective movement up the evolutionary scale through environmental design than through external intervention.* Table VIII summarizes the distinctive characteristics of these two alternative styles of life management — of evolutionary movement.

External intervention occurs when a person outside the system attempts to intervene in the system or in the person's life by doing something designed to influence, improve, change, guide, teach, or correct the system. A trainer comments on the process during a conflict in a training group; a parent rewards a child for being polite to a visitor; a minister reflects a feeling or listens empathically to a parishioner who has lost a family member through death; a manager intrudes at a critical inspection point to improve the quality of the product on the assembly; or a teacher points out an error in a solution to a problem in a classroom exercise. In each case a skilled interventionist has done something significant with the intention to improve the performance or life quality of the client-person or client-system.

The external intervention is presumed to be most effective when it is aimed at a specific behavioral objective, is performed in a skillful and sensitive manner, is part of a theoretically-sound overall intervention program designed for long-range significance, is geared to a depth diagnosis and not directed at superficial symptoms, is molecular in focus, is done with skill and understanding, and is performed in an ethical and responsible manner.

The external-intervention approach is essentially a low-trust, high-fear viewpoint. It is based upon several distrust attitudes and assumptions, among which are assumptions that:

a. the natural, uncontrolled, self-determined , free-flow environment usually found in life cannot be trusted;

b. the *system itself or the person himself or herself* cannot be trusted to come up with the most appropriate solution to problems in the person or system; and

c. only a few "certified" or professional people are qualified to join another person or system to work on a problem.

To use the environmental-design approach is to look at the

environment with a view toward understanding and changing it; or for the social system to look at its environment to see if performance or the quality of life can be improved by collaborative change.

The environmental-design viewpoint assumes that persons, groups, or institutions can determine their own lives, improve their own environments, make critical choices, learn their own skills, solve their own problems, and live in surprisingly effective ways.

Persons and institutions seem to do best when they:

a. are trusted;

b. have confidence in their own capacities to make choices, solve problems, perform tasks;

c. have freedom to succeed or fail;

d. are *with* others in deeply significant ways; and

e. see each other as resources, friends, allies — rather than as enemies, competitors, threats.

10. *Each level provides a new environment for the focus and release of new energy.* Table IX indicates some of the sources of new energy at each environmental level. The concept is that energy is always available in sufficient force for all tasks that a person or institution wishes to perform or for any life pattern that is meant to be lived. Energy is blocked, constrained, and held dormant by fear-related processes. Each new level of integration brings in a new *release of energy.*

11. *This environmental analysis can be used for perspective and for diagnosis by using any segment of the sequence* that is relevant to the system being analyzed. A few examples:

Most management systems are struggling with moving through Environments II through V, which roughly parallel Likert's System I, II, III, and IV management styles. By opening up his or her vision of viable management options in Environments VI and VII, the manager can create subsystem experiments with emergent and organic modes and thus include expanded alternatives among the live options available.

Most organizational or person environments include elements of about three adjoining phases. The range of values, assumptions, fear, impasses, and ascendent wants includes three levels. The system can tolerate this much spread and dissonance. A larger range produces too many communication problems and too much gap for empathy to bridge.

On the North American continent in the 1970's there are clear

TABLE VIII. TWO ALTERNATIVE STYLES OF LIFE MANAGEMENT
(For Teachers, Parents, Managers, Ministers, Therapists)

Key Characteristics	External intervention	Environmental design
1. Focus of initiation of change	External to person or other human system	Internal to person or other other human system
2. Direction of focus	Usually micro-focused	Usually macro-focused
3. Management required	Required skilled professional or technical manager or consultant	Low or minimal need for professional manager of process
4. Resistance level	High induced resistance	Low or negligible induced resistance
5. Diagnostic model	Medical model, with intervention and treatment geared to specific diagnosis	Emergent model, with program usually unrelated to specific diagnosis
6. Specificity of focus on outcomes	Highly specific focus on selected outcomes	General focus on unselected, emergent outcomes
7. Basic skills required	Diagnostic, remedial, interventive, and evaluative	Empathic, nurturant, creative, or other non-skill aspects of personal behavior
8. Predictability	Highly predictable when performed by skilled professional	Highly unpredictable and emergent outcomes
9. Trust level	Based on low trust of natural, uncontrolled, or self-determined environment	Based on high trust of person or system to develop from intrinsic factors
10. Level of differentiation of theory	Highly sophisticated and differentiated theory usually required or useful	Theory need not be sophisticated or differentiated
11. Focus of responsibility	Usually responsibility built into intervener, who is external to system	Responsibility built into the person or system itself, not in external agent

examples of small systems in Environments I through IX. I am aware of some *persons* who say they are living in Environment X, but I am aware of no *groups or organizations* that see themselves in this environment. The range of environments is so large that there is considerable tension in the culture. This extreme spread makes it difficult for any one large organization to make movement along the scale.

A consultant is probably most effective if his or her customary internal-environmental state is within one or two levels of the stable state of the client system. One significant contribution that a consultant can bring to another person or system is an expanded perspective gained by experiential familiarity with a wide range of environments.

One use of the scale by TORI theorists is to plan pilot or demonstration groups or organizations that give visible and convincing evidence to others that environments can be changed, that the quality of life can be radically improved, and that life in our day, with people in our culture, can be lived in Environments VI, VII, and VIII. It seems to me that the North American culture is essentially within the range of Environments III, IV, and V, with each of these three environmental, organizational, and managerial styles familiar to citizens in the culture. The response of audiences to whom I have described this 10-phase scale has been very positive, with considerable understanding and interest. My illustrations of life in each of the phases seem to make sense to my listeners. The growing familiarity with literature about life in Environments VII through X makes the task easier. For over twenty years I have been consulting with large, conservative organizations and have a reputation for working with systems *as they are,* rather than for attempting to make intrusive changes. I am therefore known for talking about organizations as they are and am able to bridge the audience-speaker gap. I believe that this analysis puts all organizational and counter-culture experiences into a common frame of reference; it provides a common theory that is spawning considerable research and demonstration projects as a groundwork for significant cultural change.

My experiences with organizations give me high confidence that significant changes are happening in North American life and that we are on the edge of a breakthrough to new and radical changes in management styles and significant cultural movement up the environmental scale.

TABLE IX. RELEASE OF NEW ENERGY INTO LIFE FLOW

Environmental phase	Primary energy released in force	Secondary energies released with special force and intensity
0 Chaos	Fear	Anger, dread, primitive emotions, flight
I Punitive	Hostility	Retaliation, jealousy, guilt, need to punish and be punished moralizing, rebellion
II Autocratic	Power	Obedience, sense of responsibility, status, sense of authority, need for order
III Benevolent	Nurturing	Love, warmth, caring, parental feelings, obligation
IV Advisory	Perspective	Vision, sense of relationship, cognitive focus, scientific views
V Participative	Consensuality	Loyalty, collaboration, persuasion, need to influence, belonging, membership feelings
VI Emergent	Involvement in community	Feeling of freedom, cooperation, sharing, broader base of perception and emotionality
VII Organic	Intuition	Empathy, heightened awareness, impulsivity, spontaneity sense of selfness
VIII Holistic	Unconscious and foreconscious	Creativity, primitive fears, rootedness, expansion of self
IX Transcendental	Altered states	Egolessness, unity of self, freedom from needs, non-sensory sources
X Cosmic	Universal and nirvanic	Ecstasy, out-of-body perspective, freedom from wants, transcendence of self, entry into infinite

How Do I Create My Own Environment?

I do this in at least five different ways.

1. *I create my own internal environment, my mindbody.* Going far beyond the earlier and promising research on psychosomatic illness, holistic medicine is discovering awesome and mind-opening evidence that one's own self-determined attitudes (what I view as trust level) trigger and sustain the dramatically destructive ailments of our tension-ridden day: headaches, hypertension, heart disease, cancer and all manner of system imbalances. In a functional and very "real" sense, I give myself hypertension. I kill myself.

Clear evidence from biofeedback and from more clinical approaches demonstrates that supposedly "involuntary" and "unconscious" processes can be brought under voluntary and conscious control. I give myself my trust and my joy. I create my life. I create my own mindbodyspirit in ways that would once have been discussed only in the wildest fantasies of science fiction.

2. *I create my own reality through projection.* Psychoanalysts use the term projection to refer to the defensive tendency of ascribing to the external world repressed mental processes which are not recognized as being of personal origin. A person, for instance, might have a delusion of persecution which is created more by internal fears than by external dangers. If we assume that "reality" is out there, then our quest for health becomes a matter of our learning to see and to live with external reality — to become "reality centered". In this view projection is seen as a mindbody error, a defense, an autistic distortion, a process to be remedied.

I am coming to see my own and other's internal reality as more and more important, valid, self-created, and subject to self choice. I create my own reality. When I see the world *as I am* and not *as it is,* I am flavoring the world with my own being. I create my world. Looked at in this light, projection becomes a positive, awesome, and creative process. What we wish, believe, and trust comes true.

When we feel good the world seems filled with warm feelings, and when we feel bad the world becomes malevolent. A less familiar process is one in which the "trusting" person sees anew with magical clarity all the hitherto unseen nuances in the world around him or her. This immense clarity may come from jogging, drugs, a religious experience, meditation, an intense TORI experience, impending death, or any number of other transforming experiences. With learning, people can bring this clarity into ordinary life.

A less well known, but now frequently documented projective process of transforming the "external environment" is to take a new and trusting look at the world. Christ walking on water, psychic surgery, the firewalkers walking in high trust through white-hot coals, the wonders performed by Indians after the sweat-lodge experience, the feats of Castaneda's Don Juan — many are the mind-expanding illustrations of trusting: of this process of creating an environment, creating a new reality, projecting self, and changing the world in which we live.

My own personal experiences of leaving my body, being in ecstasy, seeing cosmic "allness" with transcending clarity, and creating a new personal tranquillity have completely changed my view of this reality-creating process and its practical use in everyday life.

3. *I create my own external environment by contagion.* I am a common carrier. My own authentic state, given full expression, is contagious. I infect others with my euphoria, depression, joy, hate, pessimism, exuberance.

I am a part of the environment that I live in — perhaps the part that exerts the greatest influence on my environment. My effective and functional environment is my perception of what goes on around me.

The contagion is usually a very subtle process. What is communicated, what spreads the contagion, is a way of being, a gestalt, a manner, a field of energy, a way of viewing life — all of which is caught in some way by the people around me.

4. *I create my own environment by making choices.* Each of us is likely to underestimate the range of choices that is available to us. Assumptions which are born of fear limit my range of viable options. Fears of failure, rejection, embarrassment, disapproval, or retaliation restrict my awareness of alternatives.

I can choose the environment I want. I can change the topic of conversation, leave a movie in the middle, turn off my TV, quit an unpleasant job, join a new church, get a divorce, get an abortion, fire an employee, not accept an invitation, ignore a phone message, move to another part of the country, move to a new country — the list is infinite. I can choose how to feel, choose to change my body processes, change my sex with an operation or a glandular treatment, take my own life, choose my own disease, move to a desert island — there are fewer and fewer areas of un-freedom, sacrosanct alternatives that one cannot consider, or sacred cows that cannot be milked.

Belief (trust) is a powerful factor. If I *believe* that my range of options is limited, *it is*. If I *believe* that my range of options is unlimited, *it is*.

5. *I create my own environment by deliberate design.* Each of us can make conscious, planned changes in the environment of the home, school, or factory in such a way as to have a major impact upon the quality of our lives. How TORI theory might guide this designing is the subject matter of most of this book.

Relation of the EQ Evolutionary Theory to Other Fields

This evolutionary-scale theory is designed to be applicable to all professional fields that deal with people and social systems. TORI theorists and practitioners are working on the specific implications for such fields as the following:

1. *Environmental engineering and design.* The design of environments to optimize flow, defense-reduction, transcendence, sensory enrichment, or altered states changes the priorities of architects, city planners, environmental sociologists, and others interested in environmental design.

2. *Family and home development.* The home becomes a fertile garden which is designed to enrich experiences, release impulses, expand consciousness — not a place for discipline, value training, and obedience.

3. *Community development.* The possibilities for a new look at community building are discussed throughout this book. It was in the TORI weekend "communities" where we first began to see some of the awesome possibilities for community living in all institutions.

4. *Therapy and counseling.* The process of evolution through the environmental scale *is* the process of therapy. Communities geared into environmental enrichment would not need therapy and counseling in the conventional sense.

5. *Recreation.* The whole process of physical education, sports, recreation, and leisure-time enrichment is being revolutionized by the new developments in environmental design. Life itself, in an enriched environment, *is* a continual re-creating, is play in its most significant sense, and contains the re-birthing elements supposedly sought in extra-curricular activities.

6. *Management and administration.* The ten-point scale is couched in terms of management issues and extrapolates from directions started by McGregor, Argyris, Likert, and others in

revolutionizing the concepts of management. Managers would work themselves out of a professional status, as would other specialists listed here. Every person becomes his or her own environmental specialist. My life is too important to turn it over to someone else.

7. *Education and learning.* Learning becomes a central living process and would require no separate institution devoted to it. Lifelong learning *is* the process of moving along the environmental scale in a continual transcendence.

8. *Training.* At the very least, conventional training would have a new focus. Much of training is now devoted to helping people adjust to EQ levels from which life is moving away. Training might be oriented toward environmental design. How much "training" is needed is something to look at with a critical eye.

9. *Organizational development.* The scale was developed as a way of conceptualizing an organizational climate. It has direct implication for the way consultants and managers view organizations. Some of these implications will be discussed in Chapter VIII.

10. *Moral development.* One traditional view of ethics is that it is the study of "that which matters". Our TORI studies suggest that persons become "ethical" as they discover and create love for self, begin to have the energy to celebrate life, and transcend the defenses and fears that arrest and block life. In this sense ethical and psychological growth are the same. Moral development is a process of movement on the environmental-quality scale. Environmental design is an approach to the problems of moral mal-development: the drug scene, juvenile delinquency, violence, crime, rape, for instance. In TORI theory, all of these moral problems come from defense mobilization and are defensive acts, that is, anti-growth actions. The overall solution to such problems is to change the whole environmental quality in the culture. EQ I, II, and III styles, designed in part to maintain law and order, actually produce the unethical and disorderly behaviors they are designed to abolish. One of the sad (and "unethical"?) anomalies of our time is to see some holistic health centers, growth centers, schools, churches, and community-development programs managed and dominated by EQ I, II, and III styles, reenforcing the same diseases they are designed to correct.

11. *The religious community.* Many religious communities and others are designed to produce integrity, wholeness, healing, and transcending perspective in members of the church or the community. A healing look at EQ incongruities in the religious environment is

proving to be useful in consulting with such communities. This is a very promising field. Much promising EQ change is happening in church and church-related institutions.

12. *Government.* Because of the overriding significance of the macro-environment, new developments and experiments in governing are of great interest to students of the environmental-design approach. The new African nations may be a source of new data because of their disequilibrium, instability, wide range of EQ level, and search for new life.

13. *Health and medicine.* The holistic health movement forces attention of some of the health professions upon Environments VI through X. The mindbodyspirit processes are unitary. Health is a holistic concept. Fragmentation and isolation produce ill health of the body, the mind, and the spirit. We are rediscovering some of the truths that the ancients seemed to know so well and that some of today's primitive societies have retained!

14. *Personal growth.* The EQ scale has been developed as a way of integrating personal and organizational effectiveness. The TORI theorist is interested in this relationship.

15. *Group development.* Chapter VII deals with this field and the application of the EQ scale to small-group life.

16. *Volunteer work.* At worst the volunteers do what the professionals do, only less well. At best, the emerging field of volunteerism can help the culture move up the EQ scale. Too often encouraged as a natural outgrowth of Environment-III management style, volunteers, freed from the monetary aspects of extrinsic reward systems, are more open to post-V environments and the intrinsically-rewarded life. This is a very promising transitional field.

17. *Gerontology and retirement.* Retirement and the onset of "old age" can be viewed as a release from constraints, a time of new vision and freedom, a move into transcendence. The post-bondage years can release new energies for new living. Old age and death have no terrors for persons living in Environments VIII, IX and X. They are commencement years and years of entry into enriched living. If the new gospel of transcendence has any message of significance for our age-bound culture, it certainly includes this message to those approaching the transcending process of death.

18. *The alternative culture.* The strength of the alternative schools, churches, and families indicates readiness for the concept of environmental design. Part of the message is that Environments I-V

are unfulfilling, stagnating, and decreasingly relevant to modern life. Environments VI-X are the wave of the future, the source of new hope. This is a new frontier.

19. *Art, science, manufacturing, and creativity-related fields of life.* Two elements of quality performance in art, science, and industry are intrinsic motivation (the "perspiration" and courage part) and creativity (the "inspiration" and vision part). Each element is a direct function of trust as we have defined it. Each element thrives best in Environments VI through X. The heavy emphasis on discipline, order, and structure in Environments I through V in art, science and manufacturing creates a climate that constrains the development of intrinsic motivations and creativity, of courage and vision.

The order of quality in the EQ scale is the same for each of the fields discussed above. The same environment that produces high personal-growth rates produces creativity, productivity, and vitality.

In the following chapter, I will discuss the nature of TORI theory as an instrument for use by practitioners in the above fields.

Chapter 4

Vision:
Theory As a Guide to Seeing

A practical theory is powerful. When I create my own theory, it provides me with vision and perspective. Trust Level theory is especially powerful in helping me into this expansion process, because vision is a direct function of trust.

When I was teaching graduate students in psychology, the two courses I enjoyed teaching most were Theory Construction and History of Psychological Theory. True to the mainstream of that day, I was firmly convinced of the soundness of several assumptions that then seemed to be irreproachable. Among these assumptions were the following three:

1. That the physical science model was unquestionably the one to follow;

2. That "scientific" (e.g., physics and "engineering", e.g., mechanical engineering) theories and principles were of different orders of significance, and there was no question as to which was of the higher order;

3. That ontological validity was the primary criterion of quality in a theory.

There were several other assumptions that most of us made, but it is on these three assumptions that I wish to focus in introducing the content of this chapter.

During some twenty years of university teaching I made several attempts to construct theories of my own. During this process I abandoned a number of earlier assumptions, including the above three. My current assumptions go something like this:

VISION

*A theory expands my vision
and guides my discovering processes.*

1. That something quite different from a physics model is necessary in constructing an adequate theory of behavior and experience. Psychological events may differ from physical events in at least three significant ways. Psychological events are non-dichotomous; they are telic in nature, and if not telic they are at least self-determining; and they have an intrinsic quality not predictable from or determined by the environment. I understand from some of my physics friends that in the last decade a "new" physics is aborning that questions some of the same assumptions that I questioned;

2. That in psychology and in the behavioral sciences generally, a "basic" theory and an engineering theory are the same thing. All effective theory is a tri-partite affair: (a) hypothesis construction, (b) data collection, and (c) engineering test. These three processes continually interact with each other as theory is refined and developed;

3. That the most effective theory provides an instrumental function, a guiding function. *This* is the primary criterion of the quality of a theory, not ontological validity.

Trust Level (TORI) theory, as described in this book, was constructed over the years as an effort to meet my primary criteria of a satisfactory psychological theory. I will make thirteen statements about TORI theory, which is my best effort to match the criteria that I believe are most critical. Each of these statements implies an informal and "practical" criterion of the quality of a theory.

1. TORI theory is designed for application.

It is an applied theory, an "engineering" theory, designed for application to all human systems. The level of analysis, behavior, and experience is the level that is optimal for the user, the person who works with persons and human systems at that level. It is written in the language of the user. The number of variables are such as to be suited to any user. The basic four (TORI) variables are appropriately simple or complex for the practitioner to "keep in mind" without machine analysis or mnemonic aids.

The theory is suited for the user with no formal training. The person can use the theory unilaterally, without others having to know the theory or subscribe to it. The basic variables are in *all* life. It is also a whole-life theory which can be applied to all of the situations that any user faces.

The theory applies equally to the gut, the heart, and the mind of the person. When we understand this fully and apply the theory, it has integrative and wholizing properties.

The criteria overlap and each, in some ways, is a partial re-statement of the other. That is, if the theory meets any one of the subsequently following twelve criteria, it also meets the applicability criterion. The following discussions are relevant to this section as well.

2.   **TORI theory is an instrument for inquiry.**

Trust Level theory is an instrument, a tool, that serves as a general *guide to inquiry* and discovery.

It is a guide to *perception and diagnosis,* enabling the user to focus on the factors, among the multitude that operate in all human situations, that matter, that are worth examining, that contribute most to the variance, that deserve attention. Perception is always a selective process. The theory provides an initial screening. There is, of course, some limitation to this process. Selective focus means that we leave out some parts of the perceptual field.

It is a guide to *thinking and problem solving,* to analysis of the total field of reality as the theorist/practitioner sees it.

It is a guide to *action and programming,* providing a map with marked paths to effective action. It aids in the making of choices, in the planning of action steps, or in the preparing of a long-range program of social action.

A high-quality theory is, of course, not a static process; it does not lock-step the viewer, problem-solver, or actor into a program. The person using Trust Level theory is always an experimenter, an inquirer, a searcher. The theory is an aid in the search.

True inquiry is, in itself, an act of trust and faith: Trust that the universe does have some stabilities that are determinable and that personal inquiry will be effective in some significant way; confidence in the nature and validity of experience; and trust that keeps the energy high and the quest an adventure rather than a burden.

Inquiry is also, of course, a process of doubting, of caution, of safeguards, of methodological rigor, and of skepticism. It is the ebb and flow of caution and of courage that make inquiry complex and exciting.

3.   Trust Level theory is a viewpoint, a life style.

It suggests a behavioral rather than a primarily ontological option. It provides live options for what a person does rather than options regarding the nature of reality.

It is a way of looking at a problem, rather than a formula for its solution. It is a *viewpoint, rather than a prescription.* To the mother it suggests how she might look at the child rather than giving her a rule to apply to the child's behavior. For the worker and his or her boss, it suggests a relationship that might be effective, rather than a formula for the interaction. To the teacher it suggests how he or she might go about solving problems together with the pupils rather than prescribing what the teacher or pupil should do in each situation.

There are advantages to a practical theory which specifies rules for supervision, parenting, discipline, value-clarification, motivating people, or winning friends. Such theories do "tell me what to do on Monday morning" in the classroom or do give me a specific rule or prescription for each class of problem that I may meet. The inexperienced supervisor, parent, or teacher is thus reassured. Such rules are especially useful in environments I, II, and III, but become less useful as environmental quality increases. A prescriptive theory and its related techniques are useful only where fear is high and the environment primitive. As life becomes more flowing, trusting, open, self-determining, spontaneous, and rises to higher levels of being, prescriptive theories become less useful. And as life moves into higher levels of awareness and flow, we seek a theory free of prescriptions.

In the lower-level environments, persons find security in rules, in environmental consistency, in law and order, in strong leadership, in a sense of being in control, and in the certainty that rewards and punishments will follow rationally and in fair sequence on all actions that respond to or violate the rules that we have agreed upon or that we have been given.

In more trusting levels of environment, persons find security in an internal state of self-acceptance, in withness and mutuality, in the excitement of challenge, and in transcending states. Rules, guide-books, prescriptions, and interpersonal programming do not create the unexpected, the emergent, creative interdependence, and other spontaneous processes.

4.   **TORI theory is an evolving, continually-changing statement.**
The theory is a statement about and a description of life processes. It is experimental and empirical; it is always being tested. *Change* is the basic nature of living, of interaction, of process, and of being. Trusting is a catalytic force that evolves with life processes. It is not possible to confine the process within any "operational" definition that is adequate.

The theory evolves with the person who creates it for himself or herself and is a function of the evolution of the theorist, of the environment in which he or she lives, and of the situational factors of the very moment in which the theory is applied.

The person who uses TORI theory is an experimenter, continually improving in understanding and ability to test the theory itself. The theorist is continually attempting to find out what the theorist-as-person, or the theorist-as-father, or the theorist-as-manager does in real-life situations. Thus, as I discover and create my own theory, I discover and create my own life. My theory therefore becomes a statement of how I view life at the moment, how I view myself, and how I will relate to the life-process.

5.   **TORI theory is personal.**
All theory, in some sense, comes out of each person's experience in arriving at the theory. This is explicitly true in the case of TORI theory. Each person who creates/uses the TORI theory creates an idiosyncratic statement that comes out of his or her highest integration of the life experience. Naturally, a theory designed for use changes in use. Because it is always owned by the user, it is always shaped by the user. Therefore, *reality itself* is continually created by the user, and because the theory applies to the process-reality that is created in interaction, it is as live and quivering as life itself. As life changes, the theory changes.

Start with the single, guiding assumption that trusting is the central, catalytic process that infuses, colors, determines, modifies, and guides all the other life-processes. *My own life process,* then, becomes a lifelong quest to discover what trust means to me, what my trusting does to me, how it shapes my environmental state, how it determines my interactions with others and with nature — how, in short, it guides my life. I am my own single authority in this process, and no one else can tell me how this happens for me.

My own theory is my own working out of this life issue. I can state it in whatever words I need to use to convey its meaning to myself and to others. Mainly, my theory *resides in* my mindbody. It is what my mindbody does in synergizing my total system: How I see things, how I feel about life, what assumptions I make about experience, the choices I make, the integration I make of all my processes.

The application of the theory can be as cognitive, planned, deliberate, articulated, worded, or rational as I wish to make it. My experimentation can be conscious: I can make deliberate attempts to show myself to others, to tell people I am angry when I feel it, to make a deliberate choice and act on it, to experiment with my life. Such conscious efforts to be more trusting usually take the form of a variety of experimental efforts to be more personal, more open, more self-determining, and more *with* others. I can plan my program, check with others as to how they see me, search inside for my own reactions, assess my feelings about the process, persist in the effort to determine my own preferred level of openness, say, or my own manner of clarifying my wants.

On the other hand, application of the theory can be as spontaneous, unplanned, impulsive, free-form, non-conscious, unverbalized, or irrational as I wish to make it. I can let my body take over and let myself be: Go with the flow. Discover my impulses. Let the world happen. Trust that I will find my best life, my most trusting state, my deepest joy. Trust the process. My own process. Life's process.

Or I can be anywhere in between these extremes. I can invent or create my own mode of search, quest, or experimentation, for I am in charge. I am the theorist and the user.

Because *"the* TORI theory" has not been invented yet, there is no authority to tell us what it is *really* like to be trusting. Each of us is on his or her own. *I* am the probe instrument in this life experiment. I am the experimenter. I am the guinea pig. I am the data. I make the interpretations and draw the conclusions — except that there are never any conclusions.

For me, Jack, the chapter writer and the spokesman-for-the-moment for TORI theorists/users, this realization of the aloneness and the centrality of my own process and being is, at once, deeply frightening, full of dread, but also even more deeply reassuring, affirming, full of strength, full of awareness of my potential, and courage-giving.

While, *in its essence,* this is a quest I make alone, it can also be as interdependent as each of us decides to make it. Trusting means that all persons are available to me if I can learn how to contact them; that all wisdom is available to me if I can learn how to see it; that all help is there for me if I can learn how to accept it; that all love is there for me if I can be in it. I am free to make life a community. So theory construction can be, in some real sense, a communal process.

For most of us there are rhythms in our manner of searching for and creating our theory. All living is good. Sometimes it is good to reflect, to verbalize, to reason. Sometimes it is good to get out of our heads and be *in* the experience, into our trusting and into our fearing. Sometimes it is good to be outside of ourselves and watch ourselves doing the reasoning and doing the being. Sometimes it is good to be in control, sometimes out of control; to be sane at some moments, crazy at others; deeply in dread or deeply in ecstasy. It is the transcending of fearing and the experience of trusting that bring clarity and vision and enable us to *see* the theory. Trusting, the central process, gives us (a) the vision, clarity, and illumination, and (b) the courage to see the vision whole. Vision and courage are the two central components of trusting.

It is possible and useful to see the "theory" as alternatively passive and active. That is, I create the theory, but, also, the theory then creates me. It takes care of me, nourishes me, sustains me in moments of my doubt, when fear takes over. If I create the theory well enough, it resides in me to create me and care for me. In some sense I *am* my theory, and my theory *is* me. At moments of internal segmentation, when fear takes over, I can experience my theory as a kind of reified friend that comes to my aid.

This is especially true at times when I reach out in trust and meet a seemingly untrustworthy person. I trust someone, and they let me down. I am being open, and someone sees my vulnerability and uses it against me. I reach out in what I experience as love and receive in return what I experience as unjustified hate. When life seems to let me down, then my "theory", if it is strong and durable enough, if it is internalized enough, comes to my aid, putting the event or events into perspective. The theory helps me, for instance, to see that the response of the other person may not have been to my trusting at all, but to what was seen as my defensive, fearful state. I needn't conclude that trusting doesn't "work"; my particular trusting action didn't, that one time, create what I hoped for.

The structure and strength of my personal theory are functions of how I handle the fearing/trusting events of my life.

6. Trust Level theory is a unique, idiosyncratic statement.

Each person is unique. Each pair and relationship is unique. Each community is unique. As I become more trusting, this uniqueness becomes more distinct and more significant. Trusted, the person and the event take on their special qualities. Trusted, both the person and the relationship become unique.

So it is with TORI theory, which is the creation of the user. I mean this in more than a platitudinous sense. As I see persons celebrate their uniqueness, I see them grow, become stronger, more aware of their distinctive becoming, less defensive, less needing to enter battle with the world. A common parlor game among theorists, especially neo-theorists, is to put the other person's theory down by putting it into a convenient category. "Isn't what you are saying simply Platonic idealism?" Or Reichian armorizing? Or Christianity? Or Zen? Or phenomenology? Categorizing a theory, like classifying a person, is to dimish it.

Instead, each TORI user is to view his or her statement of personal theory as idiosyncratic. My theory is my peculiar, self-produced view of the world; it is *my* articulation of *my* experience. It is *not* classifiable, and any attempt at classification is to be resisted.

There is, of course, overlap in the way people who seek the trusting life experience the world and describe it. There are common elements in the experiences of TORI theorists. As a result, there is a growing body of common assumptions, common postulatory statements, shared hypotheses about trust-induction and trust-reduction, and common hunches about what works and what doesn't. But there are no categories — only commonalities.

It is useful to look at this common body of knowledge/guess/fantasy/ belief as idiosyncratic — as a special way of experiencing the world, of diagnosing, of problem solving, and of acting from a special viewpoint and using a unique set of attitudes, central variables, and assumptions. My view is that every theory of the life process is "true" (*i.e.,* is a valid way of looking at the world); each is useful for selected purposes and makes a special contribution to the field; each moves forward our general understanding of behavior, experience, and social systems. From the standpoint of the practitioner, as well as that of the theorist, the critical issue is not whether or not the theory is valid. The critical issue is: How useful is the theory for my purposes?

Each theory has been formulated by persons whose experiences grew out of a unique setting. The theory is likely to be most useful in settings similar to those from which it was derived, with the special phenomena that were under study by the theorist and in the cultural context out of which the theorist and the theory grew. Each theorist/practitioner is free to try the theory/model in his or her life situations and to judge for himself or herself which viewpoint is most useful, using the criteria that he or she selects.

I believe that, appropriately, the most significant factor in this selection is the matching or compatibility between (1) the central dynamic in the theory, and (2) the central dynamic in the user. This matching or compatibility need not be a simple relationship. In the case of TORI theory, for instance, those who use it with greatest effectiveness are those who are especially attuned to the significance of the trust/fear polarity in life. The user may have high fears, high trusts, special experiences in the clinic or in the field or in the family; the user may bear the traumatic effects of sustained or acute fear or enjoy the ameliorative effect of high trust; and there are always internal dynamics which create a fit between theory and user.

However personal and subjective the theorist/user may feel about his or her theory, each theorist/user is to some degree an eclectic, and naturally so. Each manager, therapist, or parent, at the point of deciding, intervening, or acting, uses whatever mindbody wisdom is available then and there. TORI theory is not an exclusive response — it is a potentially useful adjunct to any other theory, and any other theory can be used as an adjunct to TORI theory.

There are some common elements crossing all theories. As we gather more theory-related data, this commonality presumably will grow. For instance, the primary dynamic in Freudian analysis, in primal therapy, and in TORI theory is *fear*. The theories differ in (a) hypotheses about ways that fear is manifested and translated into other mind-body processes, and (b) derivations in terms of optimal inductions for fear-reduction. Theories differ in terms of relative emphasis placed upon the significance of fear-reduction (trust formation) as a primary factor in personal and system effectiveness. TORI theory places primary importance upon the four processes that mediate and sustain fear: (a) depersonalization and role-taking;

(b) masking and strategizing, and especially covert strategizing; (c) oughting, persuading, and manipulating; and (d) controlling and hierarchizing. TORI theory, then, would differ significantly from theories that directly or indirectly reinforce these "defending processes". Theoretical approaches illustrating this point would be: (a) procedures in psychodrama and Transactional Analysis that reinforce role behavior; (b) all theories that have strong external interventions (strategizing); (c) a wide variety of socio-economic and psychodynamic theories that imply strong programs of persuasion, parenting, and influencing; and (d) therapeutic and political theories that use control as a central process.

The degree to which an eclectic user/theorist who is using TORI theory in connection with other theories uses *role behavior* (decides to act like a manager, for instance), *strategy (e.g.,* tries to find ways to make the patient more assertive), *persuasion (e.g.,* as a consultant, tries to devise ways of making the worker more loyal or productive), and *control (e.g.,* sets boundaries for the child or the patient), depends upon a number of factors. Because in natural life all persons are to some degree fearing/defending, all of us have some component of intentional and/or unconscious elements of the above four processes in our motivations or behaviors in most situations. Therefore, someone intending to apply TORI theory has several issues to confront: How do I learn to be more trusting, less defensive, and thus have fewer defending (fear-inductive) processes to get in my way when I'm managing, parenting, or teaching? How much role-, strategy-, persuasion-, and control-oriented action do I intentionally build into life situations for which I have some formal responsibility? How important do I judge fear/trust to be, relative to other factors, in the situations in which I work and live as a professional or as a person? I might, for instance, *assume* that I truly believe that TORI theory is correct in making trust the primary variable, but unconsciously or quasi-consciously I *really* believe that power, say, is the significant factor.

7.   TORI theory is a unitary, general theory.

TORI theory is constructed to be relevant and directly applicable to *all* living systems. It is presumably equally relevant to *any* situation that a person enters. Internalizing the theory makes it possible for a person to be the "same" person in all situations, even though there might be role expectations that differ. There need not be a special theory for recreation, administration, therapy, teaching, advertising, rehabilitation, government, international relations, personal growth, parenting, being a minister, being a friend, or being a person.

If this theory is effective, one need not learn strategies appropriate to the role or modify one's behavior to fit other's expectations. One need not learn professional management techniques designed to accomplish professional goals or lead a situational, segmented life that is adjusted to the immediate circumstance, job, position, or culture. This is not to say, in any sense, that it is easy to learn such a theory-based life; but once learned, it is practical, health-producing, effective, and responsible to achieve and live such a life. It is possible to start learning *here, now,* in this culture, in whatever job one has.

It is then possible to (a) *be who I am,* in a unique, congruent, and uncluttered way, (b) *show who I am,* including all of the significant nuances of me, (c) *do what I* deeply *want* to do, making the choices and following the impulses that are most intrinsically me, and (d) *be with* other people in ways that are meaningful to me and to those I am with.

In practice, of course, all of the above happens in degree. What is significant is that persons, after some experience with living the theory in some depth, do report a high degree of effectiveness in applying the theory in a wide range of environments and professional jobs. Some people, after understanding the theory and having a confirming experience, make radical changes in life style. Others make what seem to be minor changes in attitude or behavior but report major changes in effectiveness in what they do and increased personal satisfaction in doing it.

Of great potential significance in determining the practical and immediate effectiveness of the theory is a three-year program which began in the fall of 1977. Two groups of 32 persons, representing a wide variety of professions and a number of different geographical areas in the United States and Canada, one meeting in the Central area and one meeting on the West Coast, will make three-year tests of the applicability of TORI theory. Each of the 64 professionals is planning a program in his or her organization or in a client organization to apply the theory or some major aspect of the theory. Each group of 32 will meet intermittently during the three years for a total of 31 days a year, when the programs will be planned, evaluated, and compared. In most instances, research on effectiveness will be built into the programs. Some programs will be conducted as part of the requirements for completing a doctoral dissertation. Two additional groups of similar size will begin in the summer of 1978.

From these multiple tests, we will learn much about the *general* applicability of the theory. Lorraine and I will participate in all four of these groups, as well as with the group adjunct professionals who will work with the testing groups to create modifications, changes, and additions to the general body of TORI theory.

Because of the highly personal nature of the theory, what happens to *each* of the participants in terms of personal growth and professional competence will be of central interest. The evolution of each of the four community groups of 32 through the environmental changes discussed in Chapter III will also be of critical significance. Plans are being made to fully document and describe both the personal and the community changes, and some will be reported in book form.

8.   TORI theory is congruent in structure, process, and content.

The *structure* or form of some theories is tightly ordered, formal, systematic, and logic-tight. That is, the *relationships among the statements* that make up the full statement of the theory are rigorous. The postulates and theorems of classical geometry are logic-tight. The statements in Hull's mathematico-deductive theory of rote learning are comparably rational and formal.

The *content* or substance of some theories is similarly formal and logic-tight. Within a given statement of a proposition, law, or hypothesis, the concepts are defined in terms of rigorous operations, measurable on equal-interval scales, coded in such a way as to be susceptible with relative ease to computer operations and refined to eliminate the cloudy and fuzzy edges.

The *processes* of some theories are so conceived that the progressive changes are susceptible to unitizing, in a procedure similar to calculus or at least to the "just noticeable differences" of Fechner, whose units were conceived as a phenomenological calculus. Lewin and others made compelling analyses of behavioral and experiential "process" in terms of topological space, a mathematical treatment directed toward achieving a closer approximation of the apparent non-precision of mental events.

Experience over the years has convinced me that it is illusory to try to build a behavioral and experiential system that is rational, mathematical, rigorous, and logic-tight in structure, content, and process. The search for such models is nevertheless to be encouraged. The advantages for prediction and control are obvious. However, I assume that the basic nature of experience and behavior is that it is flowing, spontaneous, emergent, fuzzy-edged, non-logical and amorphous. I see experience more as a cloud or a drop of water than a computer or a telephone switchboard, no matter how sophisticated the rational model becomes.

The structure, content, and process of TORI theory are purposefully free-flowing, cloud-like, emergent, non-rational, and fuzzy-edged. *Trust,* the major construct, is a hypothetical construct that is assumed to be general in nature, a characteristic of all personal and social systems, and related in a significant way to all experience and behavior. Any specific operational definition that I have tried to make falls short of being satisfactory for more than limited purposes.

It is possible, of course, to make a number of statements about the relationships between and among major constructs in the general system, and to make them in such a way that they are susceptible to empirical test in fairly rigorous terms and thus to use a wide range of data from existent research in the human sciences. A high level of confidence in some statements results. For example: persuasion leads to resistance; covert strategy leads to circumventive behavior; behavior that is perceived as distrusting leads to acceleration of fear and distrust, *etc.* Each of these statements is an overgeneralization. Each lacks precision and is too global to subject to rigorous test. Those who aspire to a postulate-theorem-like structure of theory would be uncomfortable with all of them.

Most "knowledge" in the behavioral sciences is in this fuzzy form. Practitioners can probably use fuzzy "theory" to advantage and improve the effectiveness of management, therapy, and teaching by the skilled use of such theory. Whether such fuzzy theory is a better basis for practitioner performance than wisdom gained from reading great literature or having profound or diverse experience is still, for me, a moot question. My confidence (trust) that such theory is very useful and that it can be made considerably more useful is such that I am devoting my life to constructing such theory.

In a significant sense, *the content of TORI theory is in the process.* What is done is less significant than how it is done. The process *is* the message. A trusting person communicates trust with body language, by the style of relating, the vibrations that are given off, the penumbral coloring, the shadow as well as, or perhaps more than, the substance. This is why it is difficult to learn TORI theory from a book, or even from a demonstration. Learning what my fears and my trusts do to me, how I learn to communicate my being rather than my role, and how I learn to show who and what I am, with all my shadows — all these learnings come from the heat of experience and love and interaction in community. These learnings are enriched by reading, by articulating theory, and by trying things out, but the core of the learning is and comes from gut experience.

So for TORI theory the distinctions among structure, content, and process are shadowy. Congruence is at the heart of the problem.

We are all familiar with incongruity of theory and practice. I recently attended a conference on holistic health in which the verbal message (the content) went on for hours with Environment VII, VIII, IX, and even X words and principles, but the procedural and relationship messages (the process and structure) were replete with Environment II, III, and IV procedures and structures. The medium was a series of lectures; the "management" of the conference was formal, structured, authoritarian, hierarchical, and benevolent. One of the papers presented in detail the techniques that would be used to teach people how to be holistic!

It is one thing for us to have some kind of high congruity in the statements, form, and even the process of the theory. It is another thing for us to achieve and to create congruity in the environments we create for ourselves.

We will not create a new and TORI-like world fit for humans through the use of non-human and non-TORI methods and processes. Testing produces the cheating. Spanking produces the delinquent child. Structuring produces unflowing people. The police state produces criminals. Therapy sometimes produces people that need to give or receive therapy. Punishing produces a system that breeds the need for more punishment. Defensive and fear-bred methods and governance produce defensive and fearful people.

The meaning of life is in the process, not in the product. A product-oriented culture will not likely produce a process-oriented people. Learning, growing, being, feeling, withing, doing, showing — all are processes. Each process rewards itself. None requires a product. None requires a reward. None requires a justification. In each case the reward and the meaning and the value are intrinsic, are in the doing, *are in the process.* The process *is* the content. The structure contains the process and *is* the message.

9. Trust Level theory is simple.

Trust Level theory aims at achieving simplicity. Nature is simple. Words, interpretations, theories, and statements tend to be complex. Complexity leads away from the natural, whole life and its processes.

Parsimony has a distinguished place in the history of good theory construction. The TORI theorist and practitioner makes an effort to eliminate all unnecessary complexity: to be stingy with assumptions, the number of concepts, the structure of the basic statement of the theory, the number of variables in the overall system, the number of variables used in diagnosis and problem-solving — all aspects of the process. What is complex about it is the statement that I have just made about simplicity!

Much of the imputed complexity used in describing behavior and experience comes from defensive processes. That is, imputing complexity is a defensive act. Scholars and philosophers increase the complexity of descriptive statements about behavior and experience in part as an effort to prove competence, cover ignorance, demonstrate articulatory powers, and win in competitive struggles with others who are competing in the word- and concept-making arena.

I believe that much of the complexity comes from unnecessary differentiation of concepts. It is possible to make progressively more precise and focused differentiations among any set of concepts or constructs. For example, it is possible to classify defense mechanisms or defensive behaviors into a seemingly overwhelming number of categories. It is also possible to classify interventions or treatments used to reduce defensiveness to an equally overwhelming number of categories. It then becomes possible to match specific treatments to specific defenses and come up with a bewildering array of matchings. One recent book on therapy suggests that the road to progress in therapy is to learn to match treatments to illnesses or defensive modes, and when we have done this we will have taken the major step in reducing mental illness! Another solution at an opposite extreme is to hypothesize that there is only one "kind" of defense that matters (*i.e.,* all defensive mechanisms are responses to internal fear states), and that one basic genre of treatment (*e.g.,* primal scream methodology; placing in an environment of optimal trust, *etc.),* or perhaps a basic few treatments will be effective or optimally effective in reducing fears underlying the defenses. Because differentiation is an easy and seductive process, and because we have so few valid data on relationships between precise treatments and precise defenses, it is possible and tempting to build a vast body of mini-theories, all of which have some evidence, some logic, or some attractiveness, about these matchings.

I prefer to take the option of simplification which, at the recognized risk of oversimplification, predisposes a search for an elegantly simple structure, the basic and elemental processes that underly the overdifferentiation.

As I have indicated earlier, there is another reason for seeking simplicity. I am searching for a theory that can be used by anyone in any situation; that can guide the user in any choice; that can be internalized, understood, and built into the mindbody. This theory will be one that allows me to act on the theory without machines for data processing, without mnemonic aids, without consultants or guides at my elbow, without notes or manuals to refer to, without complex skills that require professionalization or para-professionalization, without an esoteric language necessary for understanding or communication, without complex alternatives or variables that require complex intrapersonal data processing, without rules that risk misapplication or mechanization, and without complexity of structure.

This is certainly not to imply that simplicity, in and of itself, is valid. I would like to avoid *unnecessary* complexity. Given an alternative between two equally likely choices in theory construction, I would prefer to take the simpler of two alternatives.

One further point. We have been struggling to ferret out concepts and constructs that are redundant, that add nothing to simpler concepts which describe the behavior or the experience, that create pseudo-problems, or that predispose to reification. We are exploring doing without such redundant concepts, as well as those which arise out of misconceptions about behavior and experience. We believe we can eventually demonstrate that leadership, reward, discipline, value, supervision, role, responsibility, and authority are superfluous and, in fact, counter-productive.

10.   TORI theory has a strong experiential base.

The process of trusting one's own experience is at the heart of TORI theory. For a number of reasons, perhaps largely because behavior is more susceptible to inter-observer reliability tests than is experience, behavior has come to be trusted in modern psychology more than experience. Behaviorism has a firmer and more respectable base footing in "scientific" psychology than does phenomenology, awareness, or experience.

On the other hand, experience is surely closer to *me as person,* to trust as a construct, and to the events that I am trying to understand, predict, and join others in changing, than is behavior. Although it is possible to study trust, the self, and the social system through observable behavior, it is somehow less satisfying. It is trust, *as an experience,* that interests me.

Of the six ways set forth in Chapter III in which I chose to define the high-quality environment, five are clearly experiential constructs, though several could be defined in terms of observable behaviors. It is, of course, *possible* to describe any of the criteria in behavioral terms. The theory applies to *both* behavior and experience.

One of the contributions that psychology has made to modern life is to make us aware of the errors in, and limitations of, experience. Several generations have arrived at an increased distrust of the reliability of one's own perceptions, cognitions, motives, sensations, and inner states. Systematic inter-observer checking seems to be necessary in order to rule out the vagaries of our own internal processes. Doubt, skepticism, a healthy look askance — all are in order when one tries to determine what is real, reliable, and to be trusted. All this leads to a generalized doubt about one's own internal states — values, motives, abilities, feelings, viewpoints, sensations. It is easy to see how this atmosphere of seemingly necessary doubt provides a base of shifting sands for the TORI processes. How do I know who I am? If so much of me is unconscious, especially the most significant part, and perhaps the most *real* part, and if my perceptions and introspections can't be trusted, then whom do I turn to in my attempt to discover who I am? If I'm not sure who I am, then how do I show myself to others? Is what I seem to want what I *really* want, or are my surface wants a distortion of, even a reversal of my *real* inner wants? If, as the analysts seem to tell us, the very intensity of my perceived want proves that my inner need is just the reverse of what it seems, then where is my enduringness in all this? Where do *I* reside?

How am I, in a world brought up to distrust, with reason, the inner world of experience, to discover a strong sense of inner worth? How am I to find a faith in my own values, beliefs, and perceptions? — the strength to stake my life on my inner convictions? — a confidence that my inner feelings are genuine and worth listening to and honoring? — and a willingness to expose this inner life impulsively and without the fear-born masks of caution? How do I feel good about something I can't trust?

One of the most promising aspects of the new revolution is the centrality of the inner states. We are returning to the honoring of consciousness and sensation. Even the conservative establishment in the behavioral sciences is looking anew at *inner states,* the world of experience: altered states of consciousness, dreams, hypnotic states, drug-induced fantasy and experience, control by the will of body states and processes, hallucinatory activity, the religious experience, psychic states, cosmic and mystical states, and all manner of non-behavioral processes.

Out of all of this will come the possibility of a growing sense of trust, with a more experiential base, growing out of a wider perspective. This newer and deeper level of trust will be a firmer base than the childlike, pre-experience naivete that is potentially vulnerable to the inevitable disappointments of diverse experience. Trust that persists, fresh and whole, through the awareness of evil and error is a firm base for an enriched life. Such trust allows one to focus one's energy on the living processes rather than on the defending processes.

A full theory of human life must be based firmly on both experience and behavior.

11. Trust Level theory relates to the flow of living.

The essence of living, both experience and behavior, seems to be that *it flows.* The bodymind that functions best seems to be one that is into the flow, the continual movement of energy, the bioenergetic systems, the internal symphony of flowing processes. The mindbody is a glorious process. It is a oneness in mind, body, and spirit. It enters into synchronic and harmonious flow with other living organisms in the environment.

Some flow models seems to fit human systems best. The river of life, the stream of consciousness, the ebb and flow of feeling, the rhythms of the body. The experiences of sailing, skating, dancing, and flying seem to strike a kind of polyphony with the inner rhythms of the spirit and physical body. The primitive perceptual processes seem to fill in the voids, round off the edges of experience, and give us a world that is experientially a gestalt, made whole by the interactions between the person and the world outside the skin. The more we find out about the nervous system, the more it seems to act in flow, more like a field of energy than a computer network.

The TORI discovering processes happen, emerge, flow, and are most functional and healthy when they are unforced, when they arise out of the field of interaction between the person and the world, and when energy flows. Being, showing, becoming, and interbeing are *processes.*

Defending is stopping the flow. Putting up roadblocks. Pushing the river.

There is something about socialization and institutionalization which gets people out of the flow. People, when put in role, want to *do* something: manage, control, justify their pay or their role. I have a vivid memory of an administrative meeting at Brigham Young University when I was teaching there in the 'forties. The new part of the campus was being built on a beautiful, flowing hill. The school planners had arranged a number of concrete sidewalks in different patterns on the campus part of the hill. Soon the administration noticed that several worn trails were developing on the campus, on which students would walk in the directions they had decided to go. As a faculty member of a committee which was to solve this and other similar problems, I was party to a discussion on what we should do about these worn patterns on the lawns, and what we should do about the student violators who disobeyed the "keep off the lawn" signs. After several suggestions as to how we might stop such behavior (defend against the flow), President Harris, a man who was wise and non-defensive, suggested: "Why not simply build sidewalks over the worn patterns on the lawns?". This stopped the violations (years later I was to write about the principle that regulations produced the criminals) and speeded up the traffic between classes. Certainly not accidentally, the new sidewalk patterns were very graceful and pleasing to the eye. I am very much aware of what I have learned from experiencing trusting people like Franklin Harris, who knew very little "psychology" but knew a lot about people and about institutions. Harris was an early advocate of reducing over-management, over-regulation, over-organization, and other fear-induced accoutrements of institutional life.

There are many facets to the process of going with the flow. My ocean-playing and wave-knowing friends tell me that the surest way to drown in rip tides and other tricky patterns in the flow of the water is to fight the flow and to defend yourself against it. Going with the flow is the way to live in the flow of the water and the flow of life. As Lao Tzu said, soft conquers hard. That yielding conquers resistance, that the living process outlasts the defending process, are principles of flow.

For many years I have worked with large gatherings of from a few hundred to several thousand in number. I remember once, early on, working with a group of teen-agers, about eleven-hundred of them in an eight-day conference in Minnesota. The first time I stood up to work/play with the group, I noticed they were very restless — I could sense the pent-up animal energy. I was frightened. Petrified is perhaps a more accurate word. Following the Harris principle, I tried to tune in to what they seemed to want to do and then suggested that they do it: they translated their restlessness and animal energy into a number of quick movements that included jumping and shouting.

I had learned before then and have learned several times since that I can get a group to do almost anything provided that I don't try to get it to do what it doesn't want to do. Any group member who wants to "lead" or initiate in an effective way can tune in to what is going on in the group at a deep, organic level, translate this "want" into an activity, and suggest it. This is the only really significant service that "leadership" can provide to a group, community, or nation. But anyone who is really *tuned in to the flow,* in the community and in the self, can be very effective in channeling energy and action.

Living in the flow does not mean that I am powerless and helpless, tossed like a stick of wood on the surface of a torrent and at the mercy of accidental dangers. Deeply aware of the flow in all of us, including myself, I can join the central and organic movement that is happening. *I am a part of the community and of the flow.* If I can sense something of what we all want, I can make creative suggestions that define, create, and focus the flow. I needn't create *unnecessary* conflict. If I define my power as my ability to be me, to show me, to do what I want, and to join others in the flow, then I am always powerful. I am as powerful as my being. The expression of power is then the same as my expression of the four discovering TORI processes. "Power" then becomes an unnecessary concept, adding nothing to what is already being said in talking about the TORI processes. It is only when I define "power" as my ability to "go against the flow"; to make the defending processes effective; to detach myself, accomplish a covert strategy, persuade/manipulate, or control; or to go against life, that I become powerless. In this sense, everyone is powerless, and rightly so. Only on a very short-term and surely a dysfunctional basis is anyone able to get someone to do something they don't want to do. In this sense of power, a power trip is a bad trip for anyone. Except at a very defensive level, no one wants power. When people seek inside for "what I want to do" at any level of depth or significance, they find they want something other than power. The want for power, like many other defensive wants, is surely an illusion. Put in another way, each person has all the power he or she wants or needs all of the time: power in the sense of ability to get into the flow of the TORI processes. This is the significant meaning of the concept.

Flow is a liquid word. It has more room for the fuzzies than the pricklies. It has little room for boxes, rubrics, and logic-tight compartments. It is uncomfortable with rigid rules, square edges, arbitrary boundaries, walls, and facades — with anything that isn't natural/growing. It is organic, groovy, smooth, easy riding. It is poetry without punctuation, sinusoidal projections, kite flying, a jam session, *commedia dell'arte,* a windblown hair style, organic architecture, holistic living, a child at play, free form, freedom, being, modern dance, a book you can dip into.

Flow is a participle rather than a noun. Flowing. Perry Como singing. Finding my own rhythm. Inside.

The best theory is one that flows.

12. TORI Theory is free of technique, method, and technology.

Some theories appropriately contain a statement about technology and technique in the general principles of the theory. TORI theory is not tied in with any implications about technique. It is method-free and technique-free.

It does not suggest, demand, or create techniques. But it is open to those that may be helpful. Thus, any technique, method, experience, technology, or set of operations, procedures, interventions, or actions that increase functional trusting and/or that reduce fear levels are appropriate to TORI theory.

The above statement is true to a degree. In another sense, TORI theory has clear implications that "techniques", in and of themselves, tend to reduce trust levels. A technique is a depersonalizing process, tends to disengage the person, to put the technician in role, to remove participants from each other. Role-playing and psychodrama were instituted by Moreno and his associates for precisely this reason, that they did allow the person to disengage himself or herself from the "reality" of the situation and get into presumably safer states of "irreality". Appropriate irreality is thought to reduce the threat of the situation and make it easier to work through issues and relationships than is the greater heat of reality.

Research and experience with trust level indicate that a primary factor in increasing trust is the degree of personalness in the relationship. One problem with professional training in all of the helping and managing fields is that professionals who learn methods, techniques, strategies, and procedures — the usual tools of the trade — tend to lose themselves in the process. Their behavior becomes characterized by role-taking, and they are seen by those they manage or help as being "in role", impersonal, practiced, to some degree superficial, disinterested, and thus distant or "not present". There is a growing recognition of this distancing and depersonalizing process in professional training in psychiatry, clinical psychology, teaching, counseling, and managing.

I see a countertendency in my counsulting: Professionals, with growing experience and confidence, begin to free themselves from techniques and to enter relationships as persons. Inexperienced, insecure, and less competent persons continue to rely upon techniques as the basis for accomplishing the professional task.

There are several possibilities for weaning professionals away from the use of techniques:

(a) Devising techniques that are more personal, that allow persons to contact persons within the method.

(b) Learning a method or technique so well that the person becomes free of the technique. The person so internalizes the principles involved that relationship becomes more nearly natural and authentic.

(c) Joining the clients, patients, students, or workers as a member of a learning group and working together to create environmental designs that allow managers, parents, teachers, and therapists to become full persons within the community.

13. Trust Level theory has face validity.

There is an instant recognition by listeners and readers of the possible validity of TORI theory. Everyone has an experience with trust and fear as feelings and as powerful forces in their lives.

There is considerable advantage in viewing the theory as being valid if it is designed to be practical and has been constructed to be used. This immediate recognition has several aspects that create problems, however:

(a) The central terms are household words for which most people have a ready meaning. "Trust" has a value-laden meaning. It has a moral tone to it. We have used trust and distrust as descriptive terms meant to identify a central catalytic process. In theory, each person has a degree of distrust at each moment, triggered by a certain stimulus, and a chronic state of distrust. Similarly, there is always some fear present in each person's inner state. However, the concepts have such high connotative flavoring, with such a negative tone, that most people are likely to deny fear or distrust. It is difficult to think non-defensively about the concepts.

(b) Listeners or readers fill in the theory with many immediate assumptions, taken from common experience, about fear and trust relationships. The assumptions, laden with feelings and stereotypes, form quickly. I recall a three-hour presentation/discussion that I gave to a group of government executives in which I gave many illustrations from my experiences with government agencies, many instances which were dramatic, emotional, controversial — and which illustrated the body of trust level theory. During the talk I noticed several intense positive and negative reactions shown by members of the group. During the three hours there was considerable interaction with members of the group, with a give-and-take about issues, questions, and concerns. Two intense reactions to the presentation and interaction illustrated the process that I am referring to here: (1) one executive was angry, frustrated with me, and finally said at the end of the session: "Your theory is nothing but pure Communism, and I resent it"; (2) another executive, present during the same presentation and discussion, was somewhat bored, passive, mildly negative, and ended the session with the statement: "All you are doing is just making a pious statement about simple Christianity; I can't see that you are saying anything new." Each person was apparently bringing some intense feelings and assumptions to the session and projecting these into the emotion-laden concepts of the theory. And, of course, they were reacting to me and to my presentation and feelings about the theory.

(c) Concepts and illustrations relating to TORI theory resonate so deeply with deep-seated concerns and conflicts in most persons that guilts and self-doubts are stirred up about feelings, behaviors, and self-concepts. Trust and fear are so central to what matters that persons who really look at themselves raise concerns about selfhood and self-worth.

The theory hooks people. Community experiences, designed to allow persons several days to experience their own trust and fear, allow people plenty of time to face the intense feelings and doubts mentioned above. Participants face these in a warm, accepting climate in which they discover that everyone else has similar feelings and doubts. Living with these, sharing them with others, understanding them, exploring alternatives, and other community activities provide opportunity for self-determined learnings that are essential to the problem of human problems.

Chapter 5

Rhythm and Flow:
A Set of Guidelines

Trust enables me to get into my own rhythms, to be *in* my mindbodyspirit because I believe in myself. My theory *is* my rhythm and my flow because it is the *integration* of all of me. The full life — the trusting life — is an ebb and flow of discovering and creating. Out of these processes I create and grow my theory.

Each person discovers for himself or herself the way to create and grow a theory and how to apply it. Each person "theorizes" in a unique way.

Some people get their theory first through the head. A woman once wrote me from Hawaii saying that something I had said in a talk had appealed to her intellectually; she had applied it and changed her way of relating to her children. Others get it first through the heart or gut, having to be touched emotionally before they "see" the theory. Some seem to know what is happening to them and want to understand the process at all levels. Others seem comfortable with allowing latent processes to take over and carry the "theory" for them, sometimes with little interest in rationalizing the process or perhaps even understanding it. Sometimes the knowledge of the theory and the resultant life change may come quickly. I remember a teacher from Denver who got a sudden insight and gut-level change one afternoon in a TORI community. This was about six years ago, and he still dates his radical change in teaching method and life-style to that moment of clarity. Others may struggle with the theory and the experience for years before it "takes".

RHYTHM AND FLOW

*To trust is to be in my own rhythm
and to enter the life flow.*

Some seem to learn from introspection and self-examination. Others *do it* or let it happen. For some, learning the theory is embodied in one or more specific behaviors that mean a great deal. A principal of a school in Baltimore said that the primary learning for him was expressed in moving out from behind his desk to talk *with* a visitor or visitors sitting around a small table in the center of his office. This, for him, seemed to make the difference. Others learn a generalized perceptual viewpoint that colors all looking but may not be represented in any specific "behavioral objective". For some, TORI theory may simply enrich another theory that they use as a kind of master plan that integrates living for them. For others, TORI theory may replace other theories, providing a total and fresh view of life. Some are looking for a prescription, an answer, a set of steps to follow, something that will tell them exactly what to do on the job tomorrow. Others feel hemmed in by prescriptions and wish to be free to face or solve each issue or problem as it happens, using the theory as a viewpoint toward *ad hoc* problem solving.

Whatever one's being and learning style, the road to understanding and using TORI theory is essentially a matter of trust level. In one sense it is simply a matter of *learning* to trust. When one's trust level changes in a significant way, then all else changes.

Educating the Mindbody

The trust level of the mindbody, at any given moment, determines how personal, open, allowing, and interdependent a person will be. It is these TORI discovering processes that determine the health, productivity, and effectiveness of the person in any given situation. Learning the theory and using it means educating the mindbody, increasing the trust level. I cannot make a change in my trust level by simply choosing to do so, by willing it, or by following a strictly rational process of mindbody control. But I *can* create experiences for myself that will make significant changes in my trust level.

1. *The body.* I'm continually amazed at how much my physical state can influence my attitudes, feelings, creativity, work level, and mental states. Sometimes I think that discovering jogging was the single most important discovery of my life. Sustained bodywork has made a critical difference in my appearance, my attitude toward my body, my self-esteem, my general productivity, and my level of trust. I went through a long period of having great difficulty in getting up

enough energy to run. It was not until I discovered for myself how euphoric I would feel after running and what a permanent difference this made in me that I could fight through this lassitude barrier. The ancients seem to have known this well. There is a powerful message here that we are rediscovering. Reich taught us much about the body and its flows and its blockings, and the Neo-Reichians are educating us again to start with the body and its magic. Trust the body.

2. *Sensing and perceiving.* With the help of the growth centers and with the many-faceted revival of ancient wisdoms, we are rediscovering our senses. We are learning to see and feel with new richness, new vision. Fear-bred dogmas have restricted our seeing, touching, tasting, and smelling. A new atmosphere in the church, the school, the theatre — the *zeitgeist* — encourages exploring the senses. Learning to trust one's own perceptions comes with continued experience in a high-trust environment. It is now commonplace for persons to report, after TORI and other growth experiences, new clarity, an amazingly powerful awareness of the simple sounds, sights, and smells of life — experiences that have been dulled in normal living. A new respect for the senses and their validity is changing modern life. One learns to trust one's senses by enriching one's experiences and trying out a life style that is based upon one's trust in one's sensory experience. I learn to trust what I see and touch.

3. *The head.* It is becoming fashionable in some quarters to get out of one's head, to distrust one's reason, and to trust one's heart and gut. It seems to me, rather, that I might well learn to trust my head, and not to denigrate it. What I can learn is that *I can trust me* — I can trust what I feel, think, sense, wish, and image. I can trust my processes. My cognitions can be *integrative,* unifying, whole, personal, fused with emotionality, and close to reality. Distrust of my head, my intellect, and my words is just as dysfunctional and dehumanizing as is distrust of my heart or gut. There can be just as much fakery in one's feelings as in one's thinking. Rediscovery of the head may be the theme of the new counter-revolution that follows our current era of the feelings and the senses. In popular conception, one's "theory" is in one's head. And this makes theory a dirty word — though six-lettered. For me, one's theory is in one's body, in one's being, in one's sensing, in one's thinking. *I can thus have as much respect for my theory as I can have for me.* Trusting one's reflections and thought processes is a significant part of one's learning the theory.

4. *The heart and gut.* "Gut learning" was the fashionable word

for the acquisition of body wisdom in the early National Training Laboratories experiential T-groups. Various traditions have arrayed the mindbody elements very differently on a trustworthiness scale. Somehow to feel or touch Christ's wounds induced more trust than to hear His voice. The chakras have a clear order of priority, which is, in one sense, an order of trustworthiness. Trust your gut. Trust your heart. Trust your touch. Trust your hunches. The admonitions are legion. Having a "feel for it" is a significant test for and manifestation of my trust. Educating the feelings and emotions is a critical part of trust acquisition. This means becoming aware of feelings, experiencing their manifestations and effects, learning what they mean, and learning how to handle them.

5. *The hand.* Fear keeps us from the spontaneous, impulsive, and free life of doing and acting. We must trust ourselves in order to be comfortable when we act spontaneously. To let it all hang out is seen as very risky if we are afraid of what will hang out — and if we are afraid of reactions from others. In a high level of trust I am able to act impulsively and freely, to "let me happen", to *let me be.* I can let me be only if I trust me. There is no valid prescription. I learn to act impulsively by trying it out, testing my own reactions, determining my own tolerance for stress and ambiguity, discovering my level of freedom, and increasing this spontaneity as I determine that I can be safe. I can educate my bodymind to act spontaneously.

6. *Expressive skills.* "Skill" is sometimes seen as a nasty word. One who is skilled is one who is practiced, smooth, and, to some degree, has artifice. Skill practice is often an artificial process, especially "human relations" skills. Such skills are associated with manipulation and persuasion, with intention rather than with spontaneity. One can be skilled at giving strokes, for instance. One who "gives strokes" or offers to be "in a support group" is often distrusted more than one who simply says what he or she feels about the other person. I have found that many people become effective at human relations more readily from interaction in a "free field" in the unstructured milieu of a T-group or a TORI community than they do from structured skill practice. The trouble with most practice is that one becomes "practiced". It is useful that every person learn to achieve valid communication of thoughts, feelings, impressions, and attitudes. If one is going to work in a helping profession, for instance, it seems important that one learns the words one can use in communicating "theory", in communicating feelings, in communicating all the aspects

of one's being. One needs to learn "skills" in this positive sense: skills of problem solving, decision-making, initiating action, listening, expressing wants, and other doings that are effective in group and community action.

7. *Beyond the body.* It is clear to me that through trust we can learn to transcend the senses, the body, the feelings, and all the other expressions of the mindbodyspirit. Self-education in out-of-the-body experiences, non-sensory awareness, altered states of consciousness, and the many transcendent states that bring new trust levels, is now possible, respectable, and even common. Educating myself for transcendence and cosmic states of trust is for me the most promising avenue to trust formation. Once I get the vision and *perspective* obtained by such experiences, then trust level is seen anew in relation to states that I did not know were possible. The perspective of the Environmental-Quality scale makes possible new growth in everyday trust levels. I get an experiential base for new growth. I then *know* what it is to trust at wholly new levels, never before envisioned.

The theory states that the most-deeply organic and effective behavior for all persons is that which can be described as role-free, open and non-strategic, self-determining and proactive, and inter-dependent. Our fear-defense systems produce coping behavior inconsistent with this deeper, trusting self, that counters growth and is probably self-destructive. Educating my mindbody means that I can get enough in touch with myself so that these personal, open, want-determined, and interbeing behaviors come easily and naturally, come with little planning and thinking, come from my deepest inner self.

Experiencing My Trust Level — Learning the Theory

A person can create at least six kinds of experience that will lead to an understanding of the theory and the ability to apply it usefully in a wide range of personal and professional situations.

1. *Living in the dynamics of a free-flow system.* One advantage of the TORI community experience is that a member can experience, in depth, what happens in a free-flow, unstructured human system. It may take several experiences in a TORI community for these embedded dynamics to become visible to the eye of an observer caught in high-defense living and high-defense theory. This may be the person's first significant experience with Environmental Quality VI and VII. This is a critical change from the visible dynamics of EQ I-V climates. I am assuming that the direction of societal and evolutionary

change is toward higher-EQ levels, toward higher-trust living and free-structure dynamics. This directional change is happening at a more rapid pace than had been thought possible until quite recent developments in theory and practice.

Anyone who seriously wants to understand and use TORI theory will find it illuminating to experience the leaderless and low-structure community in depth. It is important to realize how closely tied in with EQ I-V dynamics are the current theories available to the behavioral scientist. This is especially true of behavior-modification theory, Transactional Analysis and other neo-Freudian theory, decision theory, reenforcement theory, OD theory and practice, assertiveness theory, role theory, and power theory. Not surprisingly, most available organizational and group theory grows out of experience with I-V environments. The research used to develop the theories is based upon assumptions and concepts that grow out of I-V experience and are limited by them. Trust Level theory, however, can provide a useful bridge among these diverse concepts and research studies.

2. *In-depth experience in developing a high-trust climate in a natural setting.* TORI theory is a practical theory, developed in the practical world of experience and applicable to institutions *as they are.* TORI theory is one answer to the practitioner's question: What would my organization be like if it were more trusting? This, in effect, is the question that has been asked by many innovators in our culture who develop alternative schools, alternative churches, participative businesses, communal-living ventures, cooperative nurseries, rehabilitation centers, and a multitude of experimental attempts to build high-trust institutions in the midst of what is essentially a low-trust, EQ II-IV culture.

There is no theory available that will take the place of the hot experience under the diverse pressures present when a group tries to push the evolutionary process and get a bit ahead of the trends. The principles and guidelines discussed in this chapter will "work" in the traditional establishment, but there are no guarantees, no ways of preventing the pain of learning that comes from trying things out when the action is hot.

3. *Professional-role experience in some profession or vocation where people deal with people.* Not always, but nearly so, the best positions and jobs are given to those who have had conventional training for the position. There are many advantages to hiring an imaginative person with a good people theory who will take a fresh

look at the task and perform it in a novel way. This is particularly true of a person using trust theory. Fortunately, there is an increasing number of imaginative people in positions of responsibility who are looking for unconventional people. Trust Level theory is a powerful tool that can be used in any profession, business, industry, or organization that has a large people component — and used with a high degree of effectiveness because it enables the user to move ahead of the inevitable trend.

For most persons entering a people profession or organization, it is wise to have specialized traditional training and job experience — as a clinical psychologist, an occupational therapist, a school teacher, a manager, a psychiatrist, a group worker, an industrial psychologist, an administrator, or whatever. The person has then "met a payroll", knows the techniques and methods used by competent people in the field, has seen the problems and issues that face the field worker, knows the language of the trade, and knows the feel of the cards. The TORI innovator is not working on Mars, in some safe Utopia, or in a germ-free testing laboratory, but in the everyday defensive, pressure-laden, complex world of "reality". It is in this world that TORI theory is designed to be useful.

4. *Experience at working out of a "leader role"*. I know of no satisfactory substitute for hot experience, especially a role-free, personal relationship in a high-trust milieu. Role-expectations and role-perceptions preoccupy both members and leaders when someone is appointed or elected to the leader box as manager, parent, teacher, guru, facilitator, administrator, therapist, or governor. These expectations are especially difficult to handle when the power and authority are denied, softened, or covered by pretense. The intention of the TORI theorist is to work out of the role and join the group *as a full member*.

The barriers are many: fears, beliefs that it can't happen, demands that the leader "earn the money", dependencies, needs for a scapegoat, needs of the leader to feel special, and a vast and diverse list of other fear-related factors. Many have not seen a leader successfully work out of a role and believe that it is impossible to do so. But as an increasing number of people do see it happen and participate emotionally in the powerful sense of community that follows, it will be easier for leaders and groups to achieve this leaderless state. Working through the issue is a significant learning and probably necessary for the person trying to apply TORI theory in this transition culture.

5. *Growing into transcendent and cosmic states and integrating these into one's way of being.* Familiarity with TORI theory eases the transition into transcendent and cosmic states. The rapid development of knowledge and experience with dream control, astral trips, ecstatic states, clairvoyance, drug-induced altered consciousness, meditation, faith healing, and a multitude of varied mystical and altered states, makes available to many people the possibility of transforming daily lives, raising of consciousness to new levels, and achievement of new trust levels in our society.

It is possible to create these experiences through the use of a wide variety of techniques and methods widely used in the growth movement. But emergent and self-generated experiences are more potent, whole, and life-changing. The experiences are occurring "naturally" and spontaneously in the TORI communities as people apply the theory more fully to their lives and make themselves available to new experiences as they happen. Through the understanding of such experiences, we can all make our normal lives more rich, more varied, more trusting, more ecstatic — and live more often in Environments VI-X.

6. *Experience with theory, and especially with TORI theory.* It is useful to have experience with theory, the constructs, theory-based institutions, people who live with and understand theory, the language, the unanswered questions, the research, the projections into the future, the alternatives, the misconceptions, the errors, the quacks and poseurs, the utopias, the hopes and the fears. I have a great confidence that articulated theory is useful, that it can guide social action and experimentation, that it can help integrate personal living, and that it can help us avoid the seemingly interminable repetition of error.

I certainly make no claim that TORI theory is the last word, but it is one viable alternative, one effort to apply a general theory to problems of practical living. It is one take-off place for a person to start building his or her own theory or to take another look at reconstructing the theory or theories that he or she uses. Come to think of it, it is true, of course, that everyone continually constructs a theory. Even the youngest child — especially the youngest child! Anyone who has read Piaget will never forget the importance of self-constructed theories in the child's attempts to understand the readily-available mysteries of everyday life.

TORI theory is, at once, more simple and more complex than it seems. Deliberately couched in everyday language, it may seem more simplistic than it is. TORI, like life, is very simple. Therein lies its profundity.

Guidelines for Applying the Theory

In Table X I have listed ten guidelines that may be useful to readers in getting a feel for the theory and its application. These guidelines may be used in several different ways:

a. As a kind of check list for the practitioner who is evaluating an organizational program. The user can look at the client system (church, classroom, sales department, or mental health clinic) from each of these ten viewpoints to build a diagnosis or a "treatment" program. Column Two in Table X lists the general correlates of trust level.

b. As a check list for a person who is examining his or her own growth. Column One lists ten symptoms of the growing, trusting person that change as trust level increases.

c. As a cue system for building cognitive clarity. There is no order to the list. Each statement of a guideline is another view of trust level, a restatement of the theory, another definition of trust level, another expressive symptom of organic health, a road map in looking at the effects of trust and fear, and a mini-theory of personal and organizational growth.

d. When stated in the form used in Table XI, each guideline is an alternate focus for social engineering and for system change.

In a sense, each guideline says it all. Each contains the others. The guidelines are in no sense a set of prescriptions. Each guideline defines a quest, a searching, a choice.

In each case I have tried to describe, first, how that guideline applies to the individual person, describing what I have seen happen in people who appear to be in states of high trust. I will make a general statement and then give examples of the direction that *persons* who are using the theory are taking. I will use the first person in each case in describing these people. Second, with each guideline, I will state how this guideline applies to a *social system,* first in general terms, and then with some specifics of what I have seen happen. Each person and each organization creates an individual and unique application of the principle.

1. *Being in the flow and the rhythm.*

In discovering and creating my own flow and rhythm, I am

TABLE X. TORI CHECK LIST

Applying TORI theory to the theorist/user	*Applying TORI theory to the client system*
1. Being in my rhythms. I *am* my flows and rhythms Process — not product — is it Discovering is being	**Being into system flow and rhythm** Where's the flow? Diagnosing the primary flow Not going against the river
2. Trusting my process Trusting my impulses, my body, my wants, my rhythms My body is a good cue system	**Trusting system functions** What is happening? Letting the system happen Moving into the VI-X EQ levels
3. Creating my vision I create me, and my reality I am unique; my feelings *are* I create my theory, my vision	**Creating system vision and goal** What's the mission? Creating, simplifying the mission Synergizing goal structure
4. Caring for me Nurturing me in my center Being in my essence Enjoying my divinity	**Caring for the system's uniqueness** Discovering the system's *being* Providing nurturance Celebrating differences
5. Opening me I show what I see and feel I take you into me We create overlapping circles	**Creating an open feedback system** Open space, doors, records, stockrooms, rumor systems Not channeling or constricting
6. Focussing my energy I always get what I want I can be anything I image All things are possible	**Focusing system energy and flow** What's central to our mission? Simplifying, centering the flow Focus and choice
7. Reducing my constraints My fears are illusions I constrain myself I release me	**Reducing constraints and fears** What's blocking us? Discovering leverage points Diagnosing barrier systems
8. Creating my environment I create the world around me I *always* have choice I create you, for me	**Creating the system interfaces** Who helps make us? Building creative interfaces Not fostering competition
9. Building my community We co-author our experience I build a team I emerge into the allness	**Building community in the system** Can we become a community? Seeing units as communities Moving into VI—X EQ levels

10. Sensing my allness

   Everything I need is in me

   All feelings are in me

   All my life is recapitulation

Sensing the allinall

   Everything is simple

   Everything is complex, is allness

   The organization's infinite potential

TABLE XI.

THE GUIDELINES AS THEORIES OF PERSONAL AND ORGANIZATIONAL CHANGE

The theory of model	Statement of the mini-theory
1. Freedom of flow	The healthy organism moves into its own flow, in tune with its rhythms, with an inner harmony.
2. Process trusting	The effective organism is one that allows its processes to happen, without over-management, extrinsic motivation, or over-control.
3. Cognitive-perceptual clarity	The effective system is one in which there is a shared vision and mission, viewed and conceived clearly by members who feel the importance of the vision.
4. Self-caring	The healthy system cares for itself, nurtures its central being, feels its importance, has a strong sense of identity.
5. Open system	The effective organism is an open system, with high transparency see-throughable boundaries, sharing of perceptions and feelings.
6. Focused energy	The healthy system focuses its energy on what matters, what is central to the flow.
7. Constraint reduction	The effective organism is free from undue constraints and congesting fears, has a feeling of freedom to be and do.
8. Nurturing environment	The internal and external environment of the effective system is nurturing, fostering of mutuality and cooperation.
9. In-depth community	The healthy system *feels like* a community, whose members care, and care about each other.
10. Cosmic allness	The high-trust system senses its allness, its mystical core, its eternity in the moment.

discovering myself anew in each moment. My own flow and rhythm is unique to me and *is my process*. I am always changing, flowing, being in process.

The enriched and trusting life is a flowing life. In our depths we respond with empathy and resonance to fluid forms — to dancing, skating, sailing, flying, swimming, floating, and the flowing and changing forms of life. The response to the Jonathan Livingston Seagull saga is due to something primal and to something latent that demands transcendence. And to me it is significant that the form is flowing and liquid.

Sucking, licking, breast-feeding, tasting, crying, urinating, sweating, breathing — all have an attraction quality, and especially so when one is free from inhibitions, defenses, prohibitions, taboos, and constraints — free from the discrete, boxed, metered, scaled, moralized, hard-edged, defended, evaluated, constipated, hardened, encapsulated, blocked, and solid forms of constrained life. The full life is more like a river than a concrete road. More like a cloud than a computer.

A woman who creates beautiful, flowing pieces of art on a pottery wheel once told me with zest what it was like to get "into the wheel, the clay, and the flow" of the process. When she got centered and flowing, the clay seemed to form itself, to *feel* right, to grow into a form of liquid grace. So it is with a person who discovers her own rhythms, patterns, diurnal flow, and life dance. All this is a matter of trust. If I don't have a high degree of trust I don't even *see* the flow in the wheel and the clay, or discover my rhythm.

It is important for the parent, the teacher, or the nurse to *see* the flow. This is partly a matter of perspective. Once, looking out of the window of a landing airplane, I saw thousands of people moving out of a huge stadium. With growing fascination, I watched the *flow* of the people, disembodied, abstract, undifferentiated. I was unaware of the persons as individuals. What I saw seemed rather like a river, with waves, pools, and stoppages. Just as understanding Einstein's concept of time and space is a *perspective* process, so is seeing anything. Looked at through "other eyes", the chair would become a flowing, whirling storm of atoms and would lose its chair-like form.

My experience with persons and with organizational forms is that it is useful, and more valid for our purposes, to *see* people processes in their liquid forms. For some purposes of collective prediction — perhaps in predicting traffic patterns, materials processing, mental illness, or school absences — it may be useful to rubricize, scale, and count persons and their attributes. It is *not* useful for administrators, therapists, teachers, and others who work directly with people to be seduced into these objective, classificatory, un-flow attitudes, perceptions, and behaviors. One can *choose* to see the flow.

The TORI discovering processes flow. There is a being, opening, flowering, and interbeing. The defending behaviors don't flow. They block the flow and are hard, bristly, and congesting.

Each social system is unique, has its own being. It has its own flow and rhythm. Together, in interdependence and mutuality, we discover our common form — our organization — which is more than the sum of its discrete parts. Being in this flow and this unique form is infinitely exciting.

Applying this general principle to the management of organizations, nations, and other social systems is a matter of stance, attitude, perspective, vision, and way of being. My insights about flow-centered management have come from consulting with and experiencing a few persons of vision in management — particularly in Champion Paper, Weyerhaeuser, Dow, General Motors, and the Bell System. These few are managers and executives who see things writ large, who see the organization as a living organism, and who see it with excitement and courage. They see the flow in the paper mill, in the manufacturing process, in the mobilization of resources toward movement in streams that they clearly envision.

The most effective executives perceive this clearly. They see beyond the units, the parts, the discrete elements, and experience the process as flow. They see the river. Having this perspective, they trust these processes and avoid getting lost in irrelevancies of problems that are not critical to the central flow.

It is not as easy for many of these same executives to see people processes as flowing, especially the intra-personal flow. Some depersonalize the individuals, seeing them only as parts of the larger flow. What is necessary for full growth of the executive is to put it all together, seeing the internal people processes, and the persons themselves as human and *central* aspects of the flow.

In the TORI communities we have discovered that a flowing physical environment enhances the rhythmic interaction of the persons in the community. Cushions, soft carpets, curved walls, no hard furniture — all provide an environment that enhances the flow. As the people soften and become gentle when defenses are reduced, they cuddle, touch, sometimes pile up like kittens or puppies; they dance, run, play, and flow into patterns that are soft, un-edged, liquid, and very different from the rows and linear forms of the conventional school or factory.

Management that is aware of the principle of flow tries to bring it into the organization by rearranging office and building space so that space flows with functional needs for communication, materials distribution, and other interdependencies; increasing visibility of the total operation so that all employees can see the total flow in perspective; allowing employees to discover their own work and rest rhythms rather than prescribing times for coffee breaks, and arrival and departure from work; creating a flex-time concept that is applied to many aspects of scheduling; encouraging subgroups and teams to discover their own identity and flow and rhythms; removing linear and rectangular barriers to flow that are found in regulations as well as in architecture; experimenting with moveable partitions, files, desks, and chairs; eliminating role prescriptions and job specifications that box people into hierarchial and rectangular relationships; removing norms that prevent flow; encouraging the flow of talk out of channels; encouraging people to play music and to move on impulse and to flow — anything to increase the flow and liquidity of relationships in the organization.

Productivity, creativity, and effectiveness of the organization are all enhanced when the forms of organizing come out of the emerging flows and rhythms that are natural to the organization.

2. *Trusting the process.*

As a trusting person, I trust my life processes. They contain the fullness of life. I am in them and they are in me. I am who I am. *I let me happen.* I let life happen.

When I let myself be who I am, give myself freedom to flow and happen, allow my juices to flow, I am trusting myself and my processes. When I am trusting my processes, I allow myself to play, to move into new adventures, to accept new challenges, to take risks, to go with my flow, and to keep moving ahead when I feel fear. It is precisely when there is ambiguity, uncertainty, unpredictability, when there are no guarantees, no plans, no structured techniques, that I rely upon my trusting — that I allow myself to trust my processes and go with what is happening.

My processes include my fears, uncertainties, feelings, fantasies, phobias, hunches, impulses, paranoia, flights of imagination, terror, and all of the events that go on in me. Trusting my processes means to let me be in these processes without trying to control them, direct them, or constrain them. Trusting that my free-flying way, my natural impulses, my way of being will take care of me, will pull me through, will guide me, will turn out all right.

The more one distrusts one's own processes, the more one requires a technique, a leader, a guide, a cookbook, a structure, a plan, a timetable, a reservation at the hotel, a life insurance policy, a no-cut contract, a no-risk agreement, a money-back guarantee, a buffer zone, a warning, a warm-up period, a non-title fight, a trial run, a road map, a friend in court — any hedge against the normal risks of living. The more one trusts one's own processes (competencies, perceptions, intuitions, feelings, ideas, or projections), the more one is willing to risk, to "come to play", to go all out, to seek adventure, to move toward ambiguity, to invent a new solution, to explore new worlds, to make new friends, to take on new responsibility, to accept a challenge, to take a new job, to hire an unusual employee, to develop a new product line, to pick up a hitch-hiker, or to go on a blind date. Shooting the moon — as a poker gambit or as a space adventure — is not for those who don't trust their processes.

So it is with organizations, groups, and all social systems. A system that trusts its own processes trusts the flow of life and lets it happen. Life, when trusted, will form itself. Organizations and nations grow and create their own preferred forms. Life, when free, transcends.

When organizational processes are distrusted and feared, life in the organization is over-planned, over-organized, over-managed, over-supervised, over-manipulated, and over-strategized. The *feel* of the organization is one of constriction and congestion. The distrusting can be expressed in the formal structure of rules and contracts, or it can be expressed in the informal messages conveyed by the behavior of people. It is not possible to fool the troops for long. At some level the feigners are sensed as unreal. Genuine trust is sensed, *known*.

The processes that *are* the organization *are* the message. If the processes are sound — self-determining, person-honoring, transparent, interdependent, synergistic — then the products will be sound. In the long run, of course, the processes are far more important than the products. Management, especially in a fear/emergency/fire-fighting atmosphere, has a difficult time seeing this. Fearful management is results-oriented, product-centered, and bottom-line motivated.

It is the process that counts, not the product — in sex, in play, in therapy, in friendship, in marriage, in communication, and in manufacturing.

Managements that have trusted processes have experimented with sending out blank, signed checks with orders, as Kaiser did; removed sign-in sheets and time clocks; abolished quality-control check ups; tried supervisor-less work groups; decentralized operations; tried one- or two-level management; removed all kinds of dehumanizing rules and regulations; abolished performance appraisals; done away with grades and merit pay; removed guns from policemen's hands; removed prohibition laws and drug regulations; humanized mental hospitals and prisons; removed job specifications; reduced training and communications programs; released staff and management from unnecessary functions — all manner of ways of allowing human processes to perform their magic.

The functions of goal-setting and planning are less clear. Most organizational functions are overplanned, and most goals are over-specified and overformalized. The amount of planning and goal-setting probably is a function of complexity, of group size, of amount of interdependence with correlative organizational units, and certainly of fear. My overall impression in consulting with a wide range of organizations is that too much time is spent on planning and goal-setting.

The distrusting processes (manipulating, controlling, covering, depersonalizing) are self-defeating and self-perpetuating. People who resort to control and manipulations inevitably discover that controls and manipulations become necessary. Controls and manipulations are time-consuming and costly, and they seldom work as well as had been hoped. When they don't work (the death penalty, penalties for tardiness, fines for errors, or safety rules) the tendency is to assume that the controls need to be tightened and shored up. It is very difficult and seemingly irrational to *reduce* the controls and supervision when the procedures don't work. It is difficult to get free of the assumption that the rules and controls are necessary.

3. *Creating the vision and clarity.*

I create my own unique being, my own reality, my own life mission, my own vision of what I can be. I am what I see myself to be. *I am.* I am worthy of infinite trust. I write my own life theory. My vision is as broad as I wish it to be.

Personal growth is partly a matter of cognitive and perceptual clarity. At all biological levels, fear constricts perceptual clarity and range. Trust opens up thinking and seeing.

The executives who are able to see the flow because they can stand back and view it from perspective are able to do so because they have some degree of trust derived from experience. Their trust enables them to have (a) courage, and (b) vision — the two significant elements in a trust-centered way of being. The courage to look. And the trust to take the big, long look.

Because what I am determines so much what I see, and because the seeing process is so important in my personal growth, I must learn to understand the perceptual processes and how I can enrich them. As was often illustrated in the previous chapter, my theory is integrally related to how I see my experience. Trust theory is particularly significant in this regard. Higher trust enables me to transcend my fear and look beyond what is immediately apparent.

Trust theory implies that hostile, aggressive behavior comes from defense against perceived or anticipated attack. If I can really see the hostile person as self-defending, then it is easier to react non-defensively. If I have the theory in my gut, then my reaction, even my impulsive one, is likely to be less full of anger and hurt *if I see the hostility as defense.* If I see a child's stealing as a defensive coping reaction to my punishment, I am likely to feel and react differently than if I see the stealing as a character defect or an unprovoked attack. When my theory grows out of my deepest experience and is integral to me, when it is congruent with my reasonings and understandings, then it provides a guide to my looking and thinking.

Developing my ability to perceive is a critical and fundamental process. What I see and how I see persons and events determines how I feel about them and how I will react to them. The perceiving triggers it off. I am impressed, for instance, how people who trust deeply, who understand what trusting really is and who have an resultant inner tranquillity, are able to *see through* the presenting defense layers and *see* the frightened, love-seeking inner self that resides deeply in all of us. I have seen this process so frequently that I am convinced that the inner core of each person *is* gentle and love-seeking — and not daemonic or death-seeking, as many would have us believe. In any event, the person who *sees (actually senses and perceives)* the love-seeker within reacts in ways that are less escalating and defensive than someone does who habitually sees only the ostensibly hostile behavior.

The great power of trust-inductive experiences is that this basic trust *changes* the sensing and perceiving processes. Trust theory provides a pathway for the integration of life processes at a very deep level. The person is actually creating himself or herself in the process of growth and creating, in part through the perceptual processes, the environment in which the growth occurs.

Each organization and social system creates and discovers its own mission — its vision of the present and of the future. This vision serves as a unifying and synergizing force. Just as in a significant sense each person does what he or she wants, so is it true that each organization accomplishes its mission. Its mission is its deep-lying, conscious/unconscious, inner flow and direction — the gestalted being, the synergy of all of the individual wants, fantasies, themes, and needs.

People gather together in organizations for a great variety of reasons and wants, and in the process of interacting create a great many more. They come together — in churches, businesses, clubs, professional organizations — to relieve loneliness, to find friends, to please others, to do what is expected, to build egos, to punish, to fight, to find scapegoats, to get power, to find love, to get excitement, to relieve boredom, to escape spouses and families, to change the world, to teach, to learn, to work, to do and feel all manner of things.

Somehow in amalgamating these individual and diverse wants and needs, the organization creates and discovers a mission that transcends the persons involved. The organization can become, for example, a group of evangelical zealots ruthless in making converts; a worldwide crusade for mercy and aid to the poor; a patriotic movement for murdering millions of Jewish people; a loving environment for discovering a new way of being; a work-oriented, middle-class, conservative, devoted-to-work business venture; a cruel vendetta devoted to punishing deviates and non-conformists; a professional organization devoted to preserving the good life for the selected few; or whatever the organization may become as it tries to discover itself and finds itself escalating the latent wants of the members into something that becomes a centering mission, a transcending quasi-conscious goal that everyone gets caught up in.

Organizations become what, in some part, they set out to become: the Civil Liberties Union, the Ku Klux Klan, the CIA, the Republican Party, the American Legion, Dow Chemical, the Mormons, the Quakers, or the Daughters of the American Revolution. In part they have acted out their stereotypes; in part they are reactive, responding to critics who have pushed them in ways not intended; in part they are rational, goal-setting, conscious-agenda groups; and in part they have become what they unconsciously wanted to become.

Management that has been aware of the principle of creating vision and mission has tried a variety of approaches: deep sensing sessions; career development programs centered around the central mission of the organization; hiring external consultants do in-depth interviewing of key and/or sampled persons in the organization and using these data as a base for a system-wide conference on mission-setting; company-wide theory-based seminars or experiential-training sessions built around the concept of trust and perception; semantic-differential testing programs sampling company attitudes around selected issues that are crucial to the organizational mission; a wide variety of training and "organizational development" sessions arranged to create visibility of perceptual data; ingenious ways of creating ease of entry of all employees to the offices and attention of key executives and key planning and goal-setting people; and many other types of training and communications programs.

Nevertheless, I feel that we have made very little headway in this area. We have yet to discover ways of creating mission and of involving members of large organizations so that they have a part in creating overall goals or in changing them. Feelings of isolation and impotence are common, even among those who seem to be in positions of power. In sensitivity training sessions which I have given for corporation presidents and chief officers, I have heard presidents of huge corporations comment on how impotent they felt in not being able to exert influence upon their own organizations!

4. *Caring for self and for the system's self.*

I nourish and care for me, for I am a worthy recipient of my love, an expression of the divine essence. Self-caring is a redemptive and spiritual process. Genuine love is freeing and celebrative, warming and gentling. Cared for, I am able to care for and love others and to join them in community and interdependence.

It is ironic that most of us could adequately administer to our own love need but relinquish this function to others who do it less well — therapists, parents, ministers, or friends. It is a sad commentary on the adequacy of our self-caring. We have failed to *learn how to love ourselves.*

Loving, in itself, is a nourishing process, deeply needed by all. Loving, of self and of others, is life-giving. It is the distortions of love that deprive it of its nourishing quality.

Looked at from our Trust Level analysis, loving/caring looks something like this:

a. Loving and caring is *being who I am* and being there for you as a "real" person. I can't love a role, only a person. When I have presence, I am putting my energy into being, not into defending.

Caring is not being in role, defending, or taking on the role of friend, helper, therapist, or parent. When one *takes on the stance* of the altruist, one's caring is diluted, screened, and not really available to one's self or to another.

b. Loving and caring is *communicating in depth*. Love is an expression. Love unexpressed and unfelt is not love. Love is communication, a two-way process. I show where I'm at, show my warmth and joy and anger. Loving is also learning to "read" the signs from another, a searching, a taking in, a listening to your quiet. Love is impulsive, spontaneous, natural, unpretentious, without guile. Caring is not manipulative, strategic, covert, rationed out for a purpose, careful, diluted, handed out on schedule. Love can be trusted.

c. Loving and caring is *allowing* others to be who they are. It is *self-rewarding* and does not need approval, sanction, external reward, or repayment. Love, like grace, is free: It doesn't have to be earned, deserved, or warranted. Loving caresses both the lover and the loved.

Loving is not bartering, does not demand or require repayment and reciprocation. It is not helping, protecting, parenting, or taking care of. It is not given out of loyalty, duty, or obligation. It is given and received freely.

d. Caring is *being with*. Everyone falls in love with everyone who is in an undefended state, when all parties feel *no need to defend*. Loving and trusting are the same processes.

Loving is not owning, controlling, possessing, sacrificing, depending, or sucking your strength. It is sharing, allowing, and letting be.

Self-caring, then, is a process of treating myself as I would treat a lover. It is being in me in depth. It is communicating with me, without pretense. It is letting me be who I am, without parenting, approving, punishing, or correcting myself. It is living *with* me, without defense.

None of this happens in a vacuum. I cannot, by myself, learn to love myself. Learning to care for self comes about in a caring environment that I help create. People learn to love in community. It is this strong belief that led Lorraine and me to put so much energy and high priority on developing community in our early efforts to apply

TORI theory to all aspects of personal and organizational living.

An effective organization, group, or social system is a loving and caring place. When this is so, we can learn to love the organizations we create. We love our organization as something we have created together, giving it our best efforts, our care and love. It is the *highest expression of our being together that we are able to create at the moment,* at the time. It is an expression of us.

Because we have learned distrust as a way of life, we have come to disown our organizations, to blame others for what we have created, to see our organizations, our neighborhood, and our nation as created by people "up there", those with power and influence, those with "motives", probably ulterior.

An extremely encouraging sign of the times is a growing tendency to take responsibility for our social systems. *We* are creating alternative schools, churches, and businesses; we take responsibility for them and keep them small and personal and manageable. We march on Washington, protest the Viet Nam war, create consumer cooperatives, organize to fight for women's rights, create a multitude of "self help" organizations, and do all manner of things that mean, for one thing, that we are trying to "own" our organizations.

Groups and organizations can be loving places. In Chapters VII, VIII, and IX, I will discuss some successful efforts in this direction and some principles that we have used in bringing this about.

There are many ways of applying this *self-care principle* to our professional and organizational lives. If, for instance, I am the teacher in a classroom, my first consideration is: How can I make this an environment that turns me on, that I look forward to, in which I find daily love, and where I am doing what I want to do? When I can do this for myself, the environment cannot help but be a good one for the students. There will be learning, growth, and community.

We are all familiar with classrooms in which this is not the case. If I get tired easily, dread coming to class on Monday, look forward to quitting time and the end of the week, and find that the class has responded poorly, I am not taking care of myself in the classroom. So it is with therapists in the therapy hour, parents in the home, managers in the department, or any professional. Well cared for by self, the therapist, teacher, parent, or manager is good to be around, learns to love students, children, or workers, and is likely to be highly effective.

Several organizations for whom I am a consultant are making good progress in reducing the *barriers to attainment of the caring community:* the assumption that the caring environment is impossible to attain; the assumption that loving/caring is unrelated to productivity and goal attainment; lack of experience with loving communities and caring work environments; unresolved fears of organizations and the "establishment", especially of large organizations; the assumption that unless properly supervised, people will organize themselves as the boys did in *Lord of the Flies;* scarcity of leaders, consultants, and theorists, even in education and in the churches, who believe in the attainability or relevance of the loving community; and a host of other fears and negative attitudes and assumptions that pervade modern life.

   5. *The open life and the open system.*

   I show me to you, inviting us both to come out and join the world. I take you into me and make myself available to go into you and your space. We create the overlapping circles that are transparent, translucent, and boundary-less.

   Opening of the person is both putting out and letting in. It is an opening of auras and orifices, the flowing of juices, giving out of clear messages and welcoming of incoming messages.

   Open messages are most effective when they are clear and unmixed, when they are spontaneous, and when they bubble up in the interaction. They come through best when they come early, before overplanning and overmobilization of fear, caution, and polishing up. They are heard best when they are not translated into control and punishment.

   "Leave me alone, you bastard!" is a message that contains a great deal of feeling. It shows a lot about the speaker, but it actually camouflages the basic feelings. Control, hostility, and interpretation dominate the message. It is the translated aspects of the message that create the distortion, the defense, the counter-aggression, and other negative effects of mis-communication. Messages are most effective when they are open, when *they describe me,* my feelings, and my perceptions; not when they attempt to describe you, or when they are my interpretations and analyses of you. "I am beginning to feel like a child" has a far different flavor and stimulates a different reaction than "You are acting like a parent!"

   The concept of openness is controversial; people react to it with feeling and fear. It strikes closer to where most of us live than any of the other three TORI discovering processes. Data on the TORI Self-Diagnosis Scale consistently show lower scores (less openness) on the openness scale than on any of the other three TORI measures. When I talk about the theory in detail to a new audience I consistently get more questions on openness — and more resistance, misunderstanding, and defensive projection — than on any of the other three major constructs. The interaction may be due both to my fear of openness and to the fears of others. The resistance that most of us show is in part due to our deep organic recognition of the sigificance of the concept, our fear of being opened up, and our easily-aroused guilts about covering up aspects of ourselves that we really know "should be" opened up.

At a rational level, the advantages to the person and to the system of opening up are numerous and fairly obvious:

a. Closed behavior is associated with bodily ailments, tension, and anxiety. The internal growing and healing processes are blocked. Open and non-defensive behavior has been found to reduce headaches, indigestion, blood pressure, and a variety of psychosomatic symptoms.

b. Open expression serves as a catharsis which frees good feelings. It is as if I "give my guilts away", rid myself of bad feelings, hostility, hates, and sickness-inducing thoughts.

c. Holding back is usually sensed as a negative message, for it is often negative feelings that I hold back. Openness, if clear and *focused on my feelings* rather than on your behavior, is often perceived as a positive and friendly message, even when the revealed feelings are negative.

d. Opening releases energy previously consumed in the neurotic effort to cover up which can then be used in more functional activities.

e. *Showing and telling an inadequacy changes the behavior or feeling that I experience as an inadequacy.* Showing and revealing are first steps in new growth.

f. If I am open in expression, without artifice or attempt to cover up, I don't have to remember what I told people before, and I don't get caught in the "tangled webs" that are spun by conscious or unconscious deceiving.

g. The open person is safe and has no basic need to defend. There is a sense of serenity and security about being honest and clear in one's communications. Defense starts with covering up.

h. Openness invites positive feelings, trust, and intimacy from others. Openness reduces the distance.

i. Openness breeds openness. People who are open are reciprocated with sharing and learning experiences that guide them to effective social interaction.

j. Openness is associated with and necessary to effective assertiveness and proactivity, two highly-prized behavioral values.

k. Because my feelings and negative sides are generally already known through communication processes that are surprisingly accurate, although often unconscious, my acknowledging "negative sides" by revealing them early and spontaneously builds trust and confidence.

l. Rumors and projections escalate the distortions. Early openness cuts down the rumor-escalation process and improves the data processing in the whole system.

m. The decisions in the system are of higher quality because they come out of more valid data processing in the system. Decisions that represent the genuine opinions and attitudes of people who are to carry out the decisions are apt to result in effective action.

n. Openness is one of the four most critical ingredients in the high-quality environment, discussed in Chapter III.

Effective marriages, therapeutic pairs, companies, and social systems of all kinds create open space, open communication, open forms, and open organization. Masking and filtering are for defense and protection of the fearful, not for productive living.

There are many ways of opening up the social system: open stock shelves; open space in classrooms, offices, and factories; open agendas for staff meetings; unclosed office doors; public salary schedules and correspondence files; large, open data-collection meetings; public sharing of results from questionnaires and assessment tests; open and free clothing; open elections; public and open expression of criticism and evaluation; and many ways that "free the system".

6. *Focusing energy.*

When I focus my energy in doing what I deeply want, all internal states are possible for me. When I create a clear image, energy is mobilized in amazing ways to help me actualize the image.

I have become very much aware in the past few years of how I set my own limitations, and how easily I can remove them. I produce my own energy. I tap inner resources when I get in touch with what I really want to do. This way, the distinctions between work and play disappear, energy is focused on what matters, actions are rewarding *in and of themselves.* I am into my own flow and the flow of the system, and I thus create my own life.

What is impressive in the spate of new books and articles on power, intimidation, strategy, and manipulation in management and social change is the waste of energy involved. The displacement and dissipation of energy into tangential, devious, indirect, elaborate techniques of strategy and management are impressive only because they are so wasteful. A more organic and centered way of organizational life would mean more direct, simple, natural, focused ways of doing.

People have a wide range of intrinsic motivations, and they enjoy doing many things: not only eating, breathing, having sex, and getting sensory gratification, but also working, creating, solving problems, building factories, writing books, creating symphonies, curing the sick, and producing goods. People who get in touch with what they enjoy doing, what they *want to do,* are able to find a wide variety of activities that are self-rewarding, that are pleasant in and of themselves. And often, people who are really free and tuned in to themselves are able to find activities that are magnificently exciting, perhaps ecstatic. I occasionally see an artist, an engineer, a scientist, or a carpenter who would choose to do what he or she is doing regardless of pressures to do something else. Sometimes they prefer these activities to "vacations", spending time with their families, or taking more upward-mobile positions.

Life can be very satisfying when people have discovered activities that are exciting and are doing them at a pace they choose, with people they enjoy, and under conditions that suit them. These are rarely, if ever, people whose motivations have been managed by others. When parents, teachers, managers, or ministers try to shake or change motivations of others, they usually set up some kind of formal or informal program of pay, merit badges, pats on the head, gold stars, or any other of a wide variety of rewards and punishments. These efforts to influence the behavior or character of others are often extrinsic to the processes themselves and, arbitrarily administered. So-called "behavior modification" programs are simply a sophisticated formalization of the process that most parents and managers hit on by happenstance.

Negative effects follow these extrinsic-reward (or punishment) processes. People learn to work for pay or approval rather than for the joy of doing. Rewards and punishments must be continually increased or renovated in order to maintain effectiveness. Responsibility for goal-forming, standard-setting, evaluation, and other aspects of life activities, that are best when self-determined, is *taken by someone external to the activity.* Huge amounts of useless energy are spent on these reward-related strategies that could better be spent by managers and parents on something that is more useful or enjoyable. Because the rewards seem to work, as they obviously do for a time, the myths arise *that they are necessary;* and organizations build on the false premise that extrinsic rewards are effective management tools. Most unholy is the fact that ninety per cent of the beautiful and potentially-edifying activities that people engage in are put in an onerous box called "work", a category filled with unpalatable and needing-to-be-rewarded doings that somehow aren't worth doing in their own right.

Tuning in to one's sources of energy and focusing the energy on what matters is central to one's growth. Otherwise, an energy drain diverts us from our essential being. Energy is drawn away from the discovering processes and into defending against the enemy without, when the real enemy is within. We put our energy into excellence and perfectionism, when there are really very few things that are "worth doing well". We trap ourselves into seeking irrelevant rewards — rewards for doing things that are not really what we want to do with our lives. We drain energy into all of the processes of manipulating, seeking power, persuading, leading, influencing, dominating — all diversions from the things we would do if we really got in touch with what we wanted to do, deep within us. We pour our energy into meeting the expectations of others.

Similarly, the effective organization avoids diversions and focuses energy on its central mission, on its examined wants, on its essence. Effective organizations don't drain energy into defensive maneuvers, ritualistic and inherited doings, and unexamined goals.

There are ways for inventive management to create streamlined and simple organizations that focus energy on what really matters. Such procedures as job-posting and functional and lateral mobility make it easy for people to move around and experiment with jobs and functions until they find something that turns them on and tunes them in to their deep sources of inner energy. Environmental design in this instance would mean creating an environment in which it is relatively easy for people to discover what they really enjoy doing by experimenting with new activities. Vocational counseling, interest testing, and performance testing are all useful in determing one's wants, but there is no substitute for trying things out. All effective organizations provide for ease of trying and moving into new activities. They recognize that discovering and creating one's wants, interests, and aptitudes are lifelong processes. Wants are often hidden from us until we try things. Wants continually change.

A refreshing discovery has recently been made: people *can* learn and *do* exceptionally well in several different professions and vocations. Persons and organizations change constantly in this discovering process. The resulting job mobility can be viewed by the organization as a costly and disruptive process. It is now coming to be seen as a source of new energy and creativity. John K. Wood, for instance, in *The Joy of Being Fired*, tells of his dramatic findings in connection with the mass firings of the space scientists a few years ago that followed a change in the government's space policy. He found that the firings forced many of the scientists to admit the fact that they were bored and burned out in their jobs. They discovered that they welcomed this drastic "opportunity" to seek new jobs and create new careers. Organizations do a notably poor job of creating environments in which persons can continue this creative seach for renewal and for matching life activities with the inner springs of energy.

Wood, along with many other people, helped create a precedent for people to *create* jobs rather than hunt for ones that existed. The most creative job consultants now help applicants to visualize the ideal image of the position that would be most suited to their interests and energies, and then to hunt companies or organizations that wish to provide an environment for just such a professional position.

Effective organizations are learning to put energy more effectively into their central mission: manufacturing, making products, giving service, improving product design, and creative problem-solving. And they are learning to reduce the amount of energy put into energy-draining, dysfunctional, and often counter-productive activities such as supervision, quality control, public relations, inspection systems, overly elaborate record keeping, unnecessary training and management-development programs, extrinsic-reward systems, punishment systems, security programs, and a host of other defense-related activities.

7. *Reducing constraints.*

I create the fears and forces which constrain me. What I can create, I can un-create. Fears and constraints are, in a certain very real sense, illusions. They are produced by my defensive perceptions of my world. Facing these realities can set off growth-producing processes in me. I can remove the constraints that bind me.

As a consultant I have sometimes asked members of organizations to look at what is constraining them. They will first come up with such things as tight controls, inadequate resources, lack of power and influence, unfair competition, lack of competent help, inefficient organization, labor unions, governmental regulations, restrictive corporate or central policy, public opinion, inadequate education or training, and a host of other factors which they see *in the situation.* As people discuss and examine the question, they tend to move from this kind of list to the realization that the constraints, rather than being part of the situation, exist only in their own perceptions, assumptions, attitudes, and feelings about the situation. Applying TORI theory, I have learned that these internal factors are in fact determined by one's own fears and distrusts.

Kurt Lewin found it useful to conceive of each given situation as a product of an equilibrium between two sets of forces: inducing forces and constraining forces. He recognized the valid principle that it was more effective to use energy to reduce the resisting forces than to work at increasing the inducing forces. In my experience it is clear that the initial steps are these: the recognition that the constraints are internal to me, that I have complete control over them, that they are fear-defense processes, and that the constraints are minute in comparison to the internal powers and resources that I can bring to bear upon the situation.

The environmental-quality discussion in Chapter III is relevant here. Each movement up the EQ scale is into a less constrained, more releasing environment.

Most of society's conservative and civilizing forces exist as sets of morals, guidelines, taboos, rules, conventions, prohibitions, and cautions deriving from our fears of dangers in the world of nature, and our fears of the inner nature of the person. It has been thought, "with good reason" in the experiences of history, that people are dangerous and that they need to be protected from their own inner, impulsive nature. They therefore need ethical systems, legal codes, contracts and agreements, government, security systems, and multiple checks and balances to keep their raw inner natures in control. Our fears collude with these external forces and accept pressures from outside, even augmenting them. But as trust develops and as our understanding of the many translations of fear grows, we are able to move through and beyond fear and reduce the constraints that bar our way.

So, too, the effective organization focuses energy on the reduction or removal of constraining forces upon its members. This is a basic management principle. Its full use obviously requires high trust on the part of management and a high trust level present in the organization.

Many managers, parents, and teachers reinforce an inherited constraint-induction theory with their own fears and spend considerable energy in a deliberate and rational effort to increase the reasonable and appropriate constraints upon organizational members. I recall seeing a huge sign at a YMCA swimming pool. It had a huge "NO", about four feet high, and next to this what they were saying "NO" to: running, throwing things, jumping in the water, spitting, pushing, horsing around, and jumping. I asked the director if the sign had any effect upon the kids. He said: "No, but you have to do *something* to try to control them!" He reenforced my observations about constraint management: (1) constraints seldom work, (2) they often set up resistances that increase the problems they are designed to solve, (3) they are used by management out of defense and desperation, and (4) they are used a great deal by management, especially in volunteer agencies, educational systems, and churches — just the places where they would work least well, and where this form of management is so very dissonant with the usual underlying philosophy of such institutions. The effects of punishment as a constraint are usually more damaging than the behavior that the punishment is trying to "correct" or restrain.

Because so much of traditional management theory and practice is *constraint-inductive,* it requires a quiet revolution in the organization to put into practice a *constraint-reductive* program. The central issue is one of trust level. When trust level changes, management practices change.

8. *Environmental design.*

I create the world around me, my environment, the reality I live in. I always have a choice.

This primary principle and guideline is discussed in Chapter III. Table VIII summarizes the environmental-design point of view as contrasted with that of the more traditional interventive-management style.

The effective organization creates itself as an interdependent way of life. It creates mutuality, not competitiveness; friends, not enemies. The organization creates its own neighbors as it interfaces with other organizations. As the physical and sociological environment becomes significant as a world factor, modern management has become increasingly aware of the massive effects of the cultural environment as well as of the environment internal to the organizational itself. Just as the individual creates his or her own world, the organization itself can create its own internal and external environment. The principle of environmental design indicates that effective managers *focus* upon shared efforts to *change the environment* rather than upon efforts to change individuals.

In TORI theory, environmental design centers upon four variables:

a. *Personalizing.* Providing unique psychological and physical "space" for each person. Removing role structuring in the offices, the parking lots, and the dining room. Reducing the emphasis upon tables of organization and role prescriptions. Abolishing the practice of channeling communications. Reducing categories and treating people like persons, which is what women's liberation, and racial and ethnic tensions are all about. Removing the norm that status people have titles and non-status people have none.

b. *Opening.* Discussed in Guideline Number Five.

c. *Realizing.* Increasing self-determination. Increasing the visibility of multiple options in all phases of the organization. Team-building and goal-setting, integrated into self-selection of tasks and sub-goals. Use of sociometric and pairing choices in team composition and management assignment. Use of depth psychology in goal-determination and want-creation.

d. *Interdepending.* Creating norms of teaming and cooperation. Community-building as discussed in the following section. Experimentation with matrix, grid, and other functional forms of team-formation and organization-building. Open space that allows people to see each other, interact, and discover and create interdependencies. Design of information retrieval systems that optimize interfaces among units of the organization.

9. *Community-building.*

With you, I co-author our shared experiences. None of us exists by and to ourselves. You are my sister. You are my brother. The discovery of each other in depth *in community* is a renewal process that will vitalize any organization.

I create my own community. Joining, sharing, and living in mutuality are made possible by the development of the three prior TORI discovering processes: trusting-being, opening-showing, and realizing-flowering. When I know who I am, can show me to you, and am doing what I deeply want, then I can join you in depth and shared creativity.

Moving on the EQ scale is a movement forward on the scale of community depth and strength. As we get in touch with newer dimensions of our capacity for being, of integrating more aspects of our being into our functional lives, then we are ready for higher forms of community.

For me, personally, the fourth discovering process, the *inter-depending-withing,* offers the highest form of potential satisfaction, the process that is made possible by the development in the other three processes. My greatest development has come in the TORI community experiences: my highest appreciation of my self and my own capacities; my out-of-the-body experiences; my deepest aware-nesses of trusting; my deepest religious and spiritual moments; and my own movement into cosmic states.

Any social system can become a community. Seeing itself as a community, the organization can move into whatever environmental-quality level it can visualize. We are on the brink of new discoveries about community in organization. Fresh developments in the field of group dynamics from 1947 to 1977 caused a revolution in manage-ment theory and practice. They precipitated the new discipline of "organizational development" and led to significant changes in social systems. The new developments in community-forming, pioneered by the TORI community experiences and related to other parallel developments in several disciplines, will have an even more significant impact on organizational theory and practice and on social conditions in the next thirty years.

Chapter IX discusses some of the developments in community building that grow out of Trust Level theory. Our assumptions about the potential of community are as limiting as our assumptions were thirty years ago about the "human potential" of persons, before so much was discovered in the Maslow-instigated revolution in the realm of personal growth.

10. *Sensing the cosmic allinall.*

It is difficult for me to communicate in words the effects of my cosmic and allinallness experiences and the effects of presumably similar experiences of others. The most awesome effects for me, and for people whom I have experienced personnally, include the following:

(a) An inner sense of *tranquillity,* a quieting of the inner turmoil, a realization, at the deepest times, that all need to defend has passed — that there are no enemies. No fears.

(b) A larger *perspective* on everything. Seen in relation to the allness, all tragedy and pain, indeed any feeling, is powerful *in itself*, all powerful, but *also* miniscule in relation to the infinity of life that is mine. Following my cosmic experiences, I recall looking anew at previous experiences, each of which at the time had seemed unmanageable and traumatically overwhelming — the death of my son, my divorce, my illegitimacy in a sheltered Mormon community, my sudden awareness of irreversible aging, my growing awareness of my unalterable aloneness — and realizing, with a feeling equal in immensity to the earlier feelings of existential tragedy, that each of these events was miniscule in relation to my eternal destiny and that each experience had added to the beauty that was me.

(c) A never-completely-lost *awareness of the divinity and allness in every other being.* However scarred, however scared, however flawed, each of us contains the allness and each is an aspect of divinity. Each of us *is* God. My experiences with our beautiful retarded son, Larry, who is ever my guru and teacher, taught me that we always underestimate the allness and potential in every other being. The allness is in every leaf and every animal and every child and every form of life.

(d) A new *openness to experience.* I recall with a smile my earlier provincial arrogance as a young psychology professor. The myths and hopes of operationalism, Carnapian simplistics, behaviorism, and the scientific method infected us all. I forget how many times I proved that there was nothing in psychology that couldn't be measured. I remember a long period when I wouldn't have listened to anyone who talked about some of the things that I am struggling to communicate here. My long years of consulting deprovincialized me to a degree, but my allinall experiences taught me not to ignore the most improbable, irrational, and non-replicable of reported experiences. Caution and doubt can have their useful functions, but they do keep us from new and redemptive experience. Amid the nonsense and even quackery in the newly-fermenting world are some verities that will change our lives in ways that permit no turning back.

(e) A *new appreciation for the non-rational and non-verbal.* I find, now, that it is much easier to communicate with children. Animals treat me differently. I spend less time trying to make my experiences and my motives and my feelings rational. Reason is a powerful tool, but there are more powerful ones. Trust Level theory is my effort to transcend the limits of measurement and rationality in devising theory.

I am only beginning to see some of the implications of these views for modern organizational life. Many executives and others interested in organizations share these interests, hopes, and glimmerings. I think we are beginning to "crack the cosmic egg" and open up a new vision of organizational life. I am reporting in detail in a later book in this series my own transcendental and cosmic experiences and my speculations and beliefs about the transcendental organization.

Using the Guidelines

In the remainder of the book I will use the guidelines and the sketch of the basic theory as presented in preliminary fashion in the first four chapters to examine how the theory might be applied in a variety of situations.

Chapter VI deals with counseling, therapy, marriage, friendship, and other dyadic relationships. Chapter VII deals with group therapy, family life, group-process training, team-building, and other group relationships.

Chapters VIII and X deal with organizations, management, organizational development, consulting, and the experimental organizations that we have created as both demonstrations and tests of TORI theory. TORI Associates is a non-profit prototype organization that is a radical application of TORI theory to modern organization theory. Astron Corporation is a profit-making business venture that has been created as an application of TORI theory to the "harder" realities of business life. These two major efforts will be discussed along with a number of other ventures that are in various stages of birthing.

Chapter IX is a description of community development as it applies to churches, businesses, neighborhoods, therapeutic settings, recreation, and other aspects of societal life. I will discuss the TORI community experiences as one application of TORI theory to community development.

Chapter XI discusses government and social action in relation to TORI theory. Chapter XII takes an extrapolative look at the future, a "TORI'ed" look at what might happen to us in the next generation.

TRANSPARENCY

Love means to share our space and to have nothing come between us.

Chapter 6

Transparency and Being With

To love you is to be *with* you and *in* you. To have no barriers between us. To see each other with soft eyes. We allow ourselves to be transparent with each other. We transcend our boundaries.

It is my assumption that all persons, at a deep level, want to be intimate, want to be transparent with loved ones, want to be trusting. But our self-created fears sometimes keep us apart and cloud our vision of each other.

Before we look at what moves us into a transparent interbeing relationship, let's take a look at what keeps us apart. My analysis of about two thousand hours of intensive group sessions (T-group and therapy groups) in which I was a TORI-like group "leader" indicates that the following eight factors were mentioned most often as characteristic of unsatisfying relationships between two persons:

1. People feel uncomfortable when others are dependent on them, when they are cloying, demanding, or asking for more than the other is willing to give. The other side of the relationship is also unsatisfying. Most people do not like to be dependent, to clutch, to be hungry, and to ask.

2. Most people feel discomfort in paying for a relationship or in being paid for it. Being a hireling, whore, or servant is less than satisfying. People resent being talked into things, manipulated, "invaded in my space", "sold a bill of goods", or persuaded. Most people feel uncomfortable either feeling obligated to others or having others feel obligated to them. There are only subtle differences between free-will sharing and building "obligations".

3. Most people don't like relationships that are programmed or routinized. They don't like to stay in old habits, boring patterns, or relationships that seem to be devoted to simply preserving rather than growing. We don't know how much this discomfort is a function of growth-oriented attitudes of people who seek therapy and sensitivity training. I suspect that the finding is rather general, that status-quo seekers are essentially frightened and defensive.

4. People don't like feeling disconnected, lonely, out of touch, and separate. People like to feel that they are unique and special beings, but they nevertheless want to feel related to others in some depth. A surprising number of people mention wanting to be into relationships that are spiritual, transcendent, of a new order, mystical, "real" — special in some way.

5. Many people are uncomfortable and dissatisfied with life as it is now experienced and with relationships as they now are. They seek something more exciting and adventurous. The time is ripe for change and new perspectives.

6. Coming through strong and clear is the dissatisfaction with being treated "as an object", as a segmented person (as a beautiful body, a brilliant mind, a person with a special skill), or as a non-person. People are no longer happy (if they ever were) with being treated as a hero or heroine, as a god or goddess, as a deified being — not human. Marilyn Monroe, Roger Maris, Freddie Prinze — many names come to mind of persons who received magnificent adulation and who found the process painful. Basically, we want neither to be deified nor put down — but to be treated as human and real.

7. Most people don't like to feel defensive, evaluated, or compared with others. A high number of people express strong dissatisfaction with what they experience when they take examinations, assessments for certification and licensure, or appraisals for pay increases. Considering the amount of built-in assessment in our culture, we have here many danger signals that demand attention.

8. Most people don't like to be looked at as members of a class or category, even one normally associated with prestige or adulation. Each person wants to be seen as special, unique, and not simply like other members of a class. A beautiful woman sees herself as different from other "beautiful women"; a waiter would rather be seen as a distinct person rather than as one of the service personnel; no carpenter is like any other carpenter. There is no "typical youngster". No one can relate personally to a role or a class of persons.

TABLE XII. THE MAGIC OF AN INTERBEING RELATIONSHIP

What it is like for two persons to be *with* each other	What it is like when persons are not being *with*
1. The relationship is *self-rewarding;* self-sustaining; the being motivates itself	1. Relationship needs to be managed; one or both feels need to take care of the other; one or both feel dependent; not self-rewarding
2. The relationship is *co-authored;* co-sustained; each feels: "I am creating this relationship"	2. One or both feels paid, obligated, coerced, sold, invaded, used, manipulated, persuaded, influenced
3. The relationship is *moving* up the EQ scale toward new levels of being; is growing, moving, changing, in process	3. Relationship is programmed; stabilized into familiar patterns; is preservatory; is not moving, growing
4. The relationship is *synergic;* transcendent; is an organism, an emergent whole	4. One or both feels disconnected, out of touch, lonely; the pairing does not feel like a "new reality" or a transcendent whole
5. The pairing is a *co-discovering;* an adventure; is questing or playing	5. One or both may feel bored, little excitement, wanting out, with little sense of adventure or play
6. The relationship is *personal*	6. One or both feels like an object, in role, deified, or derogated, like a non-person
7. Each of us *feels better about self* when we are together	7. One or both feels defensive, evaluated, assessed, less good about self when in the relationship
8. Each feels special, *unique,* one of a kind; feels valued for self and does not feel compared with anyone	8. One or both feels insignificant, in a category or class, under-valued, or as not special or unique

The Magic of Being Truly With Another Person

The four TORI *discovering processes* are associated with states of high trust. When people are being who they are, are showing who they are to others, and are doing what they really want to do, they are then able to join each other in an *interbeing* relationship. Unexamined and unintegrated fears create in us the discomforts listed above. The process of growth is the process of learning to transcend these fears and to have significant depth relationships.

In our culture we seek many one-on-one relationships. At first glance, it seems least threatening to seek out one other person — to build relationships one at a time. We seek companionship and warmth from friends, lovers, and spouses. We seek help from counselors and therapists in healing our mindbody wounds. We seek wisdom and learning from wise teachers, tutors, and gurus. We seek specific professional help from dentists, doctors, architects, or tax consultants. We try to find mates for golf, a movie, or a talk. We seek another person as a partner for study, work, meditation, listening to music, going to church, finding emotional support, or to share expenses.

For whatever purpose we pair, we find the partnership more satisfying and want-fulfilling if the relationship meets to some degree the criteria suggested in Table XII. Of course, relationships differ over a wide spectrum of quality. They differ in intensity, expectation, commitment, reciprocity, environmental embeddedness, and all manner of qualities. They differ also in duration, from a brief conversation with a seat-mate on a bus to a lifelong marriage.

When we take charge of our own lives and when we create our own environments, we can develop the capacity to make *interbeing relationships* of most of our links to others:

1. *The interbeing relationship is self-rewarding.* Interbeing *is.* It is like grace. It comes, in its goodness, from life, from God, from the nature of being. It fulfills itself. When our life-spaces overlap...when our life-energies fuse...when our light is the same light...when we discover the god in each other...when we cry in each other's arms... when we truly inhabit the same silence...when we love without words...when we walk in each other's mocassins...when we acknowledge the same enemy in ourselves...when we recognize the same dread...we then find it more possible to walk and talk together in communion and depth. We discover each other and share the same journey.

Such unions *are* redemptive. Such a process *is* worship. Being with others in this way *can be* therapeutic and healing. We turn to therapists only because we do not know how to discover such relationships ourselves. We fancy that we need ministers to show us how to discover such spirituality. Being together in these ways *is* loving. It rewards itself. It needs no other process for its completion, justification, or meaning. *Being with is being with is being with is being with.*

Fear is what keeps us apart. And the fear this time is most surely an illusion. There surely can be no danger — save our own fantasies — in being with another in such deep intimacy.

2. *The interbeing relationship is co-authored and created in full by each of us.* It was a long time before I really began to take responsibility for my own life — to realize that whatever happened to me was my own creation. And to realize that it was a cop-out to blame the bad things that happened to me on someone else, on my environment, or on the accidents of the universe. A similar process has been going on with me in regard to my relationships with other individuals. In the past I have allowed myself to be persuaded, to be captured — and allowed many relationships to be determined by the other person. Just as I have begun to learn that I can take full responsibility for creating my own life, I am learning how redemptive it is to take *full* responsibility for creating my relationships. And to allow the other person also to take *full* responsibility for our relationship. An interbeing relationship is one in which *both* persons share *full* responsibility for the way it is between them. This is the basis for a creative, active interchange. Neither party is able to back off and blame whatever is happening on the other person. Each can take full credit for whatever happens that is good.

In the best relationship, we both get what we want all or most of the time. There is seldom need of compromise, but we engage in a continual search for creative alternatives that are exciting to both of us. We are each active in showing our feelings, our wants, and our attitudes. We know where we stand. We don't worry about being consumed, violated, coerced, or manipulated. We are loving and being loved.

3. *The interbeing relationship is dynamic and moving, growing toward new environmental-quality levels.* Any relationship has the potential for being more than it is. Accepting each other for who each is, and where each is, both can go with the flow of the relationship. When two persons are with each other in depth, each without any

intent to change the other, a dynamic tension results that leads to continuing new growth. As I go with the flow, when I am with other persons where they are, listen intently to their being, play with their rhythms, search for the uniqueness that is in them — I discover new feelings and new emerging patterns. I am able to tap into intuitive and archetypical ways of being, and I enter into new spaces with them. When we are not programmed or pushed, we create and discover.

The relationship need never be static. Any statement about how we relate is always a statement about the past. Each moment contains new promise. Knowing that the possibilities are there creates new energy that can transform us.

The growth of a two-person relationship follows the flow of the environmental-quality framework. In EQ level I, people who are hurting and fearful are likely to misunderstand each other's advances. The love-seeking of a person desperate for affection may seem to another fearful person to be cloying, even bristly or hostile. Bragging in a search for approval can be mistaken for arrogance. A simple question may be viewed as prying. Fearing persons have many ways of punishing each other. Even the most intimate relationships regress to EQ level I under fear and mistrust.

We all know of friendships, living arrangements, and marriages which are at a dominance-submission (EQ II) level, with one person leading the dance. Trust and experience can transform these into relationships that are nourishing, benevolent (EQ III), consultative, advisory (EQ IV), or genuinely participative (EQ V). In EQ I-V relationships, one member of the pair "leads" the relationship. The leadership may vary in its EQ theme as the context varies.

It is much more common for paired relationships to move into leaderless EQ VI-X states than it is for groups or organizations to do so. An EQ VI relationship can be said to exist when neither member of the pair feels that one or the other is leading or dominant; when there is true *interbeing;* and when there is true mutuality and interdependence in choosing and decision-making.

With increase of trust, the two people will build a relationship in which empathic and intuitive communication is common (EQ VII); where there is depth integration at an unconscious or archetypical level (EQ VIII); or where they move together into transcendent and mystical states (EQ IX). I assume that relationships at EQ levels VIII, IX, and X are very rare, at least in our culture. It is possible that these relationships are more common in more primitive, less word-bound, or more mystical or spiritual societies.

4. *The interbeing relationship is itself a unique, organic whole, a transcendent reality.* Each relationship is unique, never repeated. It is to be celebrated and honored, as each of us as an individual person is honored. It is for nurturing, sustaining, gardening, and caring.

Just as I, as a person, am very different from any one of my parts or even from the sum of my parts, so is a significant pairing a new whole — a new reality that is more than the sum of you and me. Stern and the other person-centered psychologists performed a high service in reminding us to honor the person. And this honoring has been a powerful antidote to the de-personalization of our society. But this emphasis has reenforced the intense individualism of our sometimes compulsively self-determining and free-enterprise culture and has been a strong factor reenforcing our fears of intimacy and community. It is time to recognize the reality and power of paired, group, and community relationships, and to accept and honor the transcendent quality of such events. When persons are accepted and honored in their own right, they discover their richness as persons and beings in transpersonal and transcendent experiences with others.

People are often put off or even frightened by images of other-than-highly-individual living because there is fear of loss of personhood: communal or collective-living arrangements, the consuming zeal of religious orders and sects, or the de-personing dedication to national super-goals of fascistic states. Because of these frightening images, many people rightly reaffirm individualism, but they may also allow these fears to hold them back from the enriching experience of interbeing and community. The road to personal enrichment lies in learning how to live intimately and transcendentally with others. We achieve freedom, self-love, and self-determination, in the fullest sense, as we learn to live with others in deepest intimacy and community.

5. *The most-enriching relationship is a co-discovering adventure into the unknown.* We join each other to search for what we may become, to determine our being, to reach out with zest toward the ever unknown. With high trust, adventure is zestful. With high fear, the unknown and unstructured path is not inviting but constricting and defense-arousing.

The critical importance of trust is never more clearly seen than in this predisposition to adventure and play. The unknown is enticing and can seem even better than the present. Living is a process, a never-ending quest into the unknown. When we know this, we know also that holding on to what once was and which can never be again is the fear path. Boredom comes from fear. Trust helps us to welcome the ever-new moment and to look forward to ever more-promising new momemts.

6. *The fulfilling relationship is a personal one.* I am unable to think of a relationship that could not be improved by becoming more personal. Keeping things impersonal is costly in terms of any significant measure of effectiveness. Health care is improved by a more personal patient-doctor relationship. Police are safer and law and order are more effectively served when police are more personal with lawbreakers and potential lawbreakers. Military action is more effective when the traditional structured relationships between officers and enlisted men are personalized. Productivity of the factory is improved when relationships are more personal. The minister-parishioner relationship changes significantly when it becomes a person-to-person search for a spiritual path. Even in science, the desirability of "objectification" of relationships between the observer and the event is being reexamined.

7. *Each person in an interbeing relationship feels better about himself or herself when they are together.* Militant individualism is essentially a revolt against processes in the first four EQ levels — against relationships that are punishing, controlling, benevolent, or advice-giving. People who continually feel coerced, smothered, persuaded, demeaned, controlled, assessed, supervised, taught, protected, or led find it difficult to feel good about themselves. As relationships move into higher EQ levels, members discover that each person is a significant part of the environment of the other — and that this environment is most effective (for all purposes?) when it contributes to *my feeling good about myself.*

Yesterday, the day before I wrote this paragraph, I joined a group of about 20 adults for the afternoon. Susann had brought 11-month old Damon, who was playing in our midst. As we watched Damon walk confidently and trustingly up to each person to play and hug, Lana said with excitement: "Look how good he feels about himself!" We celebrated and enjoyed this expression of trust. We felt re-dedicated to its preservation and nurturing in this boy and in ourselves. This so-rare and oft-battered expression of divinity and eternity is to be found within us all.

8. *In an interbeing relationship each person feels unique, special*

and truly incomparable, not to be compared with another. Each relationship is unique. Each partner in the relationship is unique, special, not to be compared with any other being. Whenever we place ourselves in a category or box, we set up processes which diminish our specialness. This is a powerful lesson for all of us, especially parents, teachers, managers, or anyone in a position of responsibility and visibility. So many administrative and institutional processes set up comparisons among persons: grades, spelling bees, pay scales, awards and prizes, competitions, offices, hierarchies, organizational charts, parking permits, or memberships. Rewards set up as many comparison processes as punishments. "Win-win" relationships aren't better in this regard than "lose-lose" relationships. *Be-be* relationships are non-comparing processes.

The celebration of uniqueness and diversity is a mark of fulfillment and realization. What is real is to be one's self. I am who I am. I am unique. I am.

Interbeing as a Friendship Process

Many relationships are casual. They occur in passing and may involve no contact of significance. The stranger on the street, the taxi driver, the next person in line waiting to purchase something, the elevator operator, the person in the adjacent seat at the airport — we are not likely to have any significant interaction with any of them. But I know some fortunate people who know how to make these contacts memorable. They relate *personally* to almost everyone with whom they interact, even casually, for they choose to recognize the personhood in everyone — even if only with a glance or a communion of spirit. I am always impressed and warmed by this, and I realize again that it does not take time or energy to be personal. A full contact is a matter of presence, of focus, of intent. It is a matter of my being where I am.

All relationships can be mini-adventures of this kind — discoveries, a sharing of the joy in the universe . . . a touching rather than a manipulation . . . a glance of trust and not a furtive distancing . . . a warming rather than a chilling . . . an invitation and not a rebuff. Interbeing simply takes trust, not time.

It is very clear that I create my friendships and my companion-ships. I have a clear choice in the matter of being lonely or friendly. Friendship and companionship start with the intent to share my being with others.

Interbeing as Loving

Loving is something more than friendship. It is made possible as persons grow into higher levels of environmental quality. Love comes with the removal of defenses, the reduction of constraints, the quieting of possessiveness and the giving of freedom, the sensing of the essence of each other, the emergence of higher trust.

Love is being into each other's flows and rhythms. It comes when lovers trust each other's processes. It cannot be commanded or persuaded. It happens, grows, emerges.

Love is an uncomfortable foreigner in the home of the ego. Loving is released into fullness as the person grows out of needs, out of the ego, out of powering and controlling, out of sensory gratifications. Loving changes as persons move into new levels of growth. It always holds new wonders, new being. Whenever I have discovered what loving is, I have found that it was more than what I sensed it to be before the new experience. Loving is as full a process as is the fullness that the lovers bring to each other. Loving transforms the lover and the loved.

Interbeing as a Family or Home-Building Process

Whether or not there are marriage ceremonies, life is enriched by stable primary relationships, either of couples or those that exist in larger communal-living arrangements. How nourishing a home environment — one that moves into higher EQ levels — a couple can build depends on the quality of the interbeing relationship they are able to achieve.

I have observed and interviewed 21 couples who met each other for the first time while in the TORI Community Experience and who then went on to get married or decided to live together in an enduring relationship. Possibly because these people knew each other in considerable depth in one or more TORI experiences before choosing each other, the relationships are notably fulfilling ones. Factors that contribute to the positive strength of these relationships are:

1. The members of the couples have a *shared belief* in a lifestyle. Their attitudes and beliefs about the key elements in shared living are very similar. They have experienced each other's behavior in a wide variety of social situations and *know* each other's significant attitudes. The congruence between attitudes and behaviors is high. There is thus a sharing of fundamental values, perceptions, and belief systems. This underlying agreement is a stabilizing factor especially when conflict and emergencies arise.

2. Most members of the couples have a *basic trust* of each other and a valuing of trust as a key ingredient in their relationship. They do a variety of things that foster the trust.

3. These couples are *more open* than most in showing feelings, not hiding secrets, confronting differences, sharing perceptions, living open lives. The more I experience these couples the more significant I see openness to be a critical factor in family living.

4. Almost all of these people believe in the *importance of community* in life. They believe that it is important to live a TORI-like life, largely because this makes it easier to come together and create a shared, communal, and caring family life. Living interdependently is a shared value.

5. In most instances with the 42 people interviewed, the person is very much into building her or his *special, distinctive lifestyle,* very much into taking care of self — a self loving process. This is especially true of the women in the couples. These women are getting into their own freedom and learning the excitement of making new choices. Options are opening that they hadn't seen before. They are discovering that they had restricted themselves to roles that they didn't want and had allowed others, particularly men, to assign them. The TORI lifestyle and philosophy are highly congruent with the aspirations of the women's liberation movement. TORI Associates is one organization that has about an equal number of men and women involved in activities at all levels. *But* it is important that *both* the men and women in the observed couples are moving out of role, into special and unique ways of blending their own individual wants and talents into new occupational choices, careers, ways of spending leisure time, or ways of making friends.

6. For most of these individuals there is a new, *emerging integrity* that comes from listening to messages from within, rather than to messages from outside themselves. This is dramatic in many instances. They are asking — demanding — that their lives be more whole, that they put *what they are* fully into their crafts, relationships, jobs, vacation periods, education, and all aspects of living. As I'm writing this and examining my notes, I'm suddenly very much aware that I'm having difficulty in classifying and naming "aspects" of living that apply to these people. This is probably a healthy sign, for life for them flows and merges so that categories don't apply. These people seem not to work, take vacations, use leisure time, have mealtimes, work for voluntary organizations, or have schedules; rather, for *them*

living blends into all living. It flows. It is integrated and spontaneous.

7. Life for most of these individuals is *filled with feelings,* highs and lows, change, excitement, instability, discomforts, emotion, fear, fulfillment. They wouldn't want to go back to the way they were, and perhaps they wouldn't be able to.

8. All of these couples are often in *EQ VI to VIII levels.* Many are experimenting with new ways of relating that increase the number of transcendental experiences they report. They are naturally having some difficulties living in a culture that is primarily in EQ II to V levels and are experiencing problems in relating to existing professional and occupational environments and with the schools, neighborhoods, and churches as they presently are.

Interbeing as a Spiritual Process

It should not surprise us that people are expressing impatience with institutional religion. Many have turned away from organized worship and religious institutions when they found them characterized by the same fear and distrust mechanisms that they see toxifying business, government, and schools. Paradoxically, these "rebels" increasingly turn to other varieties of religious or spiritual experience — the mystical, transcendence, the prospects of afterlife and reincarnation, prayer, and healing.

I see the spiritual life as expressive of a higher level of trust. To be spiritual is to be in tune with the infinite and cosmic elements within us, to move into higher levels of environmental quality. Is there some critical demarcation between phenomena that are humanistic and those that are spiritual? Possibly not. In my own experience, probably not; my experiences lead me to believe that all being states flow into each other. They move continuously into new levels that differ only in degree from one another.

Spirituality is available to each of us. As we develop higher levels of trust we gradually transcend the barriers that at each level keep us from achieving our full spirituality: our dependence upon rationality, our wishes for sensory gratification, our ego needs, our bodily processes, even our dependence on awareness. As we grow, we get in touch with inner forces that are integrative, cosmic, and nirvanic.

Life would be so greatly enhanced if our spirituality could be integrated into all aspects of living! Unfortunately many of us relinquish the major responsibility for our spiritual life to a special professional group and to a separate institution, and then we reclaim it, more or less, for an hour or two a week.

Interbeing as Productive Work

In many ways, the place to start in building strong interbeing relationships is in the workplace. Work can have a dignity, meaning, and purpose that can center the life of the worker. People who work together at self-selected and fulfilling tasks develop strong attachments, loyalties, warmth, respect, and interdependence. This is especially true if the work is honored by the person who is engaged in it — if it provides a long-term meaning to life. I have seen this dedication and centering notably in people whose lifework is painting, creative writing, architecture, space engineering, chemistry, and other highly creative callings. Think for a moment of changing the workplace from one dominated by competition, management, and extrinsic motivation to one that fosters and nurtures synergic, self-discovering, self-rewarding, and creative work partnerships and teams. Imagine work as the medium through which people discover each other; work as having spiritual content; and work as the process which leads to transcendence.

The interbeing relationship could replace the conventional role relationship in the workplace. Interbeing relationships will be more frequent as work institutions substitute a new set of assumptions about work which differ from the present classic assumptions. We would then assume that:

1. Work can be intrinsically rewarding and need not be stimulated by differential pay.

2. Work is most productive when performed with self-selected and compatible work-mates.

3. All work relationships can be lateral rather than hierarchical, and they need not be supervised or controlled.

4. Work of all kinds is a discovery process, a quest for new solutions, new satisfactions, new personal relationships, new processes — work can be play, an adventure, a turn-on.

5. The better and deeper the relationship between work partners, the more productive the work. A good relationship is one in which each person is doing fully what he or she wants — which is the nature of creative and satisfying work. I'm talking about all activities in the market place — *everything* that needs to be done *can* be satisfying and intrinsically rewarding to work-mates.

6. Every person has a unique contribution to make to a

productive organization — each person can create a job that is uniquely suited to his or her special set of attitudes and talents.

7. Work-mates can build transcendent and higher EQ-level relationships that are as fulfilling as in any other setting, and often more so.

Interbeing as a Selling Process

Selling and marketing are processes that have become identified with our competitive, free-enterprise, capitalistic economy. Because of the manner in which we define the business world and the discipline of economics, particulary the economics of a "free market", marketing becomes a critical process in the business world. Because our society is dominated by business elements, the concepts and language of the marketplace have filtered into all aspects of our lives.

Selling is a good example. One markets oneself, sells personality, markets university programs, advertises sermons, markets growth techniques, attempts to sell ideas to others in social conversation, competes with other friends in the love market, and markets religion and the paths to salvation. It is somehow ironic to see high-pressure sales techniques used by some personal-growth programs to sell the doctrine that "one is not in this world to meet other's expectations"!

The buy-sell relationship is antithetical to the interbeing relationship. Persuasion leads to resistance, distrust, the arousal of defenses, and the distancing of the participants from each other. The experienced salesperson recognizes this defense-arousal process and learns to use a variety of techniques to reduce resistance, to simulate trustworthiness, to pretend not to be selling — processes which reduce the likelihood of an authentic relationship between buyer and seller.

There may be economic considerations that make a buy-sell system necessary in a free-enterprise culture. The costs in psychological and social terms may be so great as to warrant serious examination of the system. Can we run the economy without "selling"? In the language of the marketplace, perhaps the whole process is a "trade-off" — we put up with the distrust-sickness produced by the persuasion mode in order to distribute the goods so as to keep the system going. We are left with the question: How much production and distribution goes to pay for the mindbody distrust and fear that is created? How many units of distrust are equivalent to how many units of goods availability?

Many organizational functions as currently practiced are related to the buy-sell mode of living — public-relations, customer-relations, marketing, advertising, communications, and fund-raising. How can persons who work in these areas experience — give or receive — trust, candor, authenticity, and openness? Studies show that the distrust of such people for each other is very high. I have consulted with several clients in these fields who see the issues very much as I do. They are working hard to find reasonable solutions to problems of distrust and believe that they can be solved.

Interbeing as an Evaluation Process

One other familiar institutional process will illustrate my point further. Some activities are not congenial to the TORI interbeing processes. Evaluation is a notable example.

Much of the pressure toward evaluation in our culture comes from the business world. When I asked an educator who believed in the grading/evaluation/assessment process why schools continued to use such a dehumanizing process as giving grades, he replied: "The major reason is that the business world asks us for grades and evaluations when we send our graduates out into the world to get jobs." However, my experience with business is that most employers have little interest in or respect for the grades of prospective employees — little more than most educators do.

Another pressure to evaluate is the belief that the threat (fear) of evaluation motivates people. Students will study harder if they are tested, workers will work harder for pay and for good-performance appraisal, felons will develop better character and be constrained from criminal activities if they worry about the evaluation given them by the prison warden or parole officer, children will "do" better working for pats on the head, and Boy Scouts will learn more when working for Merit Badges. I suspect that, within limits, some of this is so — unfortunately so. If people learn, work, and live out of fear, they build up tension systems that produce sickness, guilt, and self-concepts that are tenuously based on social expectations. The more "effective" the evaluation, the more negative the effects on those evaluated.

Powerful pressures to evaluate, perhaps the most powerful, arise from the need to influence and control the people one is evaluating and the insecurity one has about the outcomes being appraised. Our felt need to evaluate or to have others evaluate us is in direct proportion to our lack of knowledge or lack of confidence about what we are doing. The more we know what we are doing and have confidence in the processes we are engaged in, the less we need evaluation.

Interbeing does not thrive in a climate of evaluation. Neither the person doing the evaluating nor the person being evaluated is comfortable with the process or with the other person in the relationship, and the two find it difficult or impossible to enter into an interbeing relationship.

Institutions in a free society must be challenged to develop processes that are self-generating, rewarding *in and of themselves,* and that require little, if any, evaluation.

Interbeing as a Managerial Process

The modern organization has been founded on the philosophy, assumptions, and life styles of EQ levels I, II, and III. Based upon the process assumptions listed earlier, a managerial and administrative class structure has arisen in organizations that makes interbeing relationships very difficult. Some of the most effective managers and executives with whom I consult are often able to break out of role, cut through the structural barriers, and relate to others at any level in the organization as unique persons. It is usually the less effective managers who get caught in the depersonalizing processes that prevent managers from seeing other organizational members as individuals of dignity and uniqueness.

Interbeing relationships are only fully possible as systems and people move toward EQ VI levels. Differential power, so significant at EQ levels I through V, is a large part of the problem. When one's "boss" can hire and fire, recommend or give pay raises or promotions, talk privately with managers another level up, make performance appraisals of one's work, and have a variety of other formal and informal powers "over" the subordinate and the environment in which he works, it is difficult to create interbeing relationships between boss and subordinate.

In Chapter VIII I will report some promising experimental attempts to reduce these many barriers. Much progress is being made, but I think that we still underestimate the psychological costs we incur in maintaining hierarchical and competitive systems. It is incredible that we continue to encourage this very powerful class system in a democratic society — a system which exacerbates the very real differences that already divide people. We ask the "second class passengers" to "step to the rear of the bus" in our airliners, where they sit in less comfortable seats, eat different meals, go to segregated bathrooms, and are generally treated like the under-class. We have executive washrooms and luxury dining rooms for the first-class people, special parking places, private secretaries, stock options, and a variety of perquisites for the upper classes and a series of down-graded lesser privileges for the various under-classes. This multi-level society is highly structured in our industrial and military organizations, and perhaps increasingly so in our religious, educational, governmental, professional, and even charitable organizations.

Years ago, when I left the provincial world of the university to consult with large organizations, I became "educated" into this world of privilege, social class, and segregated living. The privileges of power, rank, wealth, and positon are larger than I had then thought. The class differences are greater, the lines of demarcation are clearer, the class structures are even more well defined than I had imagined.

What strikes me now, as I write this, is the social cost of all these class- and power-differences, in latent hostility, enforced lowering of self-concepts, informal legislation of differences in worth of persons, structured alienation across class lines, built-in role formality, and institutionalized distrust and separation. Is it surprising that all this erupts in blackout riots in New York City? — class warfare between athletes and their upper-class management owners? — latent conflict between the governors and the governed that breaks out in such symtoms as organized cheating on income taxes to "get at the bastards in Washington"? — the prideful way the doctors pilfer from Medicare? — the sullen way the new youth boast of living off welfare? — and the constant tension and warfare between the police and the citizenry?

We joke about the "Imperial Presidency" of Nixon and the light penalties for Watergate crimes, but we all collude in nourishing the class-determined management levels in our institutions, the unnecessary management featherbedding that sustains alienating organizational structures that we inherited from the medieval church and the Prussian army.

It is especially discouraging to see this class-level alienation in religious and educational systems. If we really looked closely, the rationalizations we accept for hierarchy in the military (national security is at stake), and in business (it's the only way we can "be competitive" and make money), are probably not based upon fact, but *seem* more justifiable somehow. The justification for hierarchization in schools and churches is on even more tenuous grounds. Efficiency? Cost reduction? Complexity of the task? Such rationalizations seem especially noxious when we think of the purported aims of the churches and the schools. Do we need such alienating structures to provide an environment for people to worship God or to learn with each other?

The interbeing relationships, so central to the mission of the school and the church, are made difficult or impossible by formidable power and role specifications that accompany the increasing formalization of educational and religious institutions. The difficulties are increased by the growing trends toward more professionalization of administration, computerization, sophistication of managerial technology, and formalization of role theory.

I recently had an occasion to visit, as a consultant, the huge central offices of a large-city public school system. They reminded me of the New York offices of some of the corporations for which I consult — except that they were considerably less elegant and comfortable. The similarities were plentiful: awesome complexity, unfathomable procedural mazes, ambiguity and duplication of function, and multi-level coordination that added to the problem. But there was also obvious boredom, depersonalization, resentment, apathy, officiousness, impatience, special deference to me as an "upper-class" consultant person, and the other usual constraints. It seemed depressingly ironic that they were hiring me to find a way to make their relations "human".

Interbeing is incongruent with managing, administrating, controlling, supervising, evaluating, and governing as they are often practiced. We need to take a hard and long look at the whole concept of management of an institution, to see what forms of management are necessary in terms of organizational goals, and to see if these forms are compatible with the process of making the world more liveable by reaching higher environmental quality levels.

Interbeing as Wellness and Holistic Health

Interbeing relationships and high-trust community living mediate health and well-being. It is increasingly more difficult and relatively meaningless to separate physical, mental, and spiritual aspects of health. We are mindbodyspirits who give ourselves our health and our sickness. Practitioners in many branches of medicine, psychology, and related fields are now taking a holistic view toward health, healing, and therapy. The result will be a revolution in the health-care field.

Wellness is a holistic, developmental concept and process. The developmental aspects of wellness are described in the Environmental Quality scale. Poor health is associated with the lower EQ levels. As we move into holistic, transcendent, and cosmic processes, we move out of anxiety, psychosis, hypertension, depressions, heart attacks, all manner of physical and mental ills, and perhaps even cancer. Cancer and anxiety occur in organisms weakened by low-trust states such as self-hatred, over-control, guilt, latent conflict, repression, defensiveness, unintegratable fear, disowning our lives and our bodies, over-rationality, passivity, and congestion of the mind and the spirit.

The road to health is the discovery of interbeing and taking responsibility for living one's life at new levels of environmental quality. We may well find that persons who spend a large share of their lives in interbeing states do not get sick — in mind, body, or spirit. Anxiety or hypertension are to be treated as cues that one is not relating with trust — and are signs that one can use to reexamine relationships and to create new relationships in depth.

Taking responsibility for one's self means creating a new environment, seeking interbeing relationships, creating trusting communities, examining one's TORI processes: looking at who I am, how I'm opening myself, how I'm doing what I want, and how I'm creating interdependent relationships.

Wellness, as I view it, starts with interbeing relationships in the key areas of a person's daily life. Such relationships are at the core of the holistic health orientation, which is causing a reexamination of health-care concepts and institutions. The conventional health-care systems are sometimes even more distrust-managed and alienating than other institutions mentioned in the section above. Rationalized as necessary because we are dealing with literal life-and-death issues, the hardening of the organizational arteries in the hospital and medical clinic is notably visible. This is especially incongruent, considering that the formal aim of the hospital is to heal. It is of first importance that the atmosphere among staff be humanized. Historically, the medical setting has been class-structured and hierarchical. This must be changed.

Because of what we know about the powerful influence of the larger environment upon mindbody health, a high-priority aim of holistic-health reform must be the humanization of the hospitals. I still remember, vividly etched, the words of my mother after spending two weeks in a hospital following major surgery on her stomach:

"Jack, I would rather die than ever to come back to a hospital." It is not necessary (even in the most "intensive" ward) to depersonalize patients and each other in the name of emergencies, efficiency, and life-saving. As many hospital programs are now demonstrating, a hospital environment can be made personal, human, caring, loving — and healing, in the fine sense of the word.

Even the most efficient and modernized health care is severely under-effective when given by other than loving hands. The effects of the interpersonal environment often outweigh the effects of medical and chemical care.

Interbeing as a Therapeutic Process

Called by a wide variety of terms, provided by people with an even greater diversity of training and background, viewed with a variety of feeling-states from transference-worship to fear-hostility, therapy is on the increase. More and more people seek help from clinical psychologists, psychiatrists, social workers, counselors — but also astrologists, holistic healers, palm readers, psychic surgeons, hypnotists, nutritionists, pediatricians, vocational guidance advisers, teachers, psychics, chiropracters — anyone who offers help to troubled people.

A number of professionals find TORI theory useful as an orientation in doing therapy. My assumption is that the most therapeutic relationship between a therapist and client is an interbeing relationship as I have defined it in Table XII. The client and the therapist co-author the experience, are as personal and open with each other as they are able to be, and develop a relationship that is self-rewarding. The therapist becomes an "environmental designer", looking, with the client, at the environment they create together. Together, they move into whatever EQ levels are possible for them.

The interbeing relationship is difficult to create in a twosome where one member is paid and the other pays, where one member comes for help and the other provides it, and where one enters the relationship defining himself or herself as unwell and the other person as well. Many effective therapists are able to move beyond these initial barriers and get into a reciprocal and synergistic relationship that is growthful, nourishing, and healing for both parties.

If this TORI-like, loving relationship is indeed the most effective form of therapy, we therapists are in a sense legal prostitutes, taking pay for love. That the process works so well is a devasting commentary on our fearful, loveless, and low-EQ society. We in the helping professions are unfortunately and unintentionally something of a parasitic class, living off the ill health and dependency that is bred in an EQ II-III-IV society which we help create. These crippling dependencies are not likely to be substantially reduced by the kind of education, counseling, and therapy that we currently practice. Required, I think, is some form of "therapy" for institutions, programs similar to the ones I describe in Chapters VIII and IX, in which drastic changes are made in the prevalent environments in which we live. People living a large share of their lives at EQ levels beyond V do not need or seek therapy.

Interbeing as an Educational Process

The process of education is the process of personal and institutional development into higher levels of environmental quality. Tables V, VI, and VII show that the "educational outcomes" necessary for such life development would include processes such as the following:
- socializing
- nurturing
- consulting
- collecting and using data
- choosing and deciding
- creating our own resources
- learning to live in an emergent community
- increasing our empathy and intuition
- integrating our archetypical and unconscious processes into our conscious living
- re-capturing our extra-sensory and transcendent skills
- getting in touch with our integrative, cosmic 'and spiritual beings

Achieving these and similar outcomes need not be an inter-personal process. Persons can learn from meditation, self-hypnosis, introspection, books, television, cassettes, videotapes, teaching machines, and any number of readily available processes and resources.

However, what is likely to be the most significant learning of the processes listed above comes while building interbeing relationships with people with whom we work, play, worship, invent, sing, discover, transcend, learn, communicate, or travel. We learn to live *in the being*.

This is not to go back to the concept of "learning by doing", which had a flavor of routinized, motoric, repetitive, drill-to-perfection schooling. It is *learning by doing/feeling/being/thinking,* learning in all processes of living. The more nearly the co-learning is done in an interbeing relationship, the more significant the educational process.

The most effective two-person education process is one in which the learners are in a full interbeing relationship, co-discovering the attitudes, skills, knowledge, and abilities necessary for a full and transcending life. Can a teacher-student relationship be an interbeing one? Many effective teachers now build such relationships with students; but there are many barriers to such relationships. The "intervening" teacher, who tries to "teach" the student, is likely to learn while the student watches, as most beginning teachers discover rapidly; to build dependency in the student, especially if the teacher is skilled in doing the learning for the student; to create a fustrating and alienating environment in the classroom, as Holt and a number of other contemporary writers have pointed out so compellingly; and to create defensive resistance to the intervention strategies.

The teacher who has learned to build interbeing relationships can learn *with* the student, share a sense of wonder and excitement in the co-discovering, and create a process together that is fulfilling, even ecstatic or transcendent.

EMERGENCE

Trust makes possible the emergence
of being and essence.

Chapter 7

Emergence of the Group

Each group *emerges* as a special kind of organism, growing out of the intermeshing of the four TORI discovering processes. Each group is unique, as different from other groups as a person is from other persons. A group is more than a collection of persons, more than the sum of its parts. It has being and essence.

Some groups grow, take on life, actualize themselves, are seen by members as healthy, and provide an environment of trust. In this chapter I'll consider five kinds of groups with which I am especially familiar and in which I have lived a great deal of my life: the family group; the classroom or learning group; the therapeutic or counseling group; the sensitivity training group; and the work or management team. There are unique purposes and significantly different processes and structures in each of these five special situations, but it is the similarities that interest me most and provide the most useful content for this chapter. I respect the group I belong to, consult with, study, or learn from — just as I celebrate and honor the person. I go with the group, flow into it, savor it, *live* in it, pick up its vibrations, and try to sense its essence.

Some groups stagnate, constrict, defend, or provide an environment in which members feel less good about themselves. Such groups are seen by members as draining, boring, unhealthy, and requiring more than the members are willing to give. Some families are viewed with pain and as providing an environment that one doesn't want to return to. Some therapy groups lead to greater illness and the need for more help. Some classrooms are toxic. Some management teams hold interminable meetings, make impatient and unsatisfying decisions, create more problems than they solve, and add to the organizational burden.

Through our energies, actions, and attitudes *we create the groups we belong to* — and they, in turn, nourish or drain us.

What Do I Do When I Find Myself in Charge of a Group?

I'm writing this chapter as a message to myself and to everyone who is or will be a member of a group — and this gives me a rather large target audience. But, especially, I'm writing this for myself and for you as parents, therapists, teachers, group leaders, and managers. The theory states that such a person simply does whatever he or she would do *as a person in the group.* Of course, it isn't that simple. Parents, therapists, and managers have many pressures to assume roles and to take on special responsibilities. The pressures come from their own feelings of responsibility and from the expectations of children, clients, and workers. Removing these role pressures is an early task of the leader and the group.

In Table XIII I have summarized in checklist form the theory as it applies to the group leader who is in the process of moving from an EQ V or pre-V level to level VI and beyond. By now the specific 32 items in the table need little elaboration. For those of you who wish to follow up and read more about the theory as it applies to groups, there is an annotated list of references in the appendix. This is not intended to be a training manual for group leaders, but an elaboration of TORI theory as it applies to groups. A later book in the series is intended as a set of guidelines for experimentation.

The plan of the chapter is to discuss the theory from the standpoint of group growth and development, dealing with the major phenomena of group life as I see them. I will then discuss each of the five selected group situations: the family, the classroom, the therapy group, the training group, and the work team.

First, let me comment on a few of the items in Table XIII.

1. Again, the over-arching question that each group leader asks, in applying TORI theory, is: What would it be like if I were more trusting? The application of TORI theory is a continuing idiosyncratic process. As a therapist, parent, or teacher I continue to ask, in moments of reflection, what it means *to me, now,* to be more trusting. The function of Table XIII and of reflecting on theory is to develop

TABLE XIII. BEING WITH A GROUP
(As Parent, Teacher, Therapist, Trainer, or Manager)

I move *away* from:	I move *toward:*
1. Fulfilling my *role* as parent, teacher, or therapist	1. Being a full *person*
2. Doing what is *helpful* (my role prescription)	2. Responding to my *feelings* and perceptions (showing me)
3. Focus upon relations between *role and role* (leader-member)	3. Focus upon *relations between persons*
4. Focus upon *intervening*	4. Focus upon improving our *environment* together
5. Focus upon the family or group as *a collection* of persons	5. Focus upon family or group as a *transcendent* unit
6. Taking responsibility for me and for you	6. Taking responsibility for *our family or group*
7. Responding to what patients or children *need* (programming)	7. Responding to how *I see or feel now* (spontaneous)
8. *Modeling* appropriate or professional behaviors	8. *Sharing all* of me (showing)
9. Responding to the other as *client, student, child*	9. Responding to the other as a *unique, special person*
10. Concern for *changing* or remedying the deficient person	10. Concern for the *growth* of each of us, our being
11. Focus upon *motives,* interpretations, and inferences	11. Focus upon available and *experienced behavior* now
12. Focus upon *abstraction,* generality, or principle	12. Focus on *concrete,* primitive feelings, perceptions
13. Focus upon *values, morals, and judgments*	13. Focus upon *describing what I feel or see*
14. Focus on and concern for *then,* past and future	14. Focus on and concern for *now* (being present)
15. Description of the passive self as a *static* being	15. Focus upon each of us as a *dynamic, in-process* being
16. Focus upon *limitations* of each of us, on what we need to learn to get up to speed	16. Focus upon *strengths* and *growing edges* of each of us

I move *away* from:	I move *toward:*
17. Focus upon *rewards* and punishments	17. Focus upon *flow* and being
18. Focus upon *legality,* contract, norms, rationality	18. Focus upon *flowing* feelings and perceptions
19. Focus upon *management* and controlling the process	19. Focus upon getting *into the process,* the flow
20. Focus on terminology of fear, risk, *caution,* conserving	20. Focus on trust, *venture,* impulse, liberation
21. Focus upon *words,* semantics, speech, precision	21. Focus upon *sub-lingual* and organic integration
22. Focus upon *planning,* preparation format	22. Focus on *doing* it
23. Focus upon law, order, and *structure*	23. Focus on *de-structuring* and breaking up of patterning
24. Emphasis upon *commitment* and obligation	24. Emphasis upon wants and impulses, emergence
25. Concentration on *readiness* and present capacity	25. Preparing us for *transcending* present readiness
26. Reaching *consensus*	26. Celebrating *differences* among us
27. Concentrating on my *preferred modality,* my habits	27. Living in my *imaging,* actively creating images
28. *Accepting* my current reality	28. *Choosing* continual new realities, opening myself to transcendence
29. Listening only to my *body*	29. Listening to my *mindbodyspirit* and to all of me
30. Accepting my *EQ level*	30. Allowing myself to create *new environmental levels*
31. Living in my *current feelings* and perceptions	31. Living in the *allinall*

myself so that in meeting a new situation I can be more spontaneous and present, more together, more in tune with all of my being. I would throw away the book, as it were, when in the group and then perhaps return to the book or the table in moments of reflection and retrospective analysis. Or because trusting is an open process, I would discuss my "theory" or specific elements in it with the members of the family, class, or team. Group living at any level from EQ V through X is a collaborative and joint process of discovering. No one knows finally and absolutely the best way of being together. *Life in each group is a continuous process of discovering.*

2. The Environmental-Quality analysis in Chapter III provides a framework for any group or group leader to look at the issues. Depending upon the EQ level which determines the process, the manager or teacher asks himself, herself, or the group: How can we create a new environment that will nourish us? Here we are talking about EQ levels IV, V, and VI because leaders at EQ levels I, II, and III would not be asking these same questions. And EQ levels VI through X would not have leaders, therapists, teachers, or managers. Groups at those levels would have moved beyond the leader-related concerns dealt with in this chapter.

3. The words used in the table describing the positions which one moves away from and moves toward are intended as a list of dilemmas for reflection, rather than rules to follow. Our frame of reference is a culture facing an impasse between EQ levels III and IV, or IV and V, with some persons and groups struggling through the major impasse between V and VI, the boundary line between *leaderful* life, which is passing away as a lifestyle, and *leaderless* life, which is the wave of the future. This transition is a major societal process with far-reaching consequences. There are significant differences among TORI theorists in viewing this transition. To illustrate: in a recent flyer put out by one of the TORI International Community local groups is a statement: "We are a leaderless community, because we believe *that we are all leaders.*" To the contrary, *I* feel that we are a leaderless community because we have come to the realization that *none of us is a leader,* that leaders restrict us, and that the assumption that we need leaders is self-defeating and restrictive. This book may further productive dialogue on this and other issues.

4. One exciting and positive aspect of TORI theory is that TORI practitioners have major differences (as illustrated above) that are easily expressed and celebrated. I cite one further example. I believe

that techniques are depersonalizing and hence trust-reductive. Another recent flyer from a highly active and beautiful TORI community says: "We use no particular technique, but rather a variety of them, thus not limiting ourselves to one technique." This is certainly a major difference among us, but we must remember that each of us writes and creates his or her own theory.

5. As Item 5 in Table XIII indicates, I believe that group therapy is more than a therapist working with one individual at a time in a group setting. Most of the films and transcripts of "group therapy" that I have seen show a skilled therapist working with one person after another in a group situation. Seemingly, the hope or expectation was that therapist modeling would be effective, or that empathic observation, projective problem-solving, or some other similar process would enable the participants to benefit from the sequential therapy. I see group therapy as something very different. The group, with or without the help of a therapist, somehow creates a climate, a new environment, a new and transcendent organism that is much more than a collection of individuals or of pairs. It is this new organism that nourishes the therapy and that mediates the *interbeing* processes that *are* the therapy. What each therapist does to enhance this process is not completely clear, but clarifying the concept is a step in the right direction.

6. In Item 6 is the statement that "taking full responsibility for our family group" is a positive step in group formation. As a member of a group which is important to me, I can take full responsibility for creating our environment. I take *full* responsibility for initiating shared and collaborative processes. Anything less than full responsibility is a cop-out and allows me to blame any existing group limitations (at least, as I see them) on those members who seem to like it the way it is. This is also different from taking *any* responsibility for *any other single member* of the group, or even trying to influence other members. I take full responsibility by clearly expressing my feelings, showing me and my being, making visible my wants and preferences, and taking part in any problem-solving or creative approach to the issues or problems of the group. I can also change my wants, preferences, feelings, and even my nature as I gain more experience, achieve a deeper perspective, or engage in creative interchange. I am part of the emergence and the synergy.

7. In Item 7 I am expressing my view toward the relative ineffectiveness of motive-analysis. After years of trying to analyze my

motivations and the motivations of my patients, students, clients, and friends, I found myself going down by-paths which led nowhere. A motive is always an inference, an interpretation, a second-order and retrospective, non-existential analysis. Such an analysis usually leads to pejorative and judgmental feelings on the part of both the analyst and the person analyzed and raises defenses and the distrust level. I prefer staying with direct experience and using the concept of motive sparingly. "Motive", "need", and "value", mentioned in Item 13, are overused concepts and are best replaced with concepts closer to direct experience. The "exercises" used in "value-clarification" experiences have been used in other human-relations and psychological training. Calling choices "value judgments" adds a complicated, unnecessary, guilt-inducing, and possibly confusing step to the process of experiencing. "Value", like "leader", is a word that grows out of EQ I-V concerns and becomes less relevant in levels VI and beyond. Value-clarification experiences are probably useful in helping people move out of "value" (defense-bred) concerns and into higher EQ levels and states.

8. Item 16 highlights an especially useful concept: Functional learning comes from strengthening our present ways of being, freeing ourselves from our constraints, going with what we do and feel, being in our own rhythm and flow — *not* from getting in touch with our limitations, getting feedback on our errors, or trying to remove deficiencies. I view both education and therapy as growth processes rather than as remedial or corrective processes.

9. Item 17 points up the dilemmas of rewards and punishments. Because learning theorists long ago discovered the fairly obvious and powerful learning principle that rewarded activities are repeated and punished activities are less likely to be repeated, practitioners have used this principle to try to improve life for children, workers, clients, and other groups. Recently designated as "behavior modification", this ancient form of people control is clearly much more appropriate to EQ levels I, II, and III than to any of the higher levels. The culture may have already outgrown the need for behavior modification.

10. Item 22 refers to the trust-forming focus upon action-taking, "doing it", following impulses and spontaneity, discovering what we want to do by being into what we are doing, and other existential processes — ways that are in contrast to planning and preparation activities. The higher the fear, the greater the need for planning, pre-testing, detailing prescriptions of programs, and other rationalizing of

process. How much to plan, how much long-range visioning and imaging are functional, how much programming to do — all are issues for the TORI practitioner.

11. Item 25 refers to the growing recognition that "readiness" is a passive, fearful concept. It is retrospective and limiting to describe a person as having a readiness level. Readiness levels are states to be transcended — states that *will be* transcended by the trusting person. I am always ready for more than I was at the last moment that I looked. It is useful for me, in looking at myself, to think of readiness levels as states that I have passed through. When as a group we design for ourselves a more flowing environment, we all move past our readiness levels.

12. Item 26 refers to consensus as a concept related to EQ level. When action groups are at EQ level V, a participative mode, they often use much energy reaching consensus. This may be essential until the group moves into levels VI and VII. In a management or work team, for instance, it may be quite necessary that the group reach consensus for involvement in later action or for commitment to the planned task or action at hand. The same might apply to a family council. There are occasions when the family may wish to reach consensus: on an important family purchase, a major vacation plan, or a way of sharing the family tasks. A creative under-agenda for the family is to move beyond consensus into EQ levels VI and VII, where actions flow into each other in more natural ways, where there still is an organic or body-movement-and-rhythm agreement, but without as much of the word-processing that is so necessary at level V. In learning, sensitivity training, and therapy groups (depending upon the model being used, of course), there may be little need for consensus. Indeed, struggling for it in such groups is often a diagnostic sign of defensiveness and unproductive tension. Arriving at a consensus about how we all feel, how we see something that is happening in the group, or how we block our movement is often meaningless. It serves few significant purposes in the group and it works against the more productive aim of examining and celebrating the rich differences among us.

Groups, Like Persons, Grow

On the surface, groups seem very different from each other. Differences are so visible, persons' ways of expression are so varied, and groups start from such different places that the underlying similarities are clouded over.

I find it useful to view groups as having four basic modal concerns that are processed throughout the life of the group. Left in a free field of interaction, these four concerns, listed in Table XIV, generate intrinsic forces that reduce the concerns themselves and produce personal and group movement to fulfill the wants and natures of group members.

The *acceptance* concern has to do with the acceptance of self and others, the formation of trust of self and other members, the reduction of fears, and the achievement of *membership* in the group. The *data-flow* concern has to do with the flow of perceptual and feeling data through the person and the group, the communication system in the group, and the translation of these data into *decision-making* and choices.

The *goal-formation* concern relates to the determination of member wants, the integration of these intrinsic motivations into group actions and problem-solving, and the translation of this process into *productive work*, creativity, learning, or growing. The *control* concern has to do with our early wishes to control ourselves, the other members, and the process itself; and the translation of this protective need to control into some kind of satisfying flow of behavior, some stable and trust-able form. This process becomes the *organization* of the group, the form and structure of interdependence and mutuality.

What impresses one most about the early stages of group life are the many creative ways we devise to cover up our fears and distrusts. Column Two of Table XIV lists a few of these translations of fear. Initial fear is augmented by uncertainty, lack of structure, ambiguity, lack of clarity about the expectations others have of me, the facades we all put up to reduce any cues that might otherwise be apparent, not knowing what I will be called on to do in the group, and the evident fears of others which serve as a contagious force.

According to TORI theory, the most significant description of group life is an account of how these fears become superseded by trust. Column Three of Table XIV lists a parallel set of descriptions of how trust gradually displaces fear in these four modal-concern areas. These brief statements describe gradual trends that occur as growth happens.

Development of acceptance and membership. In the early stages of entry into a group there are many symptoms of distrust: persistent defense of one's public image; avoidance of feeling or of conflict; denial of the importance of the group or what it is doing; seeking knowledge of the roles and status of the others to determine how

TABLE XIV. DEVELOPMENT OF A GROUP

Modal concerns	Signs of early phases of development	Signs of later phases of development
Acceptance (Membership) (T)	Concern for inclusion Concern over motives Paranoia, cynicism Conformity Fear for adequacy Bartering personality Testing of acceptance Need for status Need to define role	Celebration of diversity Acceptance of motives Trust, and OK to distrust Ease in non-conformity Feelings of adequacy Being is important Letting be My space is fine Role not relevant
Data flow (Decision making) (O)	Strategy, gimmicks Facade building Caution, sense of risk False assumptions Circumvention, grapevine Deceit, dishonesty Ambiguity, projection Painful decisioning Management of data	Spontaneous expression Facade reduction Impulsive expression Realistic "theory" Conflict, confrontation Candor, frankness Clarity, directness Flowing, decisioning Flow of communication
Goal formation (Productivity) (R)	Apathy, withdrawal Resistance Persuasion, advice Extrinsic motivations Competition, rivalry Managing of motivations Atrophy of self Frenetic work Diffuse goals	Energy into work Involvement, creativity Allowing differences Intrinsic motivations Cooperative behavior Accepting motivations Re-emergence of self Satisfying work Clarity of goals
Control (Organization) (I)	Cynicism on organization Structure, channels Rules and form Bargaining, limited war Concern for controls Dependency, hostility Power struggles Concern for leadership Legalism, rationality	Fluidity of organization Informality, anarchy No need for rules Expression of wants Controls unimportant Interdependence, sharing Power irrelevant Little need for leaders Flow of feelings

dangerous the turf is; suspicion about the motivations of other people; derogation of the powers and abilities of the group; maintenance of formality of behavior; keeping others at an appropriate distance; attempts to set up rules and protective structure; and a variety of other mechanisms used to gain acceptance and reduce risk in the group. The issue is complicated, of course, because neither the person nor the group is completely aware that the concern is largely one of acceptance of self and others. Not knowing what the problem is, the group finds it difficult to work effectively. Even if I know what the "problem" is, how do I go about getting accepted by others, let alone being accepted by myself?

Members attempt to gain membership by exhibiting power or sophistication; by trying to prove adequacy; by showing knowledge of previously gained group skills; by displaying credentials in some subtle way; by pairing or handclasping with other members who seem adequate or influential; or by whatever means that seem to have worked for them in the past.

As trust grows with interaction, a number of behaviors change. Diversity becomes accepted and appreciated as potential strength. Members begin to accept attitudes and feelings in others — the same things that turned them off earlier. People gradually learn to be *personal,* rather than *in role.* People show their vulnerabilities with minimal concern for danger or hurt. Other people seem safe, seem to have acceptable and reasonable motives, feel like friends and less like potential enemies, and now seem exciting rather than threatening.

This trust transformation in the group and in most of the members seems always to occur. In some ways, it is miraculous, coming like a softening wave over the most bristly group as people discover each other for what they are, discover that people are basically safe, trustworthy, well-motivated, and human.

Data flow, decision-making, and the development of a group communication system. Movement on all four basic-concern processes occurs simultaneously, but there is an optimal sequence. Development of acceptance makes possible the opening up of feelings at a deeper level. The flow of data makes possible the integration of group-goal structures and permits the group to behave in ways that seem productive to the group. The formation of intrinsic and functional goals creates openings for the emergence of a satisfactory structure and order. This is not to say that the four processes necessarily occur in the named sequence. They flow together and enhance each other.

Honesty and candor are difficult to come by. Fear leads to caution, holding back, distortion of expression, filtering of feelings, building of polite facades, and the growth of grapevine and washroom conversation groups. In such smaller and safer subgroups the group members say what they would have liked to say, with more courage, in the larger group itself. We develop a repertoire of highly-evolved withholding skills and compensatory attitudes which sanction this filtering to ourselves and to others who might be willing to listen.

Members who have developed withholding skills are adept at fouling up the decision-making system, for if the group has difficulty in getting adequate data, it is almost impossible to make quick and effective decisions.

As trust grows, the fear-barriers that prevent candor and openness drop away. People become more expressive, impulsive, frank, and spontaneous. They say what they think and feel. They express opinions in brief and clear messages, with a minimum of preamble and apology. They make it clear how they feel. This process is what later makes EQ level VII possible and so effective.

As people become more open, conflict and confrontation occur, opening further doors to deeper communication and involvement. Congestion and blocking are reduced. Caution is less necessary. Groups get to "real" problems and issues more quickly without so much "warm up", which is usually a function of initial and unfaced fears.

The lack of open data about feelings and perceptions in natural work groups is frightening and confusing. It is also difficult to change, embedded as it is in old fears and habits, and in time-honored mechanisms so familiar that they seem natural and inevitable. When groups lack data, they obviously cannot help but make inappropriate decisions based upon incorrect assumptions: that silence means consent or dissent, that all of us like things this way, or that we must like these meetings or we wouldn't have them. A kind of unconscious conspiracy leads to hoarding of relevant feelings and opinions. The group becomes paralyzed. This collusive paralysis leads to the prevalent cynicism about all groups: that committees can't solve problems, run railroads, meet a bottom line, or do anything right.

With trust, groups learn to gather data quickly and to get out of "datalessness". They are then able to make decisions and make them more wisely than individuals could by themselves. Groups *can be* marvelous instruments of effectiveness. Some *do* run large companies, meet bottom lines, make effective decisions, and take strong actions.

Development of goal formation and various forms of productivity. Fear and distrust also result in partial data processing, which, in turn, prevents adequate integration of group goals.

Inadequate goal formation comes from lack of clear awareness of individual purposes, failure to process data, hurried agreement on partially formulated goals, lack of adequate consideration of alternatives, lack of appropriate resolution of the acceptance concern and a resulting tension that militates against productive work toward any goal, and overabstraction of the goal so that the group is not clear on what members are agreeing on.

Quality of goal-formation is a distinguishing mark of effective group action. In poor groups or in early high-fear stages of most groups, compromise goal-setting sometimes results in group members feeling that they are doing something less satisfying than they would be doing if they were alone and not in the group. Members assert that they are going along to satisfy others, to appear flexible, or to avoid being seen as stubborn or rebellious. In our early research on groups, we found a high "reservation score" in early stages of group growth. When data were later gathered by better means such as depth interviews, members who had been seen by the rest of the group as consenting were found to have a number of unverbalized, secret reservations about the decisions that were made by the group.

Apathy or frenetic work is a sign of early and unresolved tension arising from the goal-formation concern. Busywork can be mistaken for creative or productive work. It comes from duty motivations, the compulsive need to impress others, and the desire to prove to others that the group is effective. The feverish work may last for a time but has little relevance to real goals and does not lead to group commitment.

Apathy, on the other hand, is a form of resistance to goals which have been badly articulated and have not been understood. It may also come from persuasion and pushing by other members in creating goals, or from charismatic and "dynamic" people who are trying to lead the group. It may be a reaction to activities that the apathetic person has not chosen.

Groups in early stages make other kinds of goal-setting errors. Overaspiration, for instance, can create vague and distant goals which are unattainable and turn people off before group effort even begins. Casual agreement on "apple pie" and "motherhood" goals is often an escape from facing decisions about more difficult alternatives.

The processes of goal-setting are clearly related to the quality of productivity. If goals come from *deep* assessment of member wants, *open* processing of relevant data, *creative* synthesis of expressed wants and are developed in an atmosphere of high trust, the goals agreed upon are an integrating force toward cooperative behavior, satisfying and sustained work, joy in group activity, and inter-dependence.

The development of interdependence, appropriate control, and effective organization. In the early stages of group growth, fear produces demands for structure, control, rules, leadership, role clarity, channels of communication, and other means of reducing ambiguity and unpredictability. Members may ask for a timekeeper to keep members from monopolizing time. Someone may ask for ground rules. "If we take turns talking around the circle, then I will know when my time comes, and I won't have to fight to get in." Someone may ask for ordered introductions to get acquainted. As one member said: "I know what nurses are like and if I know she is a nurse, I can respond to what I know nurses will do."

When I talk about structure, I mean recognizable patterns, rules, roles, channels, controls, contracts, laws, authority, accountability, formal agreements. In another sense, there is always "structure", such as sociometric preferences, seating patterns, and communication paths.

Group members ultimately find that these apparently secure constructs are made of sand. Structures apparently play little or no part in accomplishing the conscious purposes that people have in mind when setting them up. The demand for structure is to satisfy a need for predictability, order, security, freedom from turmoil, efficiency, fairness, protection of the seemingly weak from the seemingly strong, control of apparently dangerous or disliked minorities, a rational world, a rule of law, and other seemingly reasonable states. The problem is that structure simply does not accomplish these ends, reasonable or not. Without trust, structure instead produces circum-vention, resistance, stagnation, delinquency and law-breaking, unfair-ness, new laws to correct old laws, inefficiency, disobedience, and a variety of counter-dependent behaviors. If there is high trust, structure is not necessary.

These generalizations about structure and trust seem to hold very well in small groups. Most "small" groups, as the term is used in the vast and growing literature, vary in size from six to twenty. All such small groups progress in trust over time.

As groups develop in trust they become more informal, less structured, less controlled, less concerned with power and authority, less dependent upon leadership, and more flowing and fluid in form. They show greater mutuality, sharing, and interdependence. They become more caring, orderly, safe, comfortable, and gentle, not at all like the fantasy of *Lord of the Flies* or of dangerous anarchy — the catastrophic visions of structure advocates, who view leaderlessness and emergence as "anarchy" and therefore as dangerous.

The Family as a Group

The most direct and immediately satisfying application of TORI theory is made in the home. I have seen a number of TORI practitioners apply TORI theory to home-building with their own families. Lorraine and I began using TORI theory in our home when we were married twenty-six years ago.

There have been five members of our family group. From the beginning we have tried to create a TORI-group atmosphere. Larry, our first born, died when he was 7. Blair is now 21 years of age. John is 16. All of us see each other as persons, as close room-mates living together, rather than as parents and children. We have all tried to be role-free and rule-free. We have never consciously tried to make any rules, contracts, or formal agreements.

There has been no conscious and deliberate effort in our family to "manage" the four TORI processes: to manage the role relations, communication system, motivations, or controls. We have made no conscious efforts to use rewards or punishments in the home, no deliberate efforts to influence the motivations of each other. Formal organization is almost non-existent.

We have all tried to create an environment at the EQ VI and VII levels, with an emphasis upon a lot of love, physical touching, expression of feeling, candor, openness, warmth, freedom for what everyone wanted to do, privacy when desired, empathy, listening, and as much time as possible together as a family unit. This has been the *emphasis and the intent.* The results have been very positive. There is no emphasis upon responsibility, discipline, training, teaching, rewards and punishments, morality, cautions, schedules, duty, obedience, obligations, controls, standards, and a number of classic child-rearing concepts that appear in the conventional textbooks.

Each of us, Lorraine, Blair, John, and Jack, feels good about our family, enjoys it when the family is together, and feels good in inviting friends to the home. Of course, Blair and John are now seeking more relationships outside of the home and spend an increasing amount of time with friends, and we spend less time as a family unit than either Lorraine or I would wish.

Both Lorraine and I feel very good about the way our theory has worked in the home. Of all of the things that I have done in my life I feel best about my home life, and especially about the environment we have created for ourselves. Especially, I believe that Larry, Blair, and John had the best starts in life that it was possible for Lorraine and me to help provide. I have examined the many applications of the TORI theory we have made in industry, teaching, community building, human-relations training, and consulting — and I would change a great deal of what we did in each of these applications. But in our family living, I can think of nothing major that I now would do differently as far as applying TORI theory is concerned.

Others who have tried TORI theory in the home have reported similar positive results. They have also reported difficulties, especially when first applying the theory. The trust level of the persons applying the theory is critical, of course. The members of our family *know* that we can trust each other, and we *know* that trust is a powerful and necessary ingredient — the most significant factor in the home.

Another way of putting the matter is that freedom and love are the key ingredients to living. In the clinic and in the neighborhood I have heard parents talking about their children. One woman said: "I give them freedom because I can't control the darned kids anyway, so I might as well not try." If one "gives freedom" (one can't "give" freedom, of course) with reluctance, begrudgingly, or in desperation, then the freedom is not genuine. Allowing freedom and loving family members *in a feeling of trust* is a quite different matter. TORI theory "works" for those who deeply believe that it works. To become trusting is to attain a profound organic state. One cannot simply decide to be trusting or make it a matter of will. One becomes trusting and communicates this to others by behaving in a trusting way. I become more trusting by creating an environment for myself in which I have the opportunity to see for myself that people and the world around me can be trusted.

For me, my learnings about group building in the home have been profound:

(1) It is very clear that, at least with a small family group,

leadership and parenting are not only unnecessary but get in the way of home-building and child-rearing. EQ VI and VII environments provide a very satisfying climate that is especially good for the development of children.

(2) High trust produces high trust. The dramatic and consistent finding in our home and in others where this has been tried is that children raised in this atmosphere become notably honest and frank. *When children are not punished* (particularly for telling the truth!), when they are trusted and loved, they become deeply honest with themselves and with others.

(3) What happens to children raised in a radical, high-trust environment, with no formal rewards or punishment, discipline, moral training, rules, obedience-training, or parental controls? They seem to do well in the EQ II-IV environments they find in contemporary schools, churches, businesses, athletic teams, and social institutions. One factor that operates in their favor is that they seem to have exceptionally *high self-esteem.* They feel good about themselves and have little of the defensiveness and fear of authority exhibited by children who are punished, disciplined, and trained to obey.

(4) I am especially impressed with how much Blair and John have taken responsibility for their own lives and choices. They decide what friends to make, whether or not to study, how much to watch TV, when to go to bed, what to wear, what to eat, how to spend their money, what schools to go to, and what to do with their time. They show very little dependence and remarkably little counter-dependence.

(5) One point in particular interests me as a psychologist, clinician, and personality theorist: Blair, John, and other TORI children are as close to being *guilt-free* as any persons I have ever seen. This seems to me to be of primary importance. I am very much aware of how painful and negative the effects of guilt feelings can be.

(6) Building a family on such principles makes family life remarkably pleasant and tranquil. It does not make family living trouble-free. For one thing, there are no automatic parental prerogatives that come with autocratic parenting. Up for grabs are group decisions as to where we go for a family vacation, what the main dish is to be for dinner, what program is selected on TV, who gets the car, who takes out the garbage, how loud the music gets, and a host of things that might otherwise be decided by parental "advice and consent". Freud may have been wrong about many things, and I think

that he was, but however we name the phenomenon, "sibling rivalry" is alive and well in the Gibb home. Blair and John do have fights at many levels. Their rooms also often are incredibly disorderly, and it seems they have never discovered the advantages of anal compulsivity. And they show remarkable disrespect for my sacred preferences for Chopin music! They are delightfully human.

The Classroom as a Group

I recall with amazement what a powerful experience I had in my first summer as a staff member at the National Training Laboratories sessions in 1951. There I first learned from Lee Bradford and my friends at Bethel to look at my classroom *as a group,* rather than *as a collection of learners.* I had been teaching college classes since 1937, and I had earned something of a reputation as a radical experimentalist in the classroom. I felt very good about my "teaching", but it had never occurred to me to look at the class *as a group.*

In spite of the world-wide influence of The National Training Laboratories on education, the power of this concept is still unknown to some reputable and effective educators. Some effective teachers still see the classroom as composed of multiple pairings: the teacher and Bob, the teacher and Betty, the teacher and Joe. They are familiar with the idea that there are also student-dyads and that there are classroom climates, environmental variables, and the like, but they have somehow not seen, in the gut, that the transcending and enhancing reality in the classroom is that it is a *group:* a warm, live, throbbing, transforming, powerful, overriding *organism.*

Once it is perceived, this "group" can be frightening to the teacher and to individual students. Anthropomorphized and made into a scary demon, the class may be viewed with awe. The nebulous mass of resistant faces can be frightening to both student and teacher. Group pressure seems ready to overwhelm our own strength. But joined, owned, loved, and gentled, the classroom group can instead become for student and teacher a caring place, a supportive environment, a source of deep energy, a place to look forward to being in and to resist leaving.

Once the teacher sees this new "reality" and internalizes this transcending perception, all kinds of different feelings, attitudes, and perceptions occur. The teacher is no longer the "facilitator", motivator, model, or person responsible for the standards of the class; not the method-provider, character example, target, the one responsible for helping students clarify their values or negotiate their contracts, or to re-write their life scripts. The teacher simply *joins the group,* learns and struggles, has fun and pain, tries to make sense out of the world, appreciates the universe, assimilates the traditions of our forefathers, or builds a new world. Or tries, along with the others, to do these things.

A critical difference between the effective and non-effective classroom environment is the ability of the teacher to join in the *process of inquiry,* to become genuinely interested in discovering, to get out of the role of teacher, to give up the responsibility that belongs to each student, and to create a learning environment for himself or herself. This requires a high trust in the discovering process, in the persons that are in the learning community, and in the group itself.

Again, of course, things are not all this simple. Simply changing one's perception does not accomplish all of the things that the learner/teacher/person would like to do, having accepted a professional position and the built-in responsibilities that accompany an appointment as a teacher in the contemporary system.

I have seen many teachers, at all levels of the educational system, who have accomplished this transition and are living together with other learners in classroom groups. Some of them are consciously applying TORI theory to their classroom groups. Others have not heard of Trust Level theory but obviously have an instinct for healthy group work. They are the best teachers I know; enjoyed, respected, and appreciated by students, often respected and approved by administrators. And they are appreciated by parents. These teachers are living now in a better world which they are helping to create for all of us.

The blocks that I see obstructing attempts to create a classroom group include the following:

Block 1. Running scared, and expressing this by setting up a few *controls* that hedge all bets, putting subtle pressures on the students to set "realistic" goals, trying to influence decision-making and procedures that the group sets up.

Block 2. Getting locked up in the *evaluation* processes, draining energy into grade-getting, spending time meeting organizational standards, thus using up enthusiasm and energy that might otherwise be spent in doing, being, and problem-solving.

Block 3. Spending inordinate amounts of time in *planning,* preparing, building strategy, and the procedural aspects of community building, rather than in the processes that are more closely related to direct learning: doing a project, solving a problem, making a movie, conducting a research study, discovering something.

Block 4. Getting stuck in the EQ II-IV processes that are tied up so much with authority, power, and leader-related issues. In my experience, learning groups that are effective move quickly into EQ V and VI levels.

Block 5. Avoiding the emotionality, caring, loving, touching, and person-relating processes that are so important in building a feeling of community. In working with teacher preparation programs, I have discovered no easy short-cuts to learning how to be a person in a class-room. Good teachers have a good theory, for one thing, and then try out a number of theory-directed experimental classroom experiences. The key thing that happens is that *the teacher learns* — learns to trust, to be personal, to make errors, to let the process happen, to achieve a group-focus and an environmental-design focus, and *to get comfortable in the classroom.* The prospective teacher must discover early whether or not he or she likes being with children or adults and can enjoy the people he or she is planning to join.

Block 6. Inability to have fun in the classroom or to discover joy in being a member of a learning community.

Block 7. Getting into technique orientation. There are a number of games, techniques, exercises, gimmicks, demonstrations, and programs that are prepared for the use of teachers. Teachers sometimes need to use these until they gain the experience and trust that enables them to join in the free flow of direct experience and in the creation of emergent classroom experiences. Simulation games, value-clarification exercises, the magic circle, non-verbal exercises, encounter groups, cook-book projects, and a wide variety of educational aids are useful in certain situations, particularly for inexperienced teachers, as a transition between the conventional classroom and the learning community. But they have severe limitations. They soon lose their novelty. They enable the students to *avoid taking responsibility for creating their own learning.* They are, of course, created by the program designers as outside agents and not by the community. At the worst they become time-fillers, aids that titillate the learners for a time and afford a pleasant escape from listening to the teacher, on the one hand, and to engaging in the tough task of creating their own learning community, on the other.

The learning community is, to me, a transitional form of education — a weaning from the schooling system to a culture that will soon create a learningful life environment to replace the schoolroom. Teachers who wish to be part of the revolution in education will find it necessary *to learn to learn,* learn to join others in learning, to live and learn in community, and to make learning a part of the total process of living and being. This process of change is an exciting one, well worth the occasional periods of pain and confusion that come to those of us who are learning to live in a different educational system.

The Therapeutic or Counseling Group

Along with a number of other professionals, I have found TORI theory to be a useful orientation in doing group therapy and counseling, and in consulting with self-help programs. Those who wish to examine the applications to therapy in more detail will find annotated references in the appendix. The key characteristics of the orientation are:

(1) The therapist joins the other members of the group in looking at the trust level in the environment that the group is creating, rather than intervening in the lives of the "clients" to help, counsel, or do therapy.

(2) The therapist and the clients become as "role-free" as possible. All members of the group are persons seeking a richer life at a higher EQ level, not clients being helped by a counselor or therapist. The therapist comes into the group as a person and *full member,* not as initiator, facilitator, guide, protector, counselor, or helper. He or she is in the group to learn, grow, be, discover, and create with others an emerging and sustaining environment. I have seen a number of therapists and counselors who do this very well. (T)

(3) All members of the group (including the therapist) are as open with each other as their fears permit. The therapist shares his feelings, perceptions, and problems in ways similar to those of the other members. (O)

(4) Each member of the group takes full responsibility for his or her own discovering processes, want-determination, and all aspects of his or her life. For instance, the therapist does not take responsibility for the client's getting well or even for helping this process. The group is *not a "help group",* or even a *"self-help" group,* but a group of persons being together in search of various forms of transcendence. (R)

(5) The group seeks higher levels of interbeing, awareness, and community for its members. It is assumed that the processes of interbeing and community as we have described them in this book *are*

therapeutic in and of themselves. Such life in the group or community is enriching for persons who do not see themselves as sick or as needing help. And for those who do see themselves as ill or needing remedial help, such a group or community will be healing and remedial. (I)

I am assuming that a person who can get into *interbeing relationships* such as those defined in Table XII or who is able to be in family, work, recreational, or other groups at the EQ VI or VII level is not likely to need or to seek therapy or counseling. Living in interbeing relationships, emergent groups, and TORI-like communities *is* the process of healthful being. When the four TORI discovering processes are functioning well, trust is high relative to fear, and life is healthful and fulfilling. It is because I have found TORI-like states of interbeing and community to be attainable in everyday personal and organizational living that I personally have discontinued doing therapy. Instead, I am putting my energies into working with others to create higher EQ levels in work groups, living groups, organizations, and communities — ones that I belong to or consult with.

It is a growing cultural habit for people to defer dealing with conflicts and feelings produced in work and living groups until they get to their therapy or encounter group. In doing so, they drain off energy and feelings that might have been integrated into each life situation as it came up. Admittedly, in our transitional culture, group therapy can be very useful in helping people to deal with feelings, conflicts, and choices as they occur; yet as a more direct route to healthful living, we are learning how to create work groups that encourage feeling expression, want-determination, and interdependence. People are thus equipped to deal with conflicts and feelings as they arise, thus making counseling and therapy unnecessary.

The TORI concept of therapy and counseling is not nearly so radical as it was twenty years ago, or even ten years ago; but it still differs markedly from some other theories in certain key respects. For instance, the idea of each person taking full responsibility for his or her mindbody health is now widely accepted *as a concept*. However, the concept of *teaching or training* persons to take responsibility for self seems to me to miss the essence of the issue. If *someone else* takes the responsibility for getting me to take responsibility for myself, I am deprived of a key element in the life process. In the form of so-called autogenic training, for example, the practice is essentially a form of behavior modification. That is, the therapist gives the patient the instruction to repeat a phrase which is some variation of "I take responsibility for myself" and then rewards the client for doing this. When the therapist thus becomes the pump-primer, motivator, or prestige figure that guarantees the process will work, and finally the rewarder for "satisfactory" behavior, the client is abandoning responsibility for the key elements is his or her life process.

Missing in this flow are some essential elements. To be fully responsible for self, the client *initiates* the process, invents its form, builds up internal energy to keep it going, decides how long to keep it up, and takes full personal responsibility for the *whole* sequence, or, better, the *whole flow*. TORI theorists and practitioners are interested in discovering ways in which this *full* process can become autogenic. In the TORI community experience, for instance, self-initiated membership in a trusting community creates an environment in which a person shapes his or her own initiatives, feelings, perceptions, self-generated energy, and intrinsic rewards.

One fundamental implication of the theory is this: *the most healing, remedial, and therapeutic environment is full, personal participation in a leaderless group or community which is moving up in the Environmental Quality scale, at least at the EQ VI and VII levels.* This is a more healing experience than the classic or modern therapist-aided, EQ II to V level, group-therapy environment. I believe this statement is true and that it has powerful implications for the practice of counseling and therapy.

We have learned that the TORI Community Experience, which is not therapy-oriented or self-help-oriented, is a powerful therapeutic environment and a viable alternative to the conventional therapy group. The TORI community has more viable options, more opportunity for the provisional tries at effective living, greater impact, more risk, more resources for support or challenge, and greater model diversity than two-person or group settings. A number of research studies have examined this question of effectiveness with suggestive but inconclusive results. The evidence is powerful enough to convince me that the best hope for the future of therapy-impact on the culture is to move more toward community concepts.

The Training Group

Known variously as the T-Group, the training group, the sensitivity training group, the encounter group, the process group, or by whatever name, the group has become an effective and widely-used medium for human-relations training, management and executive development, personal growth, race relations, religious education, and group work. Differing from both learning-community groups and therapy groups, the training group is focussed upon behavior change, group process (rather than content), personal growth and group growth (rather than self-help or therapy), and the total person.

I have described my concept of the training group, invented by the National Training Laboratories in 1947, in Chapter XII of *The Laboratory Method of Changing and Learning,* by Benne, Bradford, Gibb, and Lippitt. The training group is undergoing many changes that parallel those described above pertaining to learning and therapy groups.

The original technology for conducting training groups was a powerful, well-formulated orientation usually restricted, in its pure form, to process interventions. This pure form and its multitude of emerging variations have been widely and effectively used in almost any setting where persons gather together in groups. Our early formulations of TORI theory grew out of our experimentation with leaderless training groups in the early 1950's. Our research showed that leaderless T groups, therapy groups, and team-training groups were as effective as those led by professionals and in some cases more effective. This research, in turn, led to a variety of studies and demonstration projects between 1954 and 1975, which in turn led to the formulation of the EQ-level analysis presented in Chapter Three.

There are many approaches to the improvement of the training group. One has been to replace the leader with taped or instrumented instructions. The tape or instrument becomes the surrogate leader, and this process works surprisingly well. Another, derived from TORI theory, is to have groups meet on their own, without leaders, instructions, or programs. This procedure seems to work even better than using tapes or instruments. The research is well reported and highly relevant.

As with therapy groups, a professional "trainer" or "facilitator" who takes on the job of leading a training group following TORI theory would join the group as a member/learner/person, attempting to become "role-less", exactly as he or she would as a member. This is quite practical and effective, and it is now widely known as methodology.

The advantages are that both trainer and group members are able to participate in the process of the leader giving up the leadership role and struggling to become a member. Breaking out of established role-expectations is a necessary process for every person applying TORI theory as a manager, parent, teacher, staff member, therapist, politician, or in any other function in organizational life. The ambivalent feelings of the leader and the ambivalent demands of the followers/members/workers form a sea of latent turbulence that creates ambivalent feelings and ambiguity in the process of transition from leadership to membership. If my analysis of the cultural trends in contemporary society is valid, this societal transition is a central happening of our day. Hastening the transition is a job for everyone. Professionals who pioneer this process of transition are performing a significant and historical task.

The Work Team and the Management Team

The gradual transition of the work group and the management team from earlier punitive and autocratic models through higher EQ stages is accelerating as we gain knowledge and awareness.

Each manager or consultant makes his or her own determination of how rapidly to move toward full use of TORI theory in team development or in operational management. The work of McGregor, Bennis, Argyris, and Likert has been courageous and pioneering in helping the process of institutional management move through EQ levels II through V, particularly in business organizations. It is my observation that business groups are often moving more rapidly through these levels than are governmental, educational, or religious groups.

Perhaps the assumption that this transition must be gradual is over-cautious. My impression in consulting with a variety of top management groups, especially in the last three of four years, is that management is probably more ready for rapid change than is realized.

The appendix contains an experimental instrument that is a modification of the TORI Self-Diagnosis Scale. This *Diagnosing Your Team* instrument is designed to assist the consultant, manager, work group, or management team in examining the four TORI discovering processes, the key processes that will move each on the EQ scale and toward higher productivity.

It is the team itself that must determine the EQ level that is most appropriate for itself at the moment of examination. Management by objectives, in its early and more pure form, was an attempt to contrast "management by leadership" (EQ II) with "management by goal formulation", and its success is a well-accepted negation of the belief that everything has to be done by leaders and managers. Management by "acceptance and nourishing" (EQ III) has been tried many times. "Management by data flow", in one form or another, has been enhanced by developments in data processing and computer analysis (EQ IV) and has been tried in a TORI setting. It has been reported as a "consultant-less" team management concept. In several companies we were able to replace the consultant in conventional OD team-development sessions with a process in which the team formulated goals, translated them into terms that could be measured and fed into computers, and used these measures as indications of team development. Measures of process development (similar to the data on the *Diagnosing Your Team* instrument) were used along with measures of productivity and profit.

Experiences like these lay the groundwork for teams to move into EQ levels VI and VII. In practice, a number of managers and consultants who are TORI practitioners have tried joining the group as members and becoming, to the extent possible, "role-less". This has worked surprisingly well, considering the prevalence of classic management theory. Because of the greater availability of objective measures of productivity and team effectiveness in business, this application of TORI theory in business has proved more successful than it has in education, therapy, and the church. In addition, even though TORI theory is often more compatible with the implicit theory of the school, the clinic, and the church, the high fear (low trust) levels in these non-business institutions and their insecurity about outcome measures have often led them to be more cautious in experiments with group management.

Many factors contribute to the difficulty of establishing a full concept of the team *as a group,* in the full sense of the term as we are using it. Especially in the work environment we still see intense commitment to individualism and competition as a contemporary value; distrust of committees and groups as effective means of doing anything, a distrust well grounded in experience with ineffective groups; a growing awareness of one interpretation of humanistic viewpoints as a "do your own thing" and "take responsibility for your self alone" trend and ethic; the lack of available skills in group participation, decision-making, and planning; lack of convincing evidence that group management leads to productivity, profit, or creativity; and a pervasive alienation and fear of groups and "togetherness". Many of these barriers are being reduced as we gain more experience with effective and satisfying group action. The high interdependence in modern organizations makes some kind of interfacing action very necessary.

Our work has indicated that the *community* is as much more effective than the group as a model for the work organization, as the group is more effective than individual management or individual action. We will discuss this concept in the following two chapters.

Chapter 8

Simplicity and Energy Flow in the Organization

Achieving simplicity is the key to "organizing". Trust allows simplicity. With trust, we focus our energies.

For many, the word "organization" is a twelve-letter dirty word: it conjures up an image of the world of the establishment, bred of fear and distrust — a world of unnecessary, frightening, and crippling complexity, formality, depersonalization, rules, and roles.

When the critical literature looks at organizational life, one finds with disturbing frequency mention of the following diagnostic signs of organizational ineffectiveness:

— alienation, hostility
— apathy, passivity
— disrespect for authority
— rebellion, unrest
— powerlessness, impotence
— suspicion, distrust
— ebbing of morals and standards
— loneliness, depression
— tension, bodily ills
— deception, dishonesty
— regimentation, depersonalization
— plasticity, superficiality
— manipulation, covert strategy
— greed, selfishness

From my point of view, each of the above symptoms is an expression of fear and distrust, sometimes obvious and direct, often with lineage so circuitous as to be difficult to recognize.

SIMPLICITY

To trust is to create simplicity,
*   to focus the energy on what matters.*

From 1954 to 1974, as a deliberate part of a life plan, I left the university to become a full-time, private-practice consultant to organizations. Faced with the recognition that, like it or not, organizational living was a central and dramatic fact in our culture, I deliberately accepted a wide range of organizational clients in order to learn all I could about the nature of organizational life. I wanted to see what relevance, if any, my fear-trust theory had to the essence of such living.

The Fear/Distrust Cycle

The normal, pervading fears that people *bring into* organizations are exacerbated by what people usually find there: ambiguity, tight controls, latent threat, depersonalized role behavior, and the other symptoms listed above. However necessary this ambiguity and control is thought to be, it does tend to call forth increased fears and hostilities that in turn cause management to increase the controls and discipline. This reciprocal-defense cycle sustains the defensive behavior of people in key managerial positions. Management is afraid that if it does not increase the coercive, manipulative, and persuasive management procedures, the already evident undisciplined behavior will escalate and get "out of control". A self-fulfilling prophecy ensues: low-trust, high-fear theories generate more fear and distrust. This alarming state of affairs seems to confirm the earlier, only tentatively accepted assumptions of the defense theory. The lesson seems to be that if we didn't have these controls — the roles and rules of defensive management — things would get even worse. What is effectively masked, in this management-myth system, is that reduced productivity, creativity, and energy *were the result* of the very management practices that were instituted as the remedy. The remedy is worse than the disease — it *is* the disease.

This vicious defense cycle occurs in organizations particularly when fears are high and at times of emergencies, poor market conditions, pressure from top management, cultural unrest, labor pressures, heightened ambiguity, or massive change of any kind. The cycle spirals and feeds upon itself; causes energy to be directed toward dysfunctional activities; mobilizes counter forces which escalate the problems; builds a general climate of constraint; creates dependent, passive, and conforming people, and brings such people into positions of visibility and influence — the Peter principle; and sets up forces and organizational structures that sustain the fear defense.

Management and non-management alike are caught in the flow

of this *defense-oriented* cycle. The TORI discovering processes are inhibited and the TORI defending processes are fostered. The system is:
— impersonal, role-locked, detached
— covert, strategic, technique-oriented
— persuasional, manipulative, evaluative
— controlling, power-oriented, rule-focused

A Diagnostic Framework

People using TORI theory have found the following diagnostic framework helpful in examining an organization. For me the following ten leverage factors are the keys to organizational effectiveness. Among the innumerable factors that enter into the play, these are the ones that the TORI diagnostician can focus on with optimal use of energy.

1. *Role differentiation.* Classic management theory is based upon clarifying and specifying role expectations. The more clearly role prescriptions and obligations are specified, the more efficient the organization, the less the overlap, the greater the focus upon the specified task prescribed for the role. This process is the basis for the depersonalization of the system, the loss of the person, the divorce of the person from the organization and the job, and the ultimate alienation of members. It seems to me that this has always been a fundamental error in organizational theory. Increases in productivity have come in spite of this role differentiation and depersonalization. Dramatic increases in productivity are now being achieved by organizations that are turning this around and freeing the person to *be* the person and not the role.

2. *Programmed use of fear-escalation as a management tool.* Low productivity in organizations is associated with planned as well as unintentional escalation of fear as a device for managing people. "Building in a little healthy fear and respect" is a time-honored device for controlling the troops. Many managers have long used subtle procedures which heighten the fears of loss of job, loss of approval, loss of advancement, removal of benefits, isolation, reprimand, cuts in budget, or loss of emotional support. The corrosive effects of fear-induction are often difficult to see and especially difficult to associate with the fears that reduce productivity.

3. *Use of covert strategies and management techniques.* Strategy and technique build up distrust, latent resentment, and counter-forces that lead to lowered productivity and creativity. Energy is diverted into

TABLE XVI. KEY DIAGNOSTIC SIGNS OF ORGANIZATIONAL EFFECTIVENESS

TORI factor	*High-productivity focus:*	*Low-productivity focus:*
I (T)	Growth and development of the person	Role differentiation
II (T)	Raising the trust level	Programmed use of fear as a management tool
III (O)	Increasing the openness and flow	Use of covert strategies and management techniques
IV (O)	Free flow of natural communicative processes	Management and control of the communicative processes
V (R)	Fostering intrinsic motivations	Manipulation of extrinsic rewards — pay, approval, power, status
VI (R)	Fostering of the TORI discovering processes	Results, efficiency, and product orientation
VII (I)	Fostering relevant interdependencies	Use of controls, rules
VIII (I)	Maintaining simplicity of structure and "job" itself	Manipulating structure of the organization (overorganization)
IX (I)	Holistic perspective on "big picture"	Segmented, linear, and "assembly line" orientation
X (I)	Emergence of being, and the processes of joy in work	Use of management to control processes (management featherbedding)

counter-strategies and unproductive and tangential activity. Techniques are seductive. We've all heard of the executive who prided himself on always pulling the personnel folder of a subordinate just prior to meeting or interview and then subtly injecting into the conversation a bit of personal information, such as the first name of the subordinate's child, to give the impression that the executive cared so much about his associates that he remembered such things. One of the many negatives about the use of such procedures and gimmicks is illustrated by the fact that subordinates quickly discover the gimmick and laugh among themselves at the attempted deviousness of the executive. High productivity is associated with openness, candor, honesty, directness, and simplicity in relationships.

4. *Management and control of the communicative processes.* To the fearing person it soon becomes apparent that communications can be dangerous. The defensive manager learns to try to control communications. One of the hallmarks of big business is the building of huge communications empires designed to control the flow of information in the organization. The high cost of such enterprises is only a minor detriment of such programs. The builders of such communications enterprises have devised many subtle ways of controlling or attempting to control the nature and the amount of communication that flows through the system. A major cost of such manipulation is the escalation of distrust. Visible and recent examples that "news management" creates distrust occurred in the dramatic loss of trust by Presidents Johnson and Nixon when they were seen as managing the flow of information from their offices to the public. It is difficult to learn that the way to high productivity is to allow the natural flow of feelings, perceptions, and information — *all of the data.* The honest person is trusted. He or she doesn't have to advertise it.

5. *Manipulation of extrinsic rewards.* The attempts to "motivate people" and to control the motivations of subordinates are as old as the impulse to "manage" the destinies of others. The recent popularity of behavior modification has increased the use of manipulative schedules for dispensing rewards: pats on the head, pay raises, advances in position and responsibilities, a key to the executive washroom, titles, and privileges of various kinds. Differential rewards will create temporary spurts in productivity, but the long term results are detrimental to sustained creativity and self-determined productivity. In the long run, high productivity is always associated with an

atmosphere in which people have the opportunity to develop intrinsic rewards, to discover themselves and what they want to do with their lives, to determine significant and enduring internal motivations, and to make choices that get them into activities that are self-rewarding. There is no substitute for inner motivation.

6. *Results orientation and the focus upon efficiency and product.* It is a compelling and seductive argument that insists that productivity comes from the emphasis upon product. At first blush this seems obvious. The problem is that organizations that focus upon results, efficiency, and product tend to get lowered results and less product. It is a paradox that organizations which focus upon giving freedom to the self-determining worker tend to out-perform those organizations that emphasize results and efficiency. What is forgotten is that it is people who make the product, who do the work that is the "result", and who create their own efficiency. People who are engaged in activities they enjoy, who are turned on by what they are doing, who are proud of the products they are creating, who have a part in the total enterprise, and who are honored in the processes of work, tend to work hard and creatively. They produce. High productivity is created in atmospheres where the "discovering" processes are free to operate: where people are creating who they are, showing themselves to others, discovering and translating their own talents into productive work, and discovering their emotional and task interdependencies. Productivity is, in a way, serendipitous.

7. *Use of control and rule systems.* As I consult with a variety of organizations, I find that the low-productivity organizations are those that have a wide variety of control systems and make many rules. Rules create processes of circumvention. Rules create rule-breakers. Controls are made to be circumvented. Where trust is high, controls and rules are unnecessary. The presence of tight controls is a clear sign that fear and distrust are prevalent. Productivity and creativity are high when people are highly motivated to work at self-selected and self-created tasks. A good test is this: Is the worker doing pretty much what he or she would enjoy doing, whether or not he or she were being paid for it? By and large, if the workers are working simply for the pay, the organization is in trouble.

8. *Overorganization: the manipulation of organizational structure to accomplish organizational tasks.* I vividly recall a statement by a vice-president of one of the world's large organizations after being fully immersed in the third large-scale reorganization of the structure

of his organization. He told me, "The structure of the organization has very little to do with anything of importance to us." He went on to say to a large meeting of representatives of management from various levels and geographical centers that it was how people worked on problems and how they worked with each other that mattered, not the structure they worked in. It has certainly been my observation that restructuring organizations is largely a displacement of energy, an illusory process. If energy is high, motivation is intrinsic, trust is strong, and interdependency is authentic — then productivity is high, whatever the structure of the organization.

9. *Segmented, linear, and "assembly line" orientation.* For me, the key diagnostic sign has to do with how much perspective is shared by members of the organization. Productivity, creativity, and motivation are high when all or most of the members of the organization see things in a larger perspective, see how their activities are related to overall company or total-organizational goals, see what the organization is about, and are identified with the contribution the organization is making to the world picture. Perspective is a significant quality not only for the chief executive but for every participant in the organization. Tunnel vision and blind-alley work are associated with routine, high-error, and low-quality activity.

10. *Management featherbedding — overmanagement of the enterprise.* I have been trying to think, as I write this chapter, if I have ever seen an organization client-system that was not overmanaged. I have been unable to think of an instance. The more I got acquainted in depth with the enterprise, the more I could see how the organization would be improved in performance if the number of people in management were reduced, if the amount of supervisory control were lessened, if the number of levels of management were reduced, and if the number of what are usually thought of as "management acts" were reduced. As one executive client said to me, "The trouble with most managers is that they try to manage things."

One corporation with which I have worked for many years has a corporation-wide policy of frequent transfer of managers to new locations and new functions. One of the managers said in a training program: "For the first few months when we get a new boss everything goes fine and we work very effectively — until he learns our jobs, and then he starts telling us how to do them". *Overmanagement is perhaps the single most significant problem* in business, education, government, and church organizations. As trust increases, management becomes less and less necessary.

The Consultant, Executive, Superintendent, Minister

Though this is not a training manual for the practitioner, I want to look at the organization from the standpoint of the persons who take, or are given, the responsibility for "managing" or developing the organization. As must be clear from the thesis of the book, organizational health comes from a state in which everyone in the organization takes responsibility for the organization and its well being. However, there are some people who are given special functions as part of their professional "role". How do they perform these functions, for which they are paid and for which they accept "special" obligations? This book is my attempt to answer this question for myself and for others who wish to use the theory.

1. *Each organization is a unique organism, idiosyncratic, growing, learning, becoming, and being in its own way.* The organization creates its own defense, its own fears, its special environment. As a consultant, I have learned to treat each organization as unique, just as I try to think of each person as unique and try not to lay my own matrix on the organization. I try to listen, sense what is really happening, join in *as a participant,* and learn with other members of the organization what must be learned in order to live fully in that organization. Starting there, it is possible to be a very effective participant.

Coming in as an outsider to impose my values on the organization or to try to make the organization what I think it should become is a violation of the uniqueness of the organization, just as it would be if I did the same to a person. I have seen high school principals, business executives, ministers, internal consultants, and government officials make the mistake of taking a stance "above and beyond" the system and the people in it, of showing a clear disdain and/or distrust of the organization and its members. Their efforts at change are resisted and are likely to cause a massive system defense that mobilizes counter-energy. This defense mobilization is then interpreted by the well-intentioned official as corroborative of his or her disdain and distrust. I believe that TORI theory points a way out of this self-induced, difficult-to-see, and frustrating multiple bind.

2. *Collaborative efforts directed toward environmental design are one solution to this multiple-bind problem.* Environmental quality is everyone's concern. Movement on the EQ scale is the enduring issue

and the only significant long-range change that matters. Movement on the EQ scale is also highly correlated with the other immediate organizational goals: profit, productivity, organizational vitality, morale, and other criteria of organizational effectiveness. The most effective thing that the consultant or officer can do is to focus upon EQ level and environmental quality. This *perspective* enables the theorist/practitioner to transcend the tunnel focus of the fire-fighter who limits his or her effectiveness by succumbing to the attractive seductions of the "bottom line" focus and the concern with "what one does on Monday morning". It is precisely this difference in focus that points up the advantage of Trust Level theory over a more prescriptive theory which spells out the concrete steps to follow to improve the profit picture and to devise a lesson plan for Monday morning.

3. *The effective organization has a feeling of community.* In chapter IX, I will discuss the process of community building and its effect upon persons and organizations. Productivity, involvement, shared ownership, intimacy, and a feeling of participation are important aspects of the feeling that "we are living in a community".

Students of the city are saying that it is possible to create such a feeling of community even in an urban setting that has something like 7,500 people, but that it would be difficult with numbers much larger than that. This is an underdeveloped area of organizational theory. But a large organization may perhaps become a collection of overlapping small communities. These communities may be profit centers, geographically focused, and highly interdependent units where people share in as many aspects of living possible. Some of my most effective efforts in organizational consulting have occurred when I have convened a TORI Community Experience as an in-company, in-school, or in-parish experience.

4. *Many seemingly "clean" and rational organizational activities are "neurotic"/defensive responses to fear and distrust and contribute little or nothing to the "work" or productivity of the organization.* In fact, the direct cost of these activities and the indirect cost of hidden reactions in the organization are so great that these activities may be very damaging.

Experienced administrators and consultants will recognize the principle and be able to list many more examples than these: insatiable demands for quarterly reports of "progress" that are designed to check up on the project but usually require energy that is a drain from productive project work; multiple expense-voucher reports that encourage cheating; elaborate quality controls that encourage workers to shrug off personal responsibility to the control processes; budget warfare in which subordinate managers consciously upgrade demands in anticipation of retaliatory reductions by superiors; defensive and protective multiple-record keeping to ward off corporate and governmental inspections and harassment, the infamous "just-in-case" files and records; endless meetings of all manner of participants to create "involvement and participation", even though the decisions are either already made or to be made in an EQ II or III manner; and deliberate waste of paper, lights, material, and time as a "retribution" against superiors and "the organization" for intended or unintended institutional "errors".

These defensive actions arise from fears and related distrust, assumptions that then also reinforce them. From the standpoint of management, the solution to these problems is to change the defensive management practices that create the atmosphere under which these neurotic behaviors are fostered.

5. *The key question is: What would this organization be like if the members were more trusting?* Trust Level theory is an idiosyncratic process. It applies specifically to each person and to each organization. It is applied by specific people and organizations, and may differ for each situation. Applying the theory is more a matter of persons deciding what would be trusting than a matter of general application of principles. The solution to each problem is created each time by the persons and organizations involved. TORI theory provides a *viewpoint rather than a prescription.*

6. *The consultant or manager is an experimental engineer who is continually contributing to the accumulating wisdom of the organization.* Among the many managers and consultants that I have encountered, the most effective ones take a scientific-engineering approach to managerial issues. The organization learns. It makes a series of provisional tries at solutions to problems as they occur, building up a store of wisdom as to what works for this organization. The more members of the organization are involved in each informal experiment, the more effective is the provisional trying process. If the whole organizational unit is involved in all of the processes, it creates an organizational climate of empiricism and excitement: in making preliminary guesses, in planning on data collection, in discussing alternative problem solutions, in collecting data, and in generalizing about the findings. This conception of management makes managing

a highly professional process that is more than a job for technicians, rule-makers, fire-fighters, or prescription-followers.

7. *Organizations can be changed and improved in significant and dramatic ways.* I feel very positive about what is happening among contemporary organizations in North America. I have worked closely with about 300 organizations of various kinds and believe that I know many of them well. I have seen, over this twenty-year span, that organizations have become appreciably more trusting, more participative, and more open. It seems, at times, that change is awesomely slow; but the change is real and significant. And we know enough now to enable us to make great changes in how the affairs of government, education, business, and churches are conducted and goals achieved.

The TORI International Community

There are many possible avenues to creative change: new and creative organizational theory; legal action for women's rights, affirmative action, and other equal rights and opportunities reform; invention of new organizational structures; increased use of effective organizational consultants; development of the alternative and/or counter-culture organizational forms in the church, family, business, or other organizations; and the development of pilot or prototype organizations. The question remains, however: To what extent can these efforts at change succeed without fundamental reform of the political, economic, and social conditions of our culture?

TORI theorists and practitioners are active in all of these areas. I believe that the most promising approach to organizational change is in the development of the pilot or pioneering organization. For several years we have been developing a high-trust organization that is our best effort to apply TORI theory. After several years of trying out various models, we finally created in 1974 a non-profit organization, TORI Associates, Inc. We see this as a prototype of what organizations might be like in the next few decades.

We have asked the question: What would a voluntary organization look like if it were optimizing trust? We have applied the ten criteria used in Table XVI for a "high productivity" organization and, starting from "scratch", have tried to avoid the errors made by organizations that have grown under the traditional low-trust, high-fear assumptions in our culture.

1. The organization is *personal and* as *role-free* as it is possible for us to make it. There are about 10,000 members, with no role

requirements, role prescriptions, formal expectations, dues, obligations, responsibilities, titles, membership classes, or formal class
differences among persons. To meet formal and legal requirements,
the organization has been incorporated in California and enrolled with
the Internal Revenue Service as a non-profit organization. We have a
Board of Directors composed of three members who have volunteer-
ed to assume legal obligations for filing reports and taking legal
responsibility for money collected. They have no other formal powers
within the organization. There are no paid staff members. All activity
is done by volunteers as needed. Anyone is welcome to join. There is
no age, race, sex, intelligence, or other criterion for membership.
There are no dues, for these might create a barrier for some who might
not be able to afford even minimal assessments.

2. A conscious effort is made to be aware of any activity or
procedure that might change the *trust level*. There is, of course, no way
to legislate trust level. Consciousness raising has been very effective,
however. The more we learn from each other and experience living
together, the more aware we are of subtle ways in which our fears and
distrusts express themselves.

3. The organization is as *open* as we can make it. We deliberately
attempt to avoid strategies and techniques of any kind. This has
particularly significance in our organization, because many of us have
been active in the human-potential movement and in humanistic
organizations and centers, where so many of the activities are
technique-oriented. Techniques and strategies are major determiners
of distrust and depersonalization.

Persons simply join each other in any way they wish: weekends,
meals, evening get-togethers, TORI "community experiences" (described in Chapter IX), joint vacations, extended families, communal
living, cooperative nurseries, bartering occupational skills, small businesses, or other happenings. Activities are spontaneous, emergent,
and natural. Techniques are avoided unless they happen as natural
interaction. Members do not, for instance, teach each other the techniques of bioenergetics, massage, growth games, meditation, gestalt,
psychodrama, or transactional analysis, but learn to be *with* each other
in spontaneous and natural ways. Meetings, finances, publications,
inventions, records, research, and other activities are open to all
members and to the general public. Nothing is secret or private by
formal or organizational intention. All persons are free to determine
their own degrees of privacy and to make whatever choices they wish.

4. There is an active and deliberate attempt to learn to *communicate openly.* We cannot legislate free communication, but members can learn to express feelings and perceptions openly and directly. There is no conscious or deliberate attempt to legislate restriction in communication. Communication *happens.* Openness enhances trust. We are attempting to learn how to communicate freely at many levels.

5. We foster *self-determination, intrinsic motivations,* and *expression of wants.* We are attempting to create an environment in which people do only those things they find self-rewarding. No formal reward or punishment system is then necessary. No one is paid, given titles, status, power, rank, or awards. If no one wants to do something, it isn't done. This, of course, takes a bit of learning. Most of us have never lived like this before.

It is also seen as significant that the organization engages in no activities designed to influence others to do what they don't want to do. So we have no formal persuasional or influence system such as advertising, fund raising, public relations, recruiting, promotion, selling, training, teaching, or propaganda programs. These ways of being sometimes are difficult for others to grasp. It is difficult for others to understand, for instance, that we are not soliciting memberships.

Because there are no "policies", directives, or formal guidelines, there may be things that members do which are persuasion-oriented. As we gain in trust, such activities are gradually discontinued. For instance, members of the organization or of the general public are simply informed of organizational activities and are added to mailing lists if they request it. The *intent* is informational and not persuasional.

6. Emphasis is upon the TORI *discovering processes* and not upon product, efficiency, competence, or results. The general atmosphere is one in which people discover who they are, show themselves to others, do what they want, and join with others in interdependent activities. *The process is significant, not the product.*

We engage in activities that raise our own consciousness about our environment and the EQ levels. Encouragingly, many of the TORI groups report an increasing number of intuitive, transcendent, and nurturing experiences that clearly fall into the EQ levels VI through IX.

7. The organization is as *interdependent* as we are able to make

it. It is an experiment in leaderless and emergent action. In the early days we had "conveners" of the TORI community experiences. This has gradually been discontinued, and now one seldom sees any form of formal "leadership". All activities are moving into the EQ VI-X range. We have no contracts, hierarchies, rules, agreements, officers, roles, or other formal structures. This free flow has been visibly successful and is becoming more so with experience.

Fears and distrusts are often embedded, of course, in structures and norms, moralistic viewpoints, legal restrictions, certification, evaluation, rules and laws, agreements and contracts, and other traditional aspects of formal organizational life. For one thing, we have found that these elements in formal organizations are surprisingly expensive — in time, money, and bodily ailments. Our annual budget, for instance, is about $3,000 for a 10,000 member organization. Comparable budgets for organizations with similar numbers of members and similar nature of program run from $100,000 to $300,000. This aspect of the experiment is, in itself, an impressive discovery.

8. The structure is as *simple* as possible. One of the most exciting discoveries is that we can get along with stark simplicity. Our present mode of living in our whole social system is too complex. Much of the complexity is created as a response to fear — perhaps all of it. Most of the complexity results from what can be classified as planning, warning, supervising, disciplining, agreeing, selling, managing, controlling, preparing, cautioning, alerting, setting priorities, taking responsibilities, assigning and appraising, teaching, or helping. Such activities are engaged in largely because people *are afraid* that things will not go well if they don't do them. The impulse to structure comes as a response to our internal fear and distrust. *Structure is an effort to control the fear.*

9. The *whole picture* is always available to all members of the organization. That is, we *do not build in* processes that cloud or segment the view. Again, our fears constrict our vision. We do not, of course, reduce fear and increase wholeness-vision by deciding to do so. We *can* remove many structural and organizational barriers to perspective by analysis and action. The shared picture is getting broader.

10. The organization has *no management group.* As TORI theory has predicted, management is not only not necessary, but it reduces the effectiveness of the organization. In TORI Associates,

persons do things. They have ideas, suggest actions, express ideas and opinions, respond, express wants — do whatever they wish in relation to each other. Members are proactive and get together with others to get something started. There is no officer, leader, staff, or chairman to act as initiator or coordinator.

This finding reminds me of a cartoon with two boys playing on a bed, with one saying to the other: "If Daddy doesn't come up here pretty soon and get us to go to school, we'll be late!" In TORI Associates there is no Daddy. For most of us this is a strange way of life. We are learning that it is increasingly exciting, simplifying, freeing, and rewarding (it is also frustrating, at times). The glimpse of a new world is exhilarating.

We are in the process of gathering data on our experiment with this new organizational prototype. It is encouragingly successful in many ways. How applicable the design is to all organizations, or even to all non-business organizations, is as yet unanswered, but we are engaged in experimenting with the concepts and the model in a variety of other settings.

Astron Corporation

For a number of years a few of us have been struggling with various models for a high-trust business organization. It seems to me quite obvious that there are certain aspects of the competitive economic philosophy that are incompatible with a high-trust way of living. Competition, itself, seems to be both a determiner and a result of fear and distrust. While we wait for the millennium, it seems useful to try to see if we can develop a business model based on high trust that will work in a highly competitive society. I believe that we *can* develop a successful one. If my analysis is correct, there may even be some advantage to developing such a model in a competitive, low-trust society. The high-trust model is likely to be so effective that it would quickly out-perform low-trust models. A high-trust model would be of little use in a "practical" world if it required that the rest of the world be trusting!

TORI Associates has been in existence for about three years, and the description above is of the progress made in that time. Astron Corporation, on the other hand, is in the process of being created by about 90 TORI people who have explored relationships of various kinds for a few years. I will describe here the model as we see it beginning to work and will reserve for a later publication in the series a more detailed examination of the results.

I will describe the organization in the same framework as before, the ten criteria of organizational effectiveness listed in Table XVI.

1. The emphasis is on the *centrality of the person* and not the role. Astron Corporation is composed of about 90 people, professionals in various fields, who have come together as persons to conduct a business initially focussed upon publishing, consulting, and training. The intent is to apply TORI theory to these fields, to publish various materials and books illustrating TORI theory, to consult with a variety of organizations using TORI theory as a framework, to do managerial and human-relations training in a TORI way, and perhaps to build small businesses that create whatever product the individual finds exciting. In applying TORI theory, each of us is attempting to discover/create, first, whatever it is that we want to do with our lives, and, second, to do this in a way that will justify others paying us sufficient fees to constitute at least a comfortable living.

In effect, we have a federation of small businesses, joined together in a way that provides emotional support, stimulation, and whatever synergy the relationships produce. As interdependencies develop we will build whatever financial and economic relationships are feasible, always keeping the structure minimal.

As the business expands, each new person will have the same opportunity and freedom — freedom to determine what it is that the person *really wants to do*. We will attempt to invent processes that will enable each person to do this. We see this as a challenge, and as a fundamental guideline. We will attempt to work without role requirements, contracts, titles, and membership classes. Each person will be treated *as a person*.

2. There is a strong, conscious effort to maintain a *high-trust level*. This will continue to be a central guideline.

3. We are building *an open system*. We attempt to work without covert strategy and tactics. Meetings, records, inventions, salaries, arrangements, processes — all are open to each other, to clients, and to the public. A great deal of "strategy and planning" occurs as a result of defensive assumptions. We believe that we can reduce considerably the energy and expense usually devoted to defensive posturing in most business organizations.

4. We are building an *open communication system* in all possible ways. We have all participated in many TORI community experiences and have developed attitudes and behaviors that encourage the

direct and open expression of feelings, perceptions, ideas, differences, and disagreements.

5. We are fostering *self-determination, intrinsic motivations, and expression of wants.* We assume that the primary motivation for work in the organization is the enjoyment of the work that the person is doing. We do not use titles, ranks, status, or monetary rewards as motivating systems. At present all fees are set by each person with the client system or the publisher, and Astron itself pays no salaries or fees. As we develop programs or more complex institutional arrangements, we will either pay everyone the same salary or will invent some other non-competitive monetary arrangement. The primary principle is that we center upon creative work as the primary motivator and the *raison d'etre* for the organization.

All of the activities of the corporation are designed to further the TORI discovering processes, on the assumption that this way of being is producing an optimally profitable and effective business organization. As an illustration, we do not engage in formal influence or persuasional activities such as marketing, selling, promotion, public relations, or propaganda programs. We do make efforts to give out clear and direct information about services and products. The differences between information and consultation, on the one hand, and advertising and promotion, on the other hand, are subtle but very significant. *Our intent is to learn, inform and consult — not to persuade and influence.*

6. Our focus is upon the joys of *being in the process,* rather than upon results, efficiency, and product. We believe that we find fulfillment and excitement in the joys of creative work *processes,* solving problems, and creating interdepending, transcendent experiences. We also believe that these processes bring about effective products such as books, materials, and effective client organizations. Good products come out of good processes. It is the processes that are the center of focus in Astron. Focus upon process is humanizing. Focus upon product is de-humanizing.

7. The organization is as *interdependent* as we can make it. We do not force interdependence but allow it to happen. When interests and wants move in similar directions, members form teams and projects. This is now happening rather quickly.

We minimize hierarchy, rules, agreements, contracts, and legal restrictions. There is no "management", as such, and no supervision, report making, formal controls, or other conventional management "tools". We expect to keep records and controls to meet governmental and tax requirements, and to do so exactly, with no game playing and none of the usual manipulation of records in quasi-legal ways. Most management control and record systems are costly, unnecessary, and "defensive" in nature. Along with many other businesses that are doing the same thing, we intend to reduce this costly "burden".

8. We are making *the structure as simple as possible.* Here we can make considerable progress. The more "professional" the field of business management becomes, the more complicated the technology and the more complex the business systems. A massive process of self-justification is taking place. Management develops an arcane terminology, a mystical process, an elaborate methodology, and an elite fraternity. These processes of stratification, mystification, bureaucratization, and overstructuring are happening in labyrinthine ways in education, the government, and the church. Using business as a model, the church and education leaders are now justifying this disease of complexity by saying "The church is now becoming a big business", or "The schools are now becoming large enough to warrant our adopting a business model", to quote a church leader and a school leader that I heard recently. At least, in Astron, we will look hard at any new complexity to see if it is an improvement in the enterprise. The issue, of course, is a complex one! There are advantages to centralization, computer technology, and complex methodologies. Each advance in methodology exacts a price in removing persons further and further from the simple joys of interdependent and creative work. Are the advances necessarily depersonalizing? Are the advances real in terms of increased productivity and creativity? These are central issues for our pilot organization.

9. We are taking time to establish a wide perspective, to explore alternative models, to look at our assumptions, and to become clear in what we are trying to do.

10. We hope to move into EQ levels VI-VIII. We believe that we will need *no management group,* as such. Maximum emphasis will be upon the joy of creativity and work, and the resulting movement into transcendence, intuition, altered states, and the integration of previously unconscious levels of being into conscious work. We believe that the business organization can be a medium for transcendence and organic creativity. Unfortunately, partly as a result of paying people to do it, "work" has become distasteful, even noxious. Work has become something we ought to do, that must be remunerated, and that we

must do out of obligation. It has lost its self-rewarding quality.

I believe that we are creating an organization that will be profitable, successful economically, and effective. We are rediscovering the joy of work. Self-selected and self-rewarding work doesn't have to be "managed".

WONDER

When we finally really touch,
community happens — and with it
comes awe and wonder.

Chapter 9

The Wonder and Magic of Community

What I miss in today's world is a sense of community. To be *in community* is to be in touch in some deep way. With genuine communion comes the wonder and the awe of discovering each other in trust.

The search for community is heightened by the apparent alienation, unconnectedness, and superficiality of modern life. Throughout history, this search has been sustained by continuing hopes and frustrated by frequent failures. Energy for the quest has been provided by utopian activists, religious leaders, educational philosophers, political theorists, industrial reformers, and a wide variety of rehabilitative institutions.

The quest for a feeling of community has centered around three romantic or utopian hopes:

— that life be *more caring*, that people have more concern, affection, and love for each other, and that the alienation in social life be reduced;

— that life be *more intimate,* more like the family that we idealize but rarely achieve, and that closeness replace the unconnectedness that so many people experience in their normal lifes;

— that life have *greater depth,* that people *matter* to each other, and that this shared depth and meaning replace the superficiality and shallowness that is so characteristic of most social relations.

TORI theorists and practitioners have assumed that increasing the trust levels in the community would significantly increase the caring, intimacy, and depth of any community. We have tried a number of experiments in a variety of institutions. The TORI Community Experience was designed as an experiment to test this assumption and to try various ways of inducing trust and trust-related outcomes in a community.

TORI Community Experiences

Our experiments with community building began in 1965. The hypothesis was a very simple one. We assumed that if we trusted people to create their own community and could simply bring people together for a reasonable time and provide them with some space, food, and a relatively free and pleasant environment, they would create a fulfilling experience for themselves and would accomplish whatever goals they set. A decade of preliminary experiments had given us an idea of the practical problems that would arise and an awareness of the significant environmental variables that would determine the effectiveness of the overall experiment.

In the early years we provided a large hotel room, a carpeted gymnasium, a dance studio, or other open space that was as comfortable as we could make it. We charged a minimum fee ($35 for a weekend, a fee which included meals, materials, registration, and other incidentals) which paid for most of the expenses. We wanted a large enough group to simulate a "community" in a natural church, business, or school setting. We wanted at least 90 people, a group large enough to provide many of the self-management problems that congregations, companies, and neighborhood groups encounter. Size of the communities was limited to about 180, which we found to be the largest number that could communicate together easily without the use of an amplifying system. We provided a skilled volunteer who "convened" the community, provided leadership for the initial hours of group formation, helped solve some of the initial problems of housekeeping, and structured some non-verbal experiences which we had found to be useful in the initial stages of community life. We believed that such a "community-building experience" would be useful to professionals who would be creating school, church, business, and neighborhood communities.

Each participant was given a briefing sheet to be read in advance. This sheet indicated that the members of the community would be responsible for goal-setting, decision-making, community management, and the activities of the community. There would be some initial structure, but no rules, agenda, time limits, formal leadership, or curriculum — not even any furniture. At the beginning we suggested a schedule, from 8 p.m. to 11 p.m. on the opening Friday evening, a 9 a.m. to 11 p.m. session on Saturday, and a 9 a.m. to 5 p.m. session on Sunday. We wanted as long a time as we could get within the limitations of our "weekend" culture.

Our initial fears guided us to make the above decisions. We felt that we had to promise some structure in order to get enough people together to conduct the experiments. During the ten-year period between 1965 and 1975 we gradually reduced the structure as our fears were reduced and as we discovered more and more about the nature of community.

Leadership. In the initial stages of the experiment the conveners were probably useful. During the decade the amount of "convening" has gradually been reduced so that most of the community experiences now conducted in North America have no conveners at all. They are essentially leaderless gatherings of interested people who create experiences for themselves.

There was a tendency at first for informal leaders to emerge and take over the functions that would have been provided by appointed professionals. This transitional stage has been supplanted by a genuinely emergent environmental-quality level (VI) which is leaderless and residual in the processes of the community. About 12,000 participants have joined the weekend communities over the ten years, and a large number of these are now active in some way in the TORI international communities mentioned in the previous chapter.

Community composition. In the early stages the participants were adult men and women, with occasional college students attending the sessions. The groups were largely made up of the middle-class white population that attends the usual growth-center activities. Today many people come as families, with some communities being composed of about 50 per cent children. A much broader range of ethnic and socio-economic backgrounds exists in the communities. TORI weekend experiences have been held for children only, for women's groups, for the aged, for black participants and other minority groups, and for a wide range of special populations: executives, church congregations, drug patients, psychotics, disturbed children, and others. The impression now is strong that the experience is equally applicable to all persons of any culture.

Environmental design. A circular, octagonal, or nearly square space creates a centering flow, and a high-interaction seems to be a critical factor in successful community development. This flow is enhanced when there is no furniture to interfere with free and spontaneous physical movement; when members are visible to each other at most times; when there is some kind of visual boundary that defines the community space; when interaction is continuous and not broken by formal coffee breaks or evening departures for sleeping in other quarters; and when the significant happenings in the community life occur in an area that is perceptually and physically central to the community. The community then takes form, flows, develops rhythms and patterns, assumes an identity, and is experienced by members as a living organism.

This is a finding of considerable importance to community planners and designers. Community forms when the central flow of activities is visible to most of the members and when members interact with each other in the normal course of events during the day. If carpets are available for only a part of the space, for example, we find it useful to place carpets in the central rectangle of the room, leaving walking space on all four sides. Members interact in the center of the room while sitting in various free-form clusters and then interact again as they move along the visible walking spaces on the side of the room. Community gathering places are best when there are few competing attractions such as swimming pools, beaches, bars, and shopping areas. After a certain point in community-building, the people are more attractive than the alternatives. Especially in early stages, competing attractions drain energy into divergent and competing paths.

Time variables. When the emphasis is upon environmental design and leaderless emergence, time is a critical variable, especially when few of the community members have had experience with true leaderlessness. The 24 hours of intense interaction which the weekend affords is about a minimum time for the community to form into a trusting and whole organism. The communities have discovered that periods from 5 to 17 days are much more satisfying and that the greater time periods allow for fulfilling and transcendent happenings that do not usually occur in the minimal three-day period.

Focus upon natural life processes. Participants join the community to do whatever they wish, to enjoy each other as fully as they can, to make the community experience as fulfilling as they can. We do not code the experience as anything other than "life" itself. Any classification of the experience creates expectations and tends to limit the experience. People in our culture are too ready to use techniques to produce effects, rather than to encounter and fully enter life *as it happens* by allowing the natural processes of interaction to occur.

Continuity of activity. The building of community in this setting tends to happen as a continuous flow. There are no schedules, no coffee breaks, mealtimes, or rest periods. Most of the weekend experiences have been held in places where it is possible for participants to bring sleeping bags and stay in community for the total period. This "marathon" format has been especially powerful in creating connectedness among persons and reinforcing the "commuity" feeling.

Heightening of feelings and energy. One dramatic aspect of the design is the heightening of all aspects of the experience. This emerges as the participants sense and grasp their freedom. Initial fears diminish. Persons begin to discover each other. Interaction in depth occurs. Then people begin to share pain, anger, joy, boredom, alienation, excitement, warmth, love, ecstasy, and all of the realness of experience. When they are not directed or channeled by leaders or techniques, things happen with more spontaneity, are somehow "writ larger" and felt more intensely than in the usual workshop, growth experience, or encounter group. The experiences and interactions have a greater ring of naturalness and authenticity than in the usual technique-induced group experience, role playing, or simulation.

Development of unique differentiation. No script is followed and no one acts out a self-fulfilling program. The development of the community takes whatever form the processes take. Individual members will at times try to move the community in directions that meet the particular member's wants, expectations, or theories. Out of the interaction that takes place each community develops a uniqueness. Having participated as a member in more than 200 such communtities, I am impressed with their great differences as they have grown up, flowered, and reached some kind of fulfillment in the three-day weekend.

Implications for Living in Community

The global environment has a transcending influence upon the sub-systems. For ten years beginning in 1937 I taught univerity classes and did individual therapy, always concentrating on the individual person, the intrapersonal dynamics of the learner and the client, and the effects of teaching and therapy upon personal living. During the next twenty years I worked with groups, looking at events from the standpoint of group dynamics and becoming aware of how powerfully group environments affected participants. During the next ten years I experimented with the community and came to realize how powerful the larger environment of the community was relative to group and personal dynamics.

I am now moving toward looking at the larger economic and social environment at the national and world levels, and realizing how this transcends the sub-systems that are included in this larger environment. Each individual can create his or her own environment, largely by having an impact upon the system at an interpersonal level. The larger the environmental system, the less effect the individual can have upon it, though individuals can and do have significant effect upon larger systems.

For instance, the competitive economic system has a powerful and transcending effect upon all social systems in the United States, influencing values, opinions, attitudes, behavior, and feelings of persons and institutions impacted within the system. Attempts to create cooperative groups and communities meet with powerful resistive forces. Any enduring change in individuals and systems in the United States must in some way impact the total global environment.

It is possible for people to create communities that have caring, intimacy, and depth, and that differ dramatically in these character-istics from the institutions we encounter in our daily lives. Our fear/distrust assumptions allow us to see most communities as fright-ening and unchangeable. When the trust levels change significantly and we make new assumptions, the effects upon our community living are startling. We can create ongoing communities that will signifi-cantly reduce the alienation, unconnectedness, and superficiality of modern life. Our fears of large groups have little basis in reality, and we can remove them as major barriers to the achievement of a new society.

Trust level, though amazingly resistant to change, can be changed in significant amounts. Changes in the culture will come through significant and enduring changes in trust level. The TORI community experience can be a powerful instrument for massive social change. The efforts up to now have been low-key and highly experimental, but I have seen enough to know that this way of being in community is a non-manipulative and non-interventive way of achieving social change.

Holistic living is a more enduring route to community living than are more restrictive ways of being. As powerful and dramatic as are the short-run effects, the restrictive and interventive ways of living are less effective than holistic, unrestricted, "natural" ways of being. Some programs are, in part, based upon restrictive and essentially remedial training: process intervention, feeling expression, assertiveness, fight training, meditation, primal release, positive thinking, catharsis, and the like. The training and social action of the future will probably be naturalistic and holistic rather than truncated. Some segmented training has de-wholizing side effects.

Natural and whole behavior is unconstrained and spontaneous. Educational and social-action systems based upon the creation of constraints are likely to have corruptive side effects and have little permanent, organic value. Legal, moral, and educational systems built upon taboos and prohibitions have proven to be rather ineffective. The list of such taboos is long and frightening: dancing, stealing, treason, discourtesy, speeding, spitting, nudity, littering, loitering, and laughing too loudly. Because social systems built upon emergent trust are more effective than systems built upon prohibitions, the TORI community experiences are as constraint-free as is possible in our culture. As persons learn to live in such an environment, and the longer they live in one, they become more gentle, loving, considerate, caring, cooperative, neighborly, non-violent, and, of course, trusting, which is the beginning of it all. Isn't it ironic — but gratifying — to learn, as we have, that people will do naturally and spontaneously what legalists and moralists — all of the "prohibitors" — try to get them to do by means of constraint-training?

Physical touching is a very powerful and trust-producing way of relating in community. Have you noticed how tactile animals are, how they enjoy touching? We caress and fondle babies, but for the adult human animal, touching has somehow become a fear-laden and prohibited way of relating. All TORI communities discover the joyful and authentic aspects of touching. Humans have a strong and often-thwarted need to have physical contact — a kind of "skin hunger". Touching can be many things: a way of avoiding talk or eye contact; a ritual greeting; a displaced form of sexual stimulation; a form of manipulation; a form of play; or a meaningless gesture. After a few days of authentic interaction in a TORI community, touching becomes a powerful, authentic, and intimate way of expressing gentleness, caring, love, and intimacy.

The Church Community

Ministers and active lay members of various religious groups have been active, interested, and supportive members of most of the TORI community experiences. Religion at its best performs an integrative function in life. Perhaps the single most significant contribution of the TORI experiences has been a similar integrative, wholizing process. One minister said after his first TORI experience, following twenty years in the ministry: "This is the first time that I have had a genuine religious experience." Certainly a central, perhaps definitive, aspect of the religious experience for most people is the awakening of a deep trust of self, of God, and of the processes of nature.

Seeing the congregation for the first time as a "community" and realizing the many implications of this new viewpoint, several ministers have returned to their local churches and experimented with what they learned. Sometimes a three-day weekend is sufficient for a person to see the significant implications for a new ministry. Some have returned for several weekend experiences, and many have attended community sessions of five to eight days or longer.

TORI practitioners make several different approaches to the building of the church community. One is to give a TORI weekend experience to the total congregation or to the majority of the congregation. It is best not to do this until the congregation agrees to volunteer for the experience and has worked through whatever mixed feelings they have about attending. We have done this many times with large congregations and have found it highly effective. It is preferable that the minister and other key people in the congregation have had a positive prior experience with a TORI community, understand the theory well, and are TORI-oriented themselves. It is particularly important that these people be relatively trusting, open, spontaneous, and expressive people.

There are some problems. Many ministers, church educators, and church officials find it difficult to be personal, to get out of role. Ministers have been well trained to "take a ministerial role", with all that this implies: to participate formally in ceremonies and rituals, to take a caring stance in time of death or tragedy, to be a bulwark of strength for members in time of fear, and to put aside personal concerns in favor of ministering to the needs of others. Often it is difficult to find (and be) the real person of the minister under the role facade. But the church and the ministry are changing radically, and many church leaders are moving in the same direction as trust theory.

The union between the church and TORI is often a felicitous one. The emphasis upon honesty and candor, and the appreciation of the significance of the integrity of motive and inner life, both form useful bridges between the church and TORI. Many churches stress the importance of *ought* behavior and of authority-based behavior. The values of obedience, self-denial, and punishment are often implicit or explicit in the teachings of some churches and church leaders, and these are difficult to reconcile with TORI theory and practice. The continuing dialogue between religious leaders and TORI practitioners is spirited and vigorous. We are learning much about church settings and the nature of the religious exerience.

A significant bridge lies in the expression of love and warmth. Our unresolved fears keep us from expression of love and warmth, regardless of our religious beliefs. Many deeply religious people find it difficult to give physical or even verbal expression to deep caring and love. The TORI community experience has helped many of these people to understand their fears and fear-based inhibitions and has helped them to discover ways of expressing the caring that they feel — to express this for their families and for members of their congregations.

Another bridge lies in the interests of both religious and TORI communities in prayer, meditation, mystical experiences, transcendence, death and aging, healing, inner peace, and other aspects of experience that are often associated with the church. I see the current revival of interest in these phenomena in our society as a healthy and promising sign. The relation of trust formation to these experiences is obvious, and it is profound.

The Training and Development Community

The TORI community is a powerful medium for a personal-growth experience and for the learning of human-relations, as well as managerial skills and attitudes. After having participated in, observed, and led training and growth activities since 1951 in a wide variety of settings, and after having seen my own growth and that of others in the TORI communtities, I have come to believe that the TORI community is the most powerful medium for personal growth and human-relations training now available. It is a highly experimental form and changing rapidly, with great promise for evolving into newer forms as our culture changes. It is very much *in the culture* and is evolving with it.

The TORI community has many characteristics that enhance the learning processes. It is an ideal training environment for several reasons:

1. Fully autogenic learning is the most effective form of learning. In the free community, each individual has the opportunity of setting his or her own goals, making choices, creating options, responding to feedback, creating his or her own environment, making visible all aspects of the total process.

2. An optimal range of options is present. One can make a provisional try at any kind of behavior in a realistic environment, natural and life-like. One comes to accept the community as a significant segment of life. The reality factor is high.

3. The emotional climate is positive, supportive, and relatively free of risk. Though life-like, it lacks some of the risks of situations in everyday life. People can try behavior with an experimental attitude, testing one's capacities, behaviors, and reactions.

4. The potential for feedback is community-wide. One can get a full range of responses to one's social behavior. People are likely to respond caringly, openly, with honesty, in a manner that allows the feedback to be heard.

5. Behavior is more authentic in a large, open community than in a two-person setting or in a small group. Feedback is more direct and clear.

6. In the best of the communities things happen quickly, action is accelerated, feelings are intensified rather than being muted, the pace of life is quickened. There is a feeling that one can go through a lifetime of learnings, choices, dilemmas, and behavior patterns in a relatively short time.

7. Many forces combine to induce persons to take a proactive stance toward self and community. It is necessary for persons to join others in interdependence in seeking to solve the community problems that arise. Interdependent and proactive behaviors are the only ones that are functional. All this takes place in the full complexity of community dynamics. It is this kind of learning that is most necessary in a democracy, and in EQ V levels and beyond.

8. As persons have multiple experiences in these free-form communities, more and more transcendent behaviors appear, more and more EQ VIII and IX states avail themselves. Transcendent states that emerge in community are more enduring, more understandable,

and more easily integrated into life situations, than are such states when induced by intrusive techniques.

9. The skills that one learns in community are the skills that are relevant to teaching, managing, doing therapy, parenting, or taking any role in society. The training is practical and relevant.

The Learning Community

Many educational systems are experimenting with learning communities of various sizes. Schools are taking more experiential, holistic, and community approaches to the learning process.

The leaderless learning community has many obvious advantages. Because the community learns to use the resources of each member, teachers are not required. Learners assess their own needs, define the problems, suggest solutions, define the help that is needed, learn to seek relevant information, and learn to translate impulses and feelings into actions and problems solutions.

The community sets up an atmosphere that encourages risk, experimentation, choice, reliance upon individual resources, trust of self, courage to follow inner directions, free expression of feelings and differences, integration of emotionality into work and problem-solving, spontaneous and open behavior, want-determined action, and interdependence.

When the TORI community is used as a medium for education, the essence of education becomes a process of creative, joint inquiry, learning of emergent knowledge and skills, rather than a teaching-learning process. The locus of thought, action, and responsibility is in the learner rather than in the teacher. The motivation to learn comes from sources inside the learner and the process, and from intrinsic rewards and punishments within the very processes of interaction. The curriculum comes from the learner and the requirements of the process of inquiry, rather than from sources external to the learner.

Life in a learning community is a continuing, flowing process. All activities justify themselves as enriching to the moment, the process, and the goals. Classical education is seen as preparatory to later and more significant life, and thus requires constraint, goal-deferment, and discipline. In the learning community the goals are set by the learner as they emerge from the process, rather than being set by role, authority, or system. Rewards and punishments are informal, emergent, and intrinsic to the process of joint inquiry and interaction; they are not prescribed, formalized, extrinsic, or used as controls.

When we have used a TORI weekend community experience to help build a learning-community atmosphere, we have encouraged the participation of all involved in the process. We have included teachers, staff, administrators, maintenance and janitorial people, students, and school board members. At other times we have included parents, teachers, and students in a common experience. It is usually the adults who have the greatest problem in becoming personal, open, and want-determined. Unless students have become too constricted from long participation in conventional classrooms, they tend to get into the community rather easily.

An educational learning community is most effective under the following conditions:

1. The *total system is tuned in* to the philosophy, methods, values and goals of community learning. It is particularly important that the parents of the students be aware of the philosophy and activities of the community and be involved in setting goals, planning activities, and setting educational policy. It is very important for the students themselves to have a central part in all planning, policy making, and goal setting. Unfortunately, even in the most participative of learning communities, the student learners themselves are often left out of planning and policy making.

2. When the learning community is *part of a long range program* of planned change in the school system, the whole system must learn to live together cooperatively, learn the attitudes, skills, and feelings that are appropriate to community living. The whole system becomes its support base, marshalling all available forces toward the success of the experiment.

3. It is particularly important that *the teachers be clear* about the goals of the system, *share common values* such as those described in this book, and be oriented towards joining the other students in a process of joint inquiry. Distinctions usually made among conventional roles of parent, administrator, janitor, teacher and student gradually disappear, and each person becomes a learner and participant in the shared community. Everything is shared: responsibility, work, fun, goal setting, pain, and frustration. This shift can be particularly difficult for the teacher who has grown up in the conventional school system and who must learn new values, new methods, and new attitudes.

4. Research, measurement, and evaluation *are built into the process* itself, are part of the learning, and are not imposed upon the

system by external pressures. The best evaluation is that which is intrinsic.

Recreational, Social, and Professional Communities

A significant motivation for people to join country clubs, professional associations, travel clubs, family YMCA's, and vacation groups comes from a search for greater depth, intimacy, and caring in their lives. This need may be very conscious and openly expressed, or it may arise from a vague disquiet and discomfort at the unconnectedness of life. Unfortunately, the groups which people choose to meet these needs seldom do so in fulfilling ways.

The importance of discovering a feeling of community in our lives is receiving increasing recognition. Life is a flow and a rhythm. There are moments and days when each person wants privacy and aloneness. There are other moments and days when every person wants intimacy and communion with others. All meaningful activity — play, work, worship, learning, creative art — can be enriched at times when done with others *who care* and *who matter.*

The creative artist likes to show his or her work to other creative artists. The chemist or engineer seeks professional meetings to share the joys of creativity with others who are important in his or her world — those who matter. Hearing a concert or viewing a sunset is often more fulfilling when shared with people one loves. The search for intimacy and community is pervasive.

My impression from the associations I have joined as a member and the many organizations with which I have consulted is that this feeling of *community in depth* is all too rare. This is a serious gap, a cavity in our culture.

Our fears separate us and keep us from even the awareness of our need for each other. I have a vivid memory of a TORI community demonstration that I was asked to give in a large singles community. Naively, I had looked forward to this experience as one that would be warm and intimate, thinking that single people who had elected to live in community would be eager to respond to each other in depth. What I found was a large group of people who were desperately lonely, unable to touch each other physically, unable to express warmth either verbally or without words, unable to reach out on their own, and greatly dependent on the leader for initiation of activities and emotional support. At the same time, the individuals in the group seemed desperately interested in making contact in some way. My experience with most organizations differs only in degree from this one.

I have been asked many times to give demonstrations for many kinds of groups. There is usually a recognition that things would be better if "we learned to communicate with each other", or if "we were warmed up". There is usually a hope that all this can be done quickly, with a skilled leader performing his magic to help people connect in some better way. When I accept such an assignment and have only a few hours to work with the group I usually use some kinds of loosely-structured, non-verbal experiences that all groups and all ages relate to easily. The experience is often so much better than anything else they have been doing in their attempt to make connections that they are exhilarated at first. Even a glimpse of what greater intimacy might be found is exciting and positive. But true intimacy is much more difficult to attain. I have not found quick and easy roads to caring and depth.

It is possible to change radically the environment of these recreational, social, and professional groups. It requires many changes: changes in design of meetings that are autocratic, cognitive, and depersonalized; design of more flexible and versatile furniture that allows for spontaneous and fluid groupings; revision of schedules that prevent spontaneous happenings and that lock people into plans made by others long before the events that people are participating in; changes in norms, habits, and policies of the groups themselves.

Environmental design for intimacy is a major issue for all organizations. It *is* possible to design organizations and activities in such a way as to enhance caring and warmth. It is possible to create meetings, vacations, clubs, and organizations that enhance intimacy and connectedness. It is my assumption that all people want to be more caring and connected — but that they don't know how to do so, and especially don't know how to create social forms that make it possible. Just as the function of communication cannot be assigned by a corporate president to a director of communications, it is unrealistic and escapist for a social/professional organization to turn the issue of intimacy over to a social director or a cruise coordinator. Intimacy and caring are too central to the very core of the organizational being and purpose for delegation.

The Therapeutic, Healing, or Growth Community

New interest in holistic healing and organic health has encouraged attempts to build health-oriented communities. This is a very promising development: the focus upon wholeness, both in diagnosis and treatment, and on growth and development, rather than on remedial and corrective treatment, is encouraging.

New developments in holistic healing are spurring a revolution in medical and psychiatric practice. One phase that we know too little about is what are the obvious healing and growth-enhancing qualities of the communal experience itself. Too often the holistic communities are organized on EQ II to IV management principles. At worst, the community is managed and organized in autocratic and benevolent ways, relying upon esoteric techniques in the attempt to induce the healing and transcendent states that presumably accompany holistic health. Some of the best ones are holistic and organic in all significant ways.

We are moving toward a marriage of technique (in its best sense) and organizational management. My assumption is that the environment *itself* is the medium for healing, transcendence, and health. It is the atmosphere itself that enhances intuitive, caring, wholeness-oriented, transforming, and healing energy and communication. People who learn to relate to each other in these ways create the community for themselves. *The healing is in the process itself.* It is not a product produced by a process.

The Work or Business Community

Historically there have been many efforts to build community around the joys and challenge of work. The assumption is that work can be honorable, redemptive, challenging, cooperative, humanistic, and self-rewarding. Working together on tasks that are cooperatively chosen or designed, with co-workers that care and that matter, under conditions that are planned and created by the co-workers themselves, *can* be an organic and wholizing experience.

Fortunately, there is great diversity in methods, aims, and format in the attempts to build work communities. Small companies are being formed on humanistic principles, following some theory about the optimal relationship between people and work. Some large corporations are making inventive changes in decentralization, job enlargement, flexible time schedules, cooperative planning, pilot plants, and radical experiments with new management.

Urban planners are devising ways of building cities that make work easily accessible, environmentally pleasant, and integrated into humanistic and holistic living. The modern back-to-nature movement fosters attempts to live close to the land, to re-discover the simple joys of self-chosen work, to mix work with the natural environment, and to feel creative and artistic about work.

The conditions that enhance the effectiveness of these attempts are several:

1. People want to discover and create their own work tasks.

2. People generally enjoy work that is immediately relevant to their own life goals, talents, and interests. Work must have meaning that is apparent to the worker.

3. People enjoy working with compatible others, with people who care about each other, who share other aspects of life, and who form some kind of connected community.

4. If management is involved in the process of work organization, the management must move to an EQ Level that is appropriate to the level of development of the worker. Most workers want more participation in more aspects of the work than they are allowed to have. This is a complicated issue, however. False participation, ritualistic "involvement", and pseudo-choices are likely to be less humanistic than actual, honest, and out-front autocracy.

5. The work community is most effective if the largest share of the time for all workers is spent in work itself, rather than in the management, coordination, or control of work. Self-chosen work is intrinsically motivating.

6. Interdependence is important. Cooperation and teaming occur when the interconnectedness of the work tasks or projects is immediately visible. People like to feel important to each other. Under conditions of trust, people like to give help, support, and fellowship to others with whom they are working.

7. A feeling of community is a critical factor, and the work environment is best if it allows free flow of interaction, some combination of desired privacy and visibility, choice of work partners and work tasks, and multiple opportunities for interaction in personal and caring ways. Most people like to work *with* others at some point in the work process.

8. Competition in work is usually more destructive than functional. It is tempting to build in competition to improve productivity, but the gains are illusory and temporary, and the negative side-effects outweigh the apparent gains. Genuine and interdependent cooperation is a sound base for work organization.

9. There are great individual differences in all aspects of the work situation: needs for privacy, needs for help, desire for diversity in

tasks, willingness to do routine and repetitive tasks, needs for creativity, skill level, tolerance for neatness or disorder, needs for perfection, willingness to learn new tasks, willingness to conform to group pressures, and almost any work-relevant behaviors and attitudes. The work community must make provision for these differences and celebrate the diversity rather than attempt to achieve conformity.

10. Speed and efficiency are greatly overprized. A work community that puts a high premium on speed and efficiency must reorganize and replan to make room for other more significant factors. When workers are allowed freedom, they work rapidly and efficiently when it seems important to them and when conditions are favorable. Many workers take pride in speed and efficiency and will create their own internal rates and manners of work.

11. A work community is most effective when the values of the people are closely congruent with the work that is being done. People work with incredible energy and creativity upon tasks that are related to their life values: sheltering animals, achieving zero population growth, conserving natural resources, beautifying nature, conserving historical artifacts, helping the poor — whatever gives meaning and significance to their lives.

12. Pay and profit are relatively insignificant aspects of the work situation. The factors listed above are far more important in the long run. Manipulating pay and profit with the intention of creating motivation and productivity is an illusory trap. If trust and caring are high it is likely that equalizing pay or profit for all workers will tend to eliminate issues that interfere with work: jealousy of others who are seemingly paid more, and thus respected more, for work; resentment of others who fake work to get more pay; feelings of inadequacy when others are given raises or bonuses; or resentment of managerial use of pay changes as a manipulative or benevolent practice.

Residential Communities

Rapidly changing values in our society-in-transition elicit support for many experiments in living arrangements. Communes, extended families, adult communities, multiple-family living, singles apartment complexes, retirement communities, nudist colonies, tight-security guarded neighborhoods, unmarried couples, open marriages, gay communities — many forms are emerging that provide diversity and choice.

The new diversity is fortunate. We know so little about living together and have made comfortable assumptions about the universal advantages of the simple monogamous marriage and the single-family dwelling. Our present culture encourages experimentation with many models. It is likely that we will create yet a greater diversity of life styles and a wider range of choice for people seeking high-trust living arrangements.

Creating an optimal blending of privacy and joining is a critical issue. I find rather promising several attempts to build a community of from 20 to 40 families, pre-planning the building of individual family homes, all arranged in some way around a large communal room for community meals, recreation, meetings, a communal school for the children and for the adults, and other community activities. Each family would have options of privacy when they wanted it and communal activities when they wished.

Communes of varying sizes have organized around work, religion, back-to-nature living, an ideology, or sociometric preference. More common in all areas of North America are groups of three to twenty people who purchase or rent a large home and try to enrich their living in a collective way.

In all these situations a common problem is concerned with some management issues: organizing for housework, sharing finances, preparing meals, making decisions, handling grievances, mediating disputes. It is my impression that most people who join in these communal activities have liberal/romantic hopes, with little awareness of the incongruities of managing behavior and the Environmental Quality levels. They are seeking life that is appropriate to EQ Levels VI through X, but they employ familiar management patterns inherited from the autocratic/benevolent homes, factories, schools, and churches against which they are rebelling and from which they hope to escape. Hoping to achieve trust and transcend the worst of their fears, they sometimes resort to the same practices that have toxified their earlier environments: restrictive rules, penalties for infractions, linear scheduling, destructive secrecy, formalized contracts, role prescriptions, hierarchical structures, and other fear-based arrangements.

There are no easy solutions to these very practical problems. Several groups that are planning on living together are using TORI theory as a base and considering the EQ level analysis as useful for examining the environment they wish to create in the commune.

There are advantages of creating a common theory and a common set of values, working through the critical differences that lead to unproductive tension, and preserving the differences that add zest and challenge.

Trust level is even more critical in communal living arrangements than in more formal organizations. Learning to trust *is* the process of learning to live together. Recognition that it is a *learning* problem, that *the system needs to learn to be,* just as a person needs to learn to be, is a base for development.

Building a true community is not an easy matter. Well- intentioned and fairly compatible people have seemingly just as many problems creating a satisfying community as do members of a business or school organization that come together for formal purposes that are, on the surface, unrelated to forming community. Seemingly, whatever the organizational form, institutional purpose, or formal task, the *people processes* are the critical factors, and they are common to all situations where people gather. Personal, open, want-determined, and interdependent behavior is functional and trust-inductive. Impersonal, strategic, manipulative, and controlling behavior is dysfunctional and fear-escalating.

The TORI International Community

In the preceding chapter we considered the TORI international community as an organization and as a pioneering model for voluntary organizations. It is useful to consider it now as a *community*.

There are ten to eleven thousand people who participate occasionally in the activities of this community. Perhaps one thousand are continually active and consider themselves as more or less permanent members of the far-flung community.

Members feel a kinship with members in other geographic areas and often visit each other's homes, even though they may not have previously met personally. There is a common set of values and aspriations, centering around TORI theory and its many aspects and implications.

Although several groups of members live together in small communal arrangements, most interaction comes in shared vacations, meals, visits and weekends. In many of the more established communities there are communal holiday celebrations — Thanksgiving, New Year's Day, Easter, and other longer-than-weekend occasions when members can join each other with their families.

Persons bring food to share, chip in for expenses on a volunteer basis, bring friends who wish to sample the TORI life, cook communal meals, invent communal games, and join in whatever activities happen during the celebration. One community has an unstructured game called a "TORI game". There are no rules. There is usually a ball, which one can roll, carry, throw, pass, ignore or kick. The point to the game is to have activity, shared process, group hugs, spontaneous play, and the joy of movement.

A growing body of folklore, stories, indigenous poetry and songs, group games, and even rituals are aspects of the community living. The emphasis is on non-structure, non-organization, and non-technique, and there are very few formalized rituals and traditions. The general feeling is one of spontaneity and freedom of flow.

The formal organization, TORI Associates, Inc., the tax-exempt corporation, has little relevance to the activities and events in the community, where most communal activities are at the EQ VI and VII levels. It is an impressive demonstration of how much deeply-caring community activity can go on without formal organization and without formal leadership or a management group. The communes that are beginning to form among members will probably develop on a firm basis of trust and common values, with people deciding to live together after they have learned how to be together in depth and intimacy.

The path for the community has not been without frustrations and problems. An appreciable number of people have wanted to institute more formal procedures, charge dues, create membership requirements, advertise the community meetings and charge fees for the community workshops, hire administrative and secretarial staff, pay fees for member services, and try other procedures that most members feel are low-trust. There are differences of opinion on what constitutes a life of optimal trust. The community is very accepting of differences of opinion and differing behaviors. Recurring issues revolve around such behavior as smoking cigarettes, drinking liquor and wine, smoking pot, taking drugs, playing loud music, bringing pets to community weekends, chronic failure to share in costs, lack of participation in community meetings, differing patterns of relating to children, and a variety of practical issues that presumably come up in all communal and group activities. Most members feel that it is well to work through all feelings about these and other issues, prizing openness, acceptance of diversity, interdependence in depth, expression of diverse wants, and dealing forthrightly with any issue that any one member feels is important.

Some personal observations of mine are relevant. I am impressed with the changes and growth in the persons who have participated actively in the communities. People feel that they are growing and changing. I see an evolving body of practical theory that exists in the practices and behavior of people, a theory that is communicated in interaction rather than in books or even in words. This book is the first book about the theory. It is an effort to articulate some of the emerging learnings in the community, and is a communication primarily to the community members. It may also be useful and interesting to the growing number of people who write in to learn about the TORI community and who wish to participate in some way in the evolution of the theory and the practice.

My delay in writing a book about the theory has been due, in part, to my wish to see how satisfactory and effective the TORI international community is. I see it as one of the major tests of the practicality of the theory. Seeing it as dramatically successful, I now feel strong confidence that we have worked out several practical applications of the theory that are relevant to all phases of human interaction. Together with the several other applications of the theory reported in these pages, the strength of the international community is a solid and confidence-building evidence of the practicality of the theory.

Chapter 10

Releasing the Constraints: The Process of Management

To manage with trust is to join others in getting rid of the constraints that bind us — that keep us from doing what we really want to do. What we *really* want, at some level, is to have meaning in our lives, to be productive, to be creative, to join each other in the joy of work and the ecstasy of being. In fear we constrain each other. Trusting removes the constraints.

The Process of Management

Unfortunately, the very word "management" has come to signify a constraining process. Our experiences with low-trust management begin early in life. Several years ago I was called in as a professional consultant to be the neutral chairman of a national conference held in Washington D.C., on competitive sports for children under twelve years of age. It was an enlightening experience. After three days of intense and heated debate and data sharing, there was a final recorded vote on the major motion before the assembly of about 100 representatives of organizations.

The motion was made to recommend that all competitive sports for children under twelve be banned. The representatives of all of the organizations representing children voted for the motion to ban such sports. Organizations represented were the major national parent-teachers group, and psychological, educational, psychiatric, recreational, physical education, children's rights, orthopedic, and other professional groups. Every representative of these groups, without a single exception, voted for the motion to ban the sports because they

RELEASING

*To manage is to let the process happen,
to release the constraints.*

had been shown to be harmful in many ways to the young children.

Also represented were the major sports equipment manufacturers and the national media that publicize such events. Every single representative of these groups voted against the motion, and it failed — there was a larger representation from the commercial groups than from the professional groups.

The disinterested professionals had presented volumes of clear-cut evidence of damage to young children from such competitive activities, but this carried little weight against the overwhelming fact that they were immensely profitable to the athletic companies and the media. Certainly, the macro-environment is *very* powerful. We are embedded in a competitive, profit-making system. I will come back to this issue in the following chapter on social change.

The relevance here is that one major area of data dealt with the primitive and harmful management practices of the coaches, committees, parents, media, and other adults who run the athletic programs. Hours of testimony contained illustrations of what I am calling EQ I, II, and III management processes, judged by these professionals to be harmful and toxic for the children. They told of the frequent use of punishment as motivators, whimsical discipline, harmful competitiveness, a win-at-all-cost attitude of coaches, lack of participation by the children in any of the decisions about their activities, exploitation of the children for adult purposes, premature professionalization and depersonalization, and manipulative commercialization by the equipment manufacturing companies.

As the volumes of testimony indicated, these athletic programs are far from being the character-development activities they are reputed to be. Instead, they are often arenas for learning the worst practices of modern management. An example: Rule making is the norm. Rule circumvention is about equally prevalent. A typical illustration: A well known executive, who was a parent and a league official, announced to a huge, end-of-regular-season group of kids and parents: "As you know, league rules prohibit our having our All Stars practice before June 20, so we are not announcing our All Star selections until that date, when official practice will start. Meantime, we would like to ask the following 24 players to report on June 6 to play for two weeks before the All Star practice." Everyone laughed, knowing that the 24 were the players who would be announced as the All-Star selections on June 20.

Three days of such illustrations left all of the professionals who worked with youth very much convinced that the abuses in the management of organized sports for youngsters were so great as to warrant a recommendation that such organized athletics be discontinued. My impression is that in such organized sports we have groups of well-intentioned adults, willing and anxious to serve children, to provide supervised recreation, and to "keep the kids off the streets". Unfortunately, they find themselves caught in tangled webs of bad habits of parenting, traditional and unexamined management practices, distrust-bred assumptions about kids and how they learn, and complex institutional practices and rules — all of which are based upon and grow out of our earlier fears and distrusts. Parents, coach-teachers, and league officials don't *intend* to teach rule-breaking, lying, manipulative strategy, fear, and distrust. But in fact these *are* the unintentional and inevitable by-products of two highly related factors: distrusting attitudes and inadequate and false theory.

And so it is, often, with teachers, administrators, parents, counselors, ministers, managers, executives. All are caught up in a number of distrust assumptions about managing people. The message in TORI theory for all of us who manage is implicit throughout this book.

Because of the assumed centrality of management practices as determiners of environmental quality, I'd like to focus on the implications of TORI theory for the practice of management. Until groups and organizations learn to live in EQ levels VI and beyond, much of our organized life is going to be spent in environments that are determined by our leaders and our attitudes toward them. Most of you who read this book are in one or more formal "managerial roles" or are trying to prepare for one. We are caught and usually will become even more entangled in the fear/deception/manipulating web. I am going to share, below, my impressions and theory about this problem.

Centrality of Trust

My trust level is my internal regulator and what I do as a manager or parent will be a function of this changing level. Altering trust level is not a simple act of will, an act of rational choice, or a matter of understanding or insight. It is a total spiritmindbody process, a continuous re-birthing, a deeply organic process. Basic trust level is amazingly stable, but it *does* change and can be changed by the person through autogenic process. I change my trust level by creating an environment for myself that allows me to *discover* that people and processes can be trusted. Trust, like grace, comes as a gift to the spirit, but one must be prepared for it, open-minded, and willing to receive it. It is apparently a continuingly growing central process. Even Christ, often cited as a model of trusting, apparently lost His faith/trust at a moment of ultimate crisis, and His cry, "Father, why hast Thou forsaken me?", came when He wavered in His trust of the process.

The Basic Structure of Management Theory

The "content" structure of TORI management theory is some variation or corollary of the four fundamental propositions:

T: Personal behavior produces *trust;* role or depersonalized behavior produces defense.

O: Authentic *openness* produces integration of living process; covert strategy produces counter-strategy and circumvention.

R: Internal *realization* results in high productivity; persuasion produces resistance and disintegration.

I: *Interdependence* produces synergy; control produces dependency/rebellion.

Put another way, "managing people" means to relate in some enhancing, non-constraining way to the following processes:

T: Inner *trust*, emotionality, acceptance, inclusion, membership, growth of selfhood and being.

O: *Open* communication, flow of "hard" data and data about perceptions and feelings, input and output.

R: *Realizing* of potential, goal formation, productivity, work, creativity, performance, motivation, problem solving.

I: *Interdependence,* control, organization, structure, flow, form, relationships, interbeing.

The teacher or administrator who is relatively trusting is likely to "manage" emotionality, communication, goal formation, and organizing by being more personal, open, allowing, and interdepending. The manager who is relatively less trusting will be more depersonalizing, strategic and closed, persuasive, and controlling.

One way to apply TORI theory is for a parent or manager to conduct a continuing series of mini-experiments with life — being as personal, open, allowing, or interdepending as he or she *is able to be in the immediate situation,* granting his or her fear level (perceived risk).

Life, for the TORI-oriented manager, is a continuing discovery, a learning process, an experimentation, an experience with trust formation. A primary criterion of managed-system effectiveness is:

Are managers learning from what they are doing?

All management problems can be classified under one of the four processes listed above. The technical aspects of relating to such problems as materials acquisition, floor space, manufacturing, distribution, and finance are important technical issues. But *the* critical and overriding *management* issues concern *how managers relate to the people* who in turn relate to these technical problems. The key question is: How do managers relate to emotionality (T), communication (O), motivation (R), and interdependence (I)?

Managing Environmental Quality

The EQ level in churches, homes, businesses, schools, and agencies is, with few exceptions, in the EQ II, III, and IV range. The manager's job, it seems to me, requires him to function at a higher level — to provide some kind of answer to the question: How can I learn to live in some fulfilling way in the environment/institution I'm in? Another concurrent question is: How can I join with others collaboratively to change this environment? It is important to me to live, at peace with myself, in *the world I am in.* If I can learn to relate to the world I'm in with authenticity, in a personal, open, allowing, and interdepending way, then I and the world will change.

If I want to use TORI theory in a diagnostic and reflective way in looking at my organization and my task, I must look at the fears and the distrusts in the system and how they express themselves and at the trust in the system and how it is expressed. For instance, a frequent pattern in our contemporary culture is a bi-modal distribution of attitudes about environmental quality. There is a vigorous and vocal majority of people who believe in EQ II and III levels as a model of management. They believe in a clear, direct, and responsible authoritarianism as the most efficient, realistic, and attainable pattern of life. This autocratic group believes in a muted and reasonable use of power, with the most expert, qualified, skilled, and intelligent citizenry serving as leaders — a balance wheel against the vagaries and instabilities of societal events.

Another group, clearly a minority, believe in EQ V and VI levels as a model of enlightened management. They believe that people have the capacities and skills necessary to make their own decisions, to create their own lives, to make responsible choices, to engage in productive and creative work, and to join with each other to create, together, their schools, homes, businesses, and churches.

Both of these groups are highly diverse and these two statements are greatly oversimplified. But the statements represent a significant issue of our time: *How do institutions that are essentially autocratic and benevolent move toward participative and emergent environments?*

The following two tables present a schematic analysis of these two bi-modal environments. Table XVII presents an analysis of the *autocratic and benevolent* styles of environment, their predominantly defensive character structure, and the effects of these styles upon the system and the people in the system. Roles are structured, delineated, and prescribed, and result in the draining of energy into defense, the creation of a general atmosphere of paranoia and various forms of protective collusion. Masking and covert strategies are programmed into the system, resulting in secrecy, energy drained away from productive activity into counter-strategy and circumvention, and great difficulties in using any kind of decision-making process other than issuing directives from the top. Motivations are managed by manipulating extrinsic reward systems, which results in multiple forms of resistance to doing productive and creative work. Processes are controlled by rules, laws, and power, resulting in a wide variety of forms of dependence and counter-dependence.

Table XVIII presents analysis of *participative* and *emergent* environments, which allow for the rise of the discovering processes in such a way that the primary tone of the organization or group is non-defensive. Personal behavior leads to trusting and caring. Open, disclosing behavior leads to integration of emotionality into work rather than into circumventive strategies. Allowing behavior results in personal and system goal integration of intrinsic motivations. Interdepending behavior leads to emerging patterns of synergy and cooperation.

EQ level IV, which is advisory in nature, is a relatively neutral transitional stage between these two opposing poles in our culture. The expansion of the data base and the bridging between management and labor mute the reactive and defensive processes stirred up by authoritarian practices and lay the groundwork for later stages of participation and authentic collaboration. "Scientific" management is a way station between autocracy and creative emergence.

TABLE XVII. AUTOCRATIC AND BENEVOLENT MANAGEMENT (EQ II, III)
(Managing, Teaching, Counseling, Parenting, Ministering)

Defending Processes	Manager-Teacher-Counselor-Parent Way of Being	Modal Effects of This Way of Being Upon the Person, Team, Community, or Nation
Depersonalizing		
Boxing-Coding	Fear/Distrust	Draining of life energy into defense
Role-ing	Role behavior	Escalation of fears and distrusts
Observing	Role prescriptions	Increased feelings of suspicion, paranoia
Detaching	Role demands	Protective pairing, collusion, subgroups
Appraising	Punitive feelings	Fear of therapy, exposure, hurt, danger
	Defending	Distortion of perceptions
Masking		
Closing	Covert strategy	Energy into counter-strategy, circumvention
Covering	Facade building	Emphasis upon secrecy, need for privacy
Distancing	Use of techniques	Distortion of communication upward, downward
Pushing away	Programming communications	Feelings of alienation, sadness, withdrawal
Screening	Filtering	Difficulty in consensual decision making
	Secrecy	Suppression of negative feelings
Oughting		
Denial of self, own wants	Persuasion	Resistance, apathy, passivity, disinterest
Value orientation	Manipulating extrinsic rewards	"Neurotic", displaced, unnecessary work
Parenting	Performance appraisal	Distal-proximal flow, against the river
	Competence orientation	Energy diverted into meeting expectations
	Taking responsibility	Emphasis upon authority and responsibility
		Unrealistic, overaspirational goals
Depending		
Controlling	Power and control focus	Symbolic and displaced fighting
Submitting	Rule-making	Resistance to authority, latent hostility
Dominating	Boundary setting	Ambivalence, impotence, blaming others
Leading	Paternalism or abdication, non-directive	Bargaining, barter reactions to power
Rebelling	Legalism	Conforming to expectations and power
		Demands for structure, rules, order

TABLE XVIII. PARTICIPATIVE AND EMERGENT MANAGEMENT (EQ V, VI)

(Managing, Teaching, Counseling, Parenting, Ministering)

Discovering Processes	Manager-Teacher-Counselor-Parent Way of Being	Modal Effects of This Way of Being Upon the Person, Team, Community, or Nation
Trusting-Being	Trusting	Increase in personal, non-role behavior
Warming	Being a person	Sensing uniqueness of self and others
Centering	Leaving role	Feelings of excitement, awareness, zest
Personing	Caring	Increase in self-caring, caring for others
Acceptance	Spontaneity	Increased confidence in own work product
Self-regard	Proactive being	Increased diversity, exploration, disorder
Opening	Showing feelings	Increase in flow
Letting in	Disclosing of self	Reciprocal feedback, openness, disclosure
Communing	Authentic behavior	Integration of emotionality into work
Listening	Empathy	Consensus more easily reached or not
Showing	Impulsiveness	necessary
Free	Non-cautious	Freedom with negative feelings
Realizing	Allowing	Escalation of intrinsic motivations
Actualizing	Letting be	Goal integration and directionality
Wanting	Showing own wants	Increased autogenesis, proactive norms
Asserting	Problem solving	Owning of work, eagerness, work orientation
Expanding	Proactivity	Increasing congruence of work and play
Exploring	Searching	Reduced emphasis on power, competition
Interdepending	Joining	Increased interdependence, cooperation
Joining	With-behavior	Emergence of inner control and norm system
Sharing	Co-learning	Integration of conflict into co-effort
Integrating	Informalizing	Reduced concern for structure and forms
Synergizing	Non-controlling	Allocation of work by interest, consensus
Being with	Self-oriented	Flexibility, proximo-distality of flow

Determining One's Own Internal Environmental Quality

As stated in Chapter III, the EQ scale is a description of personal growth, as well as of organizational growth. It is my observation that most persons and institutions have a functional span of about three EQ levels. There is a level that we have largely moved away from, one that is the primary mode of the present, and a third that seems plausible, possible, and attainable in a reasonable length of time.

There is also a significant experiential range: a range of environmental alternatives which a person, a group, or an organization has experienced in depth so that decisions and images are reality-oriented, communicable, and clear. For instance, many persons have never really experienced groups of any size in which leaders did not provide the major source of energy and organization, and so in their minds EQ levels VI through X exist only in some vague conceptual realm and are not really viable options or action images. On the other hand, some modern children raised in progressive homes and schools may never have experienced an EQ level I or II environment and know about them only through reading or hearsay. Many students of management see as viable alternatives only the four EQ levels II through V, roughly paralleling the familiar Likert Systems I, II, III, and IV management styles. For many people, talk about EQ levels IX and X, about transcendent and cosmic phenomena, is unfamiliar, threatening, or too much like science fiction to take seriously as living options for today's world.

It is important for any person who attempts to apply Trust Level theory to get in touch with his or her own developmental level, preferred mode of interacting, fears and anxieties about certain levels, experiential gaps, range of clear images, and value systems. I am assuming that each of us can do this with some useful degree of accuracy. While to some degree one can choose a management style, it is my observation that each person lives best in an environment that is relatively congruent with his or her own values, modal behavior, attitudes, customary habits, and deep-lying proclivities.

I believe that there is a natural growth of persons and institutions along the EQ scale. *Defense level* is correlated with EQ level in an inverse way. The more we reduce our defenses, the more we and our culture move up the EQ scale. When we and our organizations learn to understand and accept who we are or what they are, defenses are reduced, and feelings of trust move the system on the scale. For example, when autocracy becomes a way of life and people are more trusting of it, there is a natural tendency to become compassionate and benevolent. When, at the organic EQ level, empathic and intuitive modes of living become familiar and integrated into life, there is a natural tendency for integration to occur at other levels and for the inner wellsprings of quasi-conscious energy and creativity to become incorporated into living.

One aspect of this process is consciousness raising. As people become aware of new EQ levels, of new freedoms, of new potential, or new trends, there is a tendency to grow and to realize or actualize inner images.

Whatever I can image clearly I can accomplish or be.

Clear and vivid imagery of a new EQ level is a potent step in its attainment.

Self Management in Persons and Systems

Growth is an inner-outer process. Effective persons and organizations are centered. Directions, motives, movement, feelings — all come from the center of the being of the person, of the group, or of the organization; they then move to the outer edges, and then on to external relations.

The manager who contributes to the myth that he or she "manages" the system, sets its goals, makes its decisions, or creates its process, is creating trouble. Being, data flow, goal formation, and interdependence, the four TORI variables, are *system variables,* emerge from the innards, and are needs of the system itself. The sensitive manager (like any other effective system member) senses what people want, diagnoses the emerging goals, sees the process that is developing, and then contributes to the process as best he or she can. This process of management creates strong, dynamic organizations that are inner-directed, and it creates persons who are centered *and* interdependent.

Effective managers, ministers, therapists, teachers, and parents are continually in the process of working themselves out of a job. They live and work in ways that strengthen the system itself; they increase the visibility of interdependencies, and in the process they become less essential to the organization or the family. Inexperienced, insecure, or defensive managers or parents do not recognize this process and often act in ways to make themselves indispensable. In fact, new managers often try to do something managerial to justify their additional salary and status.

The Control System

A fundamental error of the manager, parent, or person in role is to get tied up in the control system. The attempt to control another person sets up counterforces that are detrimental to the system. Managers *can* help to set up processes that control *other processes.* One can control the flow of goods, the processing of data, and the use of space; but persons and systems are healthier if it is the aims, conditions, data, or the other needs of the system that control people.

There are many ways of exerting control or attempting to. These may be conscious or unconscious, intentional or unintentional. A parent or teacher who expresses an opinion, makes a suggestion, or utters an offhand remark may be creating a relationship that exerts a subtle control over the child or student.

Defensiveness and Regression on the EQ Scale

Defensiveness is the countervailing dynamic of trust level. Any manager can increase the effectiveness of the system by doing whatever is possible to remove forces that increase defensiveness. Among the frequent factors that increase defensiveness, and the concomitant, counter-productive defending process of role-ing, clos-ing, oughting, and controlling are:

1. *Fears* of all kinds. These are the generic force of the defense systems. "Managerial behavior" produces fears of disapproval, evalua-tion, depersonalization, failure, inadequacy, and a whole host of feelings associated with the fear of father figures.

2. *Pressure and tension.* Inexperienced and fearful managers may deliberately increase pressures on the false but prevalent assumption that increasing the inducing forces on people will increase motivation. Management at all levels applies pressure from above to increase fear/tension/activity below.

3. *Competition.* An atmosphere of competition results in continuous attack on the perceived adequacy of people, and the resulting need to defend.

4. *Evaluation.* Children, students, workers, members of the congregation, and patients, all respond with defense when they see themselves being evaluated *now* or threatened with evaluation in the *future.* Whatever positive effects may come from the threat of evaluation, they are surely counter-balanced by the negative effects of the defensive behaviors produced.

5. *Strategy.* People who feel themselves in the ambiguity of an

atmosphere filled with strategy, especially covert strategy, are continually focused on counter-strategy. The defense-oriented energy spent on devising strategies and counter-strategies is probably the single most powerful contribution to lowered productivity in tightly-managed operations.

6. *Physical danger.* Imaginary or perceived physical dangers contribute to defensiveness. Children who have been punished are particularly susceptible to physical threats. Defensive managerial postures are especially aroused (and rationalized) when there are poisons in the hospital or home cabinets, violent prisoners in the yard, deep waters near the summer camp, dangerous machinery in the plant.

When defense levels are aroused, managers regress to lower EQ levels. When fear and defense are mild, regression goes back one or two levels. The higher the fear and defense, the further down the scale the person goes. If fear is high enough, almost anyone, whatever his or her theory, will go back to power and/or punishment.

Regression is particularly prevalent when the theory is not well internalized and embedded in the being and habits of the manager. The frightened mother who feels insecure about her child-rearing practices is easily aroused to spank or lash out. The threatened supervisor whose theory is inadequate for most emergencies will resort to punishment when pushed.

Regression is reduced when the environmental quality is well-integrated into articulated theory, well-established assumptions, congruent values, emotional support, and clear choices.

The Management Dilemma in a Transitional Society

Many managers, ministers, parents, and administrators see themselves caught in the middle of a set of conflicting pressures and forces. Expectations are strong and conflicting: the expectations of bosses, boards, subordinates, neighbors, customers, the congregation. Books on management, child rearing, church education, and administration proliferate and conflict with each other. It is almost literally true that if a parent or manager decides upon a clear course of action, he or she can find an authoritative book with a theory to rationalize the action.

Even if I as a manager wish to do so, it is impossible to meet all the conflicting demands of parents, relatives, superiors, boards, workers, or others who may have legitimate, or see themselves as having legitimate demands on me.

A working solution that seems to be successful for many TORI practitioners in resolving these dilemmas is to follow some such sequence as the following:

(1) As the manager or parent or minister I start by looking into myself, creating my own theory and learning what EQ level is comfortable for me in my surroundings, where I live and work. I take care of me and my emotional and psychological needs, discovering what relationships are most fulfilling for me with my family, team, or congregation.

(2) I make determined efforts to create a climate of trust and freedom in my family, group, or team. It is important to share our fears and trusts openly with each other, to tell each other what we want for ourselves and for the group, to be as personal with each other as our fears permit, and to explore the ways in which we want to be interdependent. As the leader, I may be seen by the family or the team as having some kinds of responsibilities above and beyond those of other team or family members. It is best to deal openly with this issue and to create a solution agreeable to the members and to authorities that interface with me. Intra-team and intra-family relationships are usually considerably easier to work through than interface issues. If the division head insists that I, as the responsible manager, am responsible for failure of my management team to meet a production deadline, my team and I have an issue to work through with each other and with the division head. If the school authorities decide that I, as a parent, am responsible for seeing that my children go to school regularly and on time, my family and I have an issue to work on with each other and with the school authorities.

The TORI parent or manager who has worked through a theory in some manner approximating the processes listed in Table X will have little trouble with these first two steps in building a theory and creating a compatible and trusting work group or family group. The process is exciting and stimulating.

Any face-to-face group or family can achieve whatever EQ level the group can clearly form into a concrete image that the group wants to achieve. I am not saying that there will be no problems. There will likely be anger, differences, conflict, rivalry, jealousy, resentment, and frequent negative and disturbing feelings. There will also be love, support, understanding, empathy, encouragement, joy, and many positive and encouraging feelings. The *processes* of discovering each other, of fighting and coming into conflict, of loving and caring, of celebrating and transcending differences, of creating trust — these are the real fabric of living and being. This is at the center of the family, the church, the business, or the school: trusting the magic of the discovering processes.

(3) As I am creating my own theory and sharing in the building of the team or family, I make an effort to relate to the organization and community in a trust-building way. The key is to keep my courage and my vision — to keep my faith. A high-trust family or a high-trust team is a support environment for all its members, including the parents and the team manager. The intimacy and closeness that come with interaction-in-trust increase the trust among team members. This trusting environment often contrasts with the seemingly distant and impersonal environment of the surrounding organization or neighborhood. Upper management, other teams, and the family neighborhood members may not understand our motives, our life style, or our daily rhythms as well as we do. Our team or family is sure to be more TORI-like, more close, more personal, and more free than the surrounding organization and neighborhood.

It is my observation that the interface between a TORI team or family and the surrounding environment will be supportive and positive if the team or family members are authentically personal, open, want-determined, and interdependent in relating to the surrounding environment. All members of the team relate to other members of the organization and can contribute to the overall climate of trust. The manager or parent is more likely to have critical interfaces with significant others, particularly in an authority-oriented climate. I know no magic formulae, but I have observed that most TORI-like managers and parents have a trust of others that makes it possible to relate to the outside world in a trust-escalating way.

(4) While fulfilling whatever functions are required by the organization, the government, and the public, I do whatever I can to *join the team or the family as a member and full person* and enter into all the tasks, functions, and activities that define the group and the task. This process is not an abdication. It is not passive, non-directive, or confined in any way, but is an active joining and sharing.

In the discussion of management and role in the various chapters in this book I have taken a strong position on leaderlessness and emergence. As managers, ministers, administrators, parents, and therapists, we are useful only as we are needed by dependent people who are not fulfilling their potential as free, proactive, whole, and organic beings. We will no longer be needed by people who recognize that they don't need us. It is useful and necessary for us to hasten this process of consciousness raising, for a function of the therapist, parent, and leader is to reduce dependency. As we make the rapid transition into an emergent culture and as the team or family grows into new EQ levels, the *role* of manager, parent, minister, or administrator will gradually disappear. During the transition the persons in these roles can be aware of this process and be a significant force in the evolution of society toward an emergent life.

Why Be a Manager?

In our upward-mobile culture, people who want to advance often seek to move away from *doing* and move into managing others who do. An opposite trend — by those who are returning to the soil, to nature, and to crafts — is motivated by a recognition of the joys of "work", defined in a very broad sense.

The motives that lead one to become a manager, therapist, minister, helper, administrator, teacher, or executive, come to some degree from the following cluster: desire for prestige, power, money, control, influence, status, and avoidance of the meniality of "work". Our analysis shows that these motivations are clearly associated with lower EQ levels. They are in fact illusory, of little enduring satisfaction to actualized people, and they disappear as people grow into higher states of growth and environmental quality. These motivations are not associated with high environmental-quality levels.

People assume these roles for many other reasons: excitement, creativity, a wish to make contributions to society, and a desire to help people, among others; but persons can learn to satisfy these motivations in non-role ways as the society changes.

As we create a more holistic society there will be less need for people to work on the basis of motivations that are essentially defensive in character. People who want power, control, influence, and status usually want these states as *a defense against fears* of being impotent, insignificant, inferior, or under the arbitrary control of others. It is my observation that these power/control/status drives diminish or disappear when people move into holistic or transcendental states, as people lose the defensiveness that supports and feeds these drives.

When people get in touch with deep intrinsic motivations to *do,* create, be, discover, experience, transcend, give, commune, *feel,* they are able to create a personal and occupational life filled with these self-created and self-discovered wants and satisfactions. Consequences follow:

1. Such people find satisfaction on the job, create few problems for the organization, and do not need others to manage or lead them or give them therapy. Their own processes are healthy and life-giving.

2. Full involvement in this kind of life makes it possible for such people to reach holistic and transcendent states without the artificial aids of techniques or special methods. They create their own transcendence.

The Changing World of Assumptions

Defensive management in the early EQ levels is buttressed by a set of assumptions that change as managers develop more trust of the people they manage. The more defensive the parent, teacher, manager, minister, or administrator, the more likely is he or she to make some of these assumptions:

1. Deep down, most people don't really know what is best for them.

2. Most people don't really know what they want to do and need skilled help in such determination.

3. If most people are left alone, without expert help, their lives will be disorganized, immoral, have little creativity or productivity, and be of mediocre quality.

4. Those with higher motivations, a larger perspective, greater skills, and more intelligence must take leadership in bettering society, in running a mill, in setting a moral example, or in setting adequate goals.

5. People need training in communication and if left alone without adequate and skilled help, are likely to express themselves poorly, listen inattentively, and create difficulties for themselves.

6. The majority of people is not highly motivated and, if not supervised properly or given inspiration by expert leaders, will be rather lazy, do relatively shoddy work, and seek the easiest and least challenging tasks.

7. Most people show little interest in real learning and need skilled help in developing learning interests, required skills, goal-setting experience, and appropriate habits of study.

These assumptions are self-fulfilling. The more firmly the

manager believes them, the more likely is he or she to act in ways that prove them to be true. Many parents, teachers, and managers act in these ways toward children, students, and workers. Perhaps more significant is the fact that many children, students, and workers make these same assumptions about themselves and about the others around them.

I believe that these assumptions are *not* true. The world, in my experience, is more like the following:

(1) Deep down, most people *know* what is good for them. In fact, each person is the best judge of himself or herself and is the best expert on his or her own life. People, in an environment of trust, discover this.

(2) Most people really do know what they want to do. Many times, through fear and distrust, people do not *express* what they want. These same fears and lack of trust keep them from *doing* what they want to do.

(3) When "left alone" and when given *full* responsibility for themselves, most people are highly goal-directed, ethical, creative, and productive. This has been demonstrated over and over in experimental programs with groups that were thought by many to be the least likely to take such responsibility: prisoners, mental patients, juvenile delinquents, and others with poor track records in life. What is required is a group of persons with enough courage (trust) to give each other full, *unqualified*, trust. So many parents, teachers, and managers give a kind of probationary and contingent trust, which is only a pseudo-trust and is recognized as such. Contingent trust is often frightening and difficult to deal with.

(4) Most people are competent, skilled, intelligent, and motivated enough to provide their own leadership, initiate their own actions, build their own morals, and run their own lives.

(5) Most people know how to communicate very well. Many times they allow themselves to be immobilized by fear and distrust and shut themselves off from expressing themselves or from listening to others.

(6) Most people enjoy self-chosen work and in fact will choose the most challenging and significant work available. What's more, they will do it very well, for they like to do well. They accept challenge, tackle worthy tasks, and perform with quality. This reality is often covered up in the defensive climates that one can find in many homes, schools, and factories. "Work" that is not worth doing is not worth

doing well, as Maslow put it. Work that is arbitrarily assigned, meaningless, irrelevant, unrelated to inner goals, or given punitively is resisted by most people. Students, children, and workers who do such work with understandably low motivation are then seen as lazy or incompetent, as "poor students" or "poor workers".

(7) Most people are curious and experimental. They enjoy learning new things and have wide interests, setting "real" goals rather than artificial ones and studying avidly when they move into autogenic learning processes — when they are in charge of *their own* learning.

Such assumptions are woven into the fabric of our theories about people and life. Each person has a complex inter-weaving of attitudes, feelings, perceptions, assumptions, beliefs, and habits that we have called his or her "theory" of living. This theory and these embedded assumptions grow and change with experience. They are highly related to the EQ level. People live in, create, and are nurtured by the EQ level that is most suited to their current inner nature. This inner nature and theory of living both grow and change with experience. Both the inner nature and the theory can be changed by the person. How this change occurs is a major issue of this book. The learning theory calls for new directions in management development for teachers, parents, and other managers of the processes of living.

Management Development

One's theory of management growing emerges from the EQ level of one's life. To oversimplify:

In a punitive environment, people would be subtly punished for having the "wrong" assumptions about people, and behavior modification programs would be set up to change the assumptions or to attempt to do so. In a purely autocratic environment, people would be instructed to manage differently, given the correct assumptions, or told how to set up situations that would produce new assumptions.

In a benevolent environment, new managers might be given differential warmth and approval for having the correct assumptions and behavior, be carefully protected from incorrect experiences, and be helped to learn new assumptions. In EQ level IV, the training program might be highly rational and persuasive, with information and new data given as the base of the training program. People would be taught new assumptions.

A participative program might include a learning community in which new or potential managers would work together to create learning experiences, set common learning goals, and attempt to discover their own theories and assumptions.

In EQ levels VI though X there would be no need for a formal training program for new and potential leaders. The need for managers, teachers, and "parenting" parents would gradually disappear. People would know how to create new experiences and new states of being and would go about doing so. The environment itself would be the medium for learning and development.

CREATING

The world around us is continually in the process of being created anew.

Chapter 11

Social Change: Discovering and Creating a New World

Discovering and creating are twin, interflowing processes of social change. Change is universal and continuous. Persons, groups, and societies change most rapidly through the evolution of Environmental Quality levels when trust is high, for trust allows us to join each other in creating a better world.

We can apply the same theory to overall cultural change that we use in trying to understand all other human process, that *trust level is the key leverage variable in world change.* Enduring change in the social order is in direct relation to that social order's upward movement on the Environmental Quality scale, as progressively higher levels of trust are achieved by its individuals and its organizations. Trust level results from significant changes in the four basic TORI discovering processes. These propositions are as central to political, economic, and social change as they are to changes in the family, the business, and the school.

The Diagnosis

From the perspective of the EQ analysis, the world is in more of a fluid state than ever before. In the United States and in certainly the majority of industrial nations, most institutions can be classified as benevolent, advisory, participative, or emergent environments, EQ levels III through VI. There remain vestigial elements of EQ I and II in some families, schools, prisons, and athletic programs, and to a certain extent in all of our institutions. But we also have many images through our reading or our experiences of individuals and groups reaching EQ levels VII through X. Most of us, in our daily lives, live in relationships at levels III through VI.

A number of analysts have pointed out that the *dominant themes* of our day are fear, distrust, and defense in various guises. We have in recent history passed through times when the dominant themes of EQ levels I and II — punishment, retribution, power, control, obedience, and rebellion — were the key themes of institutions in which and with which we lived.

But new consciousness levels bring higher levels of trust, lessening our need for defense and increasing our dissatisfaction with a world of power, punishment, and coercion. Nurturing, participative sharing, communication in depth, and shared search for freedom occur more frequently. These are the marks of EQ levels III through VI.

To some extent, defenses and distrust have gone underground: They are now often disguised and less easily recognized for what they are. Fear and distrust, tyranny, coercion, oppressive scheming, and enslavement appear reincarnate in the form of four modern and deadly sins: *role-taking, covert strategy, persuasion, and leadership.*

The sickness of our day is embodied in these four "defending" processes and their many variants. Does this sound harsh? Let me explain.

Role-taking or *depersonalization* is endemic to our culture. The hot-cold, hating-loving, redemptively-unique person is lost in "assuming appropriate roles". When I am a "parent" dealing with a "child", I am no longer a person being with another person. Even though I happen to be a superintendent, I needn't *be* a superintendent. A teacher playing the role of teacher cannot be an effective teacher. The sadness of Watergate is epitomized in the process through which *the person* Richard Nixon once was finally disappeared into *the role* of the "imperial presidency". And the "lesson" of Watergate is not that one wicked man led us into this calamity, but that we have created a culture in which we are depersonalizing each other, joining in an alienating process in which roles are relating to roles relating in turn to still other roles. Nixon is a symbol of the age, a flowering of our theme, an object lesson, a warning signal that screams: "Let's look at what we are doing to each other!" It was no accident that we elected this kind of person to represent us to the world.

Role-taking is a potent and seductive process. In some informative experiments at Stanford a few years ago, the students taking the roles of guards became so hostile and punishing to the students taking the roles of prisoners that a role-taking experiment studying prison behavior had to be discontinued prematurely. Role prescriptions that we give ourselves and that others give us tend to lock us into depersonalizing behavior. A patient classified as a paranoidal schizophrenic in a mental hospital will tend to act out what the patient thinks such people do, and hospital personnel get into the same perceptual patterns. The sickness is reenforced by the role percep- tions.

The stabilization, stereotypy, and preservation of roles are major targets of the women's movement. Seeing oneself and being seen in the role of female starts early in life. According to a Georgetown study, female children under two years of age were administered 50 per cent more over-the-counter drugs than male children. The study found that this role-taking and role-giving persisted into adulthood: women took more over-the-counter drugs than men, even when sickness rates were similar.

Covert strategy is the identifying mark of the closed life The fearing and distrusting person thinks strategically in an effort to respond to a variety of fears: fears of revealing feelings and opinions that might cause disquiet or retaliation; or fears that unplanned, unstrategized, and implusive actions might not "win friends and influence people". The more fearful we are, the more we feel it is necessary to devise a strategy to "deal with" the other person. The more we are into a role, the more likely we are to come up with a strategy, a device, a technique, a gimmick, a plan, or a management tool. *And the more we do this the more we induce distrust.*

Some roles are noted for the use of strategy and resultant distrust: psychologist, lawyer, salesperson, advertiser, public relations expert. Whenever I've asked people to tell me what it means to "use psychology", their answers indicate that it means to "trick people" or to manipulate them. Two recent studies of the legal profession indicate that the more experience people have with lawyers, the more they come to distrust the law. The reporter of one of the studies recommended that, as a result of this finding, the legal profession ought to hire public-relations experts to create a better "image of the law"!

The creation of distrust is in direct ratio to the rise of strategy. Again, the Watergate phenomena are relevant. It was characteristic of Nixon and his co-conspirators to engage in what seemed like interminable secret-strategy sesssions. It is diagnostically significant in looking at our contemporary culture that a frequent statement of the lesson of Watergate was: They should have destroyed the tapes.

Or that it was poor strategy to have made them in the first place. The more penetrating lesson is that covert strategizing is a sickness that characterizes our culture. It is a sickness that retards cultural and social growth to newer levels of fulfillment.

Persuasion is the attempt to manage other people's motivations and is a hidden sickness of cultures in the EQ III, IV, and V ranges. Advertising, public relations, performance appraisal, merit pay, and other institutionalized forms of motivation management are so woven into our culture that they are a way of life — integrated into our values like motherhood, patriotism, and competition. Most institutions hire public-relations people, advertisers, propagandists, and lobbyists to try to change people's motivations: to get them to want new things, to want to go to our church, to buy our cigarettes, to want to join the army, to want the girdle we sell, to want to vote for our candidate, or to want to believe what we want them to believe. These professionals engage in a constant battle of subtle distortion, seductive massaging of the truth, selective laundering of the data, expert manipulation of symbols, incessant bombardment of the senses, and the use of a wide variety of media messages directed toward the manipulation of our motivations.

Persuasion is the antithesis of inquiry. Our legal system, for instance, is historically rooted in the "adversary" system, which pits the parties against each other in the attempt to persuade the jury of the merits of opposing sides, in contrast to an objective and dis-passionate inquiry into the "truth" of the matter. This process of prosecution and defense is in direct contrast to one of discovering. It is easy for this adversary mode to get into politics, the church, medicine, education, and other institutions. Forensic medicine is a growing field. Doctoral students "defend their theses". Hardsell ministers market the gospel message. The President feels he has to "sell" the idea that there is an energy shortage.

This constant and pervading climate of persuasion results in a generalized resistance to the assault of such messages, a cynicism about the motivations of people who are assumed to be distorting their messages in some way to influence, manipulate, or control us. It is assumed that ministers, teachers, counselors, lawyers, psychologists, store clerks, and used car salesmen all have hidden motives, and that is is necessary to respond to what everyone says with suspicion and distrust. This neurotic buy-sell culture feeds the growing cynicism and paranoia of our day. It is an unhealthy atmosphere in which fulfilling relations are difficult to achieve and sustain.

Leadership is the fourth process embedded in our defensive culture that masquerades as a positive attribute of persons, organizations, and societies. Leadership is defined in most of the textbooks as the process of getting other people to do what you want them to do: the management of the actions of other people. Leadership in an elite group and reliance by underlings that the elite will perform the vital functions of the society are the key, defining marks of the EQ levels I through V. The transcendence of leadership and the building of processes that do not depend upon leadership are doorways to higher states of being, to greater fulfillment, and to higher levels of productivity and spirituality. A critical step in the growth of the person is the movement away from dependence upon the leadership of another person. The key to the future lies in increasing the number of instances of emergent leaderless groups in education, business, therapy, and all phases of life. The key to changing environmental quality is the growing trust in ourselves *as individuals,* and also *as groups and communities.*

I remember a white manager in the presence of a black manager characterizing the black "march on Washington" as "surprisingly" orderly and responsible, *i.e.,* "the blacks must have had good leadership". The black person expressed indignation; his inference correctly interpreted the white person's derogation of black people's ability to act responsibly on their own. One of the most resistant forces against growth is the assumption that we need "leadership" to motivate, protect, encourage, nurture, and organize us. We give away our own dignity and worth when we make this assumption and allow "leaders" to influence, dominate, control, and take power over us.

These four camouflaged defending processes are so easily rationalized, appear to be so innocent and even righteous, and are so interwoven in the culture of the home, the church, the school, and even the mental hygiene clinic, that it is difficult to recognize these as the toxic diseases that they are and to see the effects these processes have on the erosion of trust level.

The Less Effective Processes of Societal Change

The processes and methodologies that people use to achieve social change are, not surprisingly, appropriate to their EQ level. The problem often is that the methods are more appropriate to the level we have passed through, or are now passing through, than to the level *we are moving into.* As a result the methods and processes tend to be forces that act to *preserve* outmoded forms, attitudes, and environmental qualities. Change efforts can be far more effective if they are appropriate to the world we are trying to create rather than to the world we are trying to grow out of.

1. *Use of punishment.* Of all ways of inducing change, probably the least effective is punishment. Considering the ineffectiveness of punishment as a tool for changing behavior, it is surprising how prevalent it still is in our institutions. It is used in the home, in the classroom, and on the athletic field. Children are spanked and scolded; privileges are withheld; fines and other penalties are assessed for errors, broken rules, and inappropriate role behavior. Children are abused not only in anger, but also in calm and deliberate application of parenting and managing philosophy.

Punishment is widely used through the law enforcement and the penal systems, with little effect other than increasing the problems that it is designed to solve. Typical is the finding regarding the Delaware whipping law, an unbelievably primitive provision which prescribed public whipping for a number of serious crimes. Several studies analyzing incidence of punishable crimes during periods when this law was in effect and when it was rescinded indicate that the punishment did not diminish incidence of crimes the whipping was intended to deter.

Even more serious are the ancillary effects which punishment visits upon everyone involved in the process. A study of black and white children at a summer camp sponsored by a social-change organization found clear evidence that dislike of the other race was higher among children who came from homes where punishment was commonly used. The contrary was found in the attitudes of children who came from homes where punishment was little used.

2. *Use of power* is primarily an EQ level II process. Power depends upon its unequal distribution for effectiveness. Powerful parents can get children to make some changes. Teachers with power can sometimes get students to act in certain ways. But the side effects are often so negative as to offset whatever beneficial social change the power-based action may have produced. Warfare, both in its hot form and its cold form, is a last-resort, fear-induced, EQ II process that reenforces autocracy in form and substance and creates enduring side-effects that are often, if not always, more harmful than the immediate effects of the war itself.

The effectiveness of legal action is a function both of power and of trust. At primitive stages there is so little trust that a life under law is unattainable. As trust grows and social needs are clarified, laws evolve as a codification of mutual trust. Presumably, with advances into higher EQ levels laws will not be necesary. In our current society, the application of law depends upon the use of power — the power of the majority, the courts, the police, and the punitive system.

Movements for "woman power", "black power", and "brown power" are responses to the Level-II nature of our culture and of the Level-II philosophy of the power-seekers. "Personal power", "encounter group", "fight training", and "assertiveness training" approaches often use militant or quasi-militaristic terminology and concepts and tend to lock participants and the social system into lower EQ levels. All of these may be necessary as safety-valves to release the aggressions that accumulate in a power- and control-centered culture They are barriers to the movement of the culture toward significant levels of new trust and new environmental quality.

3. *Use of covert strategy.* A common theme in many change efforts is *strategy.* A hidden strategy is necessary in hot or cold war. The less trust between antagonists, the more useful a strategy is in labor-management negotiations, a divorce-court battle, a lawsuit, or a conference between opposing churches. The necessity for strategy disappears as trust level rises. The more one trusts the process and the other party, the less one has to plan and prepare a strategy when going to ask a favor, make a proposal of marriage, request a loan from a banker, or ask the boss for a raise. The more one fears, the more important it is that the strategy or plan be clever, devious, or overwhelming. It is not accidental that the terms strategy and tactics are derived from the military.

Strategy is a Level-II, III, and IV process. But many efforts to achieve the states that characterize Levels VI, VII, VIII, and IX are also basically strategic in nature, relying upon devious or hidden techniques for their effectiveness. When the *methodology* is appropriate to Levels II and III and the *aim* is to reach states that characterize higher environmental levels, the results are predictably very mixed. The closed and devious strategies of *est,* Ringer's *Winning Through Intimidation,* and other such techniques are inappropriate to their stated aims and will have no enduring effect on growth toward higher trust levels.

When one examines the handbooks of some social-change

activists, what is most striking is the low-trust techniques that are employed. They are often elitist ("We know what the people need"), devious and strategic, esoteric, distrusting ("People need to be trained by our staff in order for them to achieve their ends"), power-oriented ("You need to develop a strategy that gets first to those in power"), depersonalized, ends-oriented rather than people-oriented. They are appropriate to the defensive EQ levels, but not to growth.

4. *Use of moralistic and evangelical methods.* The use of a moralistic viewpoint in relating to either the methods or the aims of social change is effective for those who seek to manipulate others through the use of fear. It induces or revives guilt, induces neurotic dilemmas over right and wrong, and creates a feeling of general inadequacy. It springs from an autocratic or persuasive change effort. Values emerge from experience and are related to the predominant EQ level of the culture. To base a change effort on the assumption that one EQ level is of higher moral or ethical value than another is ineffective. Values and morals change along with the EQ level. They emerge with growth and are related to trust level. All enduring values parallel the TORI discovering processes and follow the same development as the EQ levels. The four TORI values are love, honesty, integrity, and interdependence, the same four that we find in most enduring religious and psychological systems. TORI theory is simply a description of these central processes.

The More Effective Processes of Societal Change

I am defining effective social change as movement on the Environmental Quality scale. Processes that cause significant and enduring change in EQ level result from forces that are intrinsic to the culture at that level.

It is much easier to see the limitations of the change-induction methods that are level-fixated and ineffective than it is to discover what an effective change method might be. My experience is necessarily limited to the EQ levels of institutions in which I have participated, but my vision is not. Let me try to spell out what TORI theory indicates would be major criteria for and characteristics of an effective change effort.

1. *The effort must provide a new perspective and vision for the culture.*

For me, the greatest significance of the EQ analysis in Chapter III is the perspective that it creates. When I see a long-range extrapolation of current events in my life, I am able to *see* my life differently and to make choices in the light of this broad perspective. Seen in the vision of a longer time-line, the alternatives of my life are more clear. I know what I want. I know where I'm at and where I want to go. Conversely, when in fear I see the immediate choice *only in the moment,* I am torn by many ambiguous alternatives. Though I believe in living fully in the moment, I also believe in rhythms and flows in my life, often living *fully in the moment* and "flowing into choices", as it were. At other times I live *fully in my reflections* and speculations, in a sense living in eternity, or at least in what is my experience of eternity, timelessness, and perspective. I enjoy each of these experiences. For me it is important to see my life experiences in the perspective of a long time-line.

I believe that it is important for the culture to move in harmony with its basic rhythm. Unless it is so, the culture is dissonant and cannot perceive itself in its times of fullness or see itself in its moments of perspective. TORI theory provides one frame of vision, one way of integrating these diverse elements in the continuing rhythm of life. I find that in discussing societal change with groups, this extrapolative frame of reference — the EQ analysis — provides a basis for impressive agreement among people about the social changes they would like to see.

For example, most people dislike participating in the selling and advertising process, either as a seller or a buyer. I have yet to hear a person who had other than negative reactions to movies or news on television being interrupted frequently with advertisements. Haven't you heard, as I have, people talking about advertising and selling in this way? — "I hate it, but I suppose someone has to do it if we are going to keep the free enterprise system going." — "I hate to have a salesperson call on the phone or come to the door, but I put up with it because I guess they have to make a living." — or "People must like to see advertisements on TV, or we wouldn't have so many of them". I have yet to hear anyone, taking a long view of the process, who felt that buying and selling was a positive process *in and of itself.* Punishment, covert strategy, persuasion, and leadership are seen by many persons as *necessary evils* when they are looked at in the context of immediate social conditions. When looked at in the context of a larger world view or of a long-range perspective on human growth, these processes should and, someday will, be left behind us.

The process, the form, and the substance/content of trust level theory are all congruent in providing one perspective on social change. The deeper the trust, the wider the perspective of the viewer/theorist who is looking at social change. To be effective, a social-change effort must be embedded in a long-range perspective of some kind. Most social change programs never achieve their goals because of lack of an adequate theoretical base, fears brought on by a sense of emergency, pressures from the establishment, short-range financing, and other similar factors which limit vision, lead to opportunism, and produce limited results.

2. *The effort must be discovery-oriented.*

Life is a process of continual discovery. An effective social-change effort is an attempt to discover something, not an attempt to prove or to demonstrate something. It is research in the best sense. The change process itself *is* the research — the quest. One lesson of the Hawthorne studies is that when people are engaged in what they perceive as a discovering process, they *are* more productive, creative, and fulfilled. It is the discovering, *per se,* that makes it productive.

A simplistic model of doing social-change research is to compare two methods: one that is thought to be less effective, usually the conventional or present way of doing it; and one that it is believed may be more effective. If the "experiment" is well-planned and well-controlled, and the alternative methods are well-defined, the difference in measurement of the results can be attributed to differences in the two methods. There are, fortunately, better ways than this of doing research.

The focus of an effective change effort is upon *discovering* a way of producing pollution-free automobiles, of planning a balanced urban environment, of creating a more redemptive social milieu for retired people, of setting up a school that stimulates learning, or of creating a happier organization.

Again, it is necessary to stress that the quality of the *process* of discovering is more important than the *product* of the social-change effort. The process must be humane. The people participating are paramount, for enduring and effective societal change does *not* come out of a dehumanizing process. As far as we as TORI theorists are concerned, this people-process *is* the product: What results at the end of the change process — a better car, neighborhood, or school —is only a by-product of change in people. The process *is,* in a real sense, the product.

The president of one of my client organizations once asked me to help him sell the employees of the company on the advantages of a beautiful new building that the company had planned and built for the corporate headquarters. I told him that his *process* of social change was creating the change problems that he was experiencing and that he was involving me at an unfortunate point in the change process. The building itself was an incredibly effective building, with open space, multiple-option forms and furniture, and it incorporated the best ideas that skilled architects were able to provide.

I told my client that an effective change process is person-centered, open, self-determing, and interdependent. His change process met none of these four TORI criteria. The *persons* who were going to use the space had not entered into the planning — the planners planned around the *roles* that would be performed and provided, in an inventive way, to be sure, *for the roles*. The space was open, but the process of planning was closed and strategic; the planning had been a fairly secretive and private process, with a small group of experts making the decisions. The persons who were going to use the space were scarcely consulted. A centralized filing system and a centralized typing pool were created, based upon well-established systems-design principles and work-management processes. Principles of function interdependence were considered in depth. Principles of interdependence of people-in-the-work-situation were largely ignored.

The *intentions* of the president and his executive team were to create an EQ III-IV management system. The employees *experienced* it as an EQ II system. The *process* had clearly been at the EQ-II level. *The process had a built-in persuasion stage* — it required "selling". And the selling led to resistance — several years, in fact, of multi-level resistance to the new building. This incredibly costly resistance was not to the change, *per se*, nor to the new working plans, nor to the well-designed building, but to *how* the change was made. There had been too little communication before and during the planning and designing of the building, and too little involvement in the process. Instead, the *selling process* was communicated after the change was complete. The process is the message in either case.

Had the total change effort been genuinely directed from the beginning toward *discovery* — toward discovering how to create space that would be efficient and would lead to more effective corporate activities — it would have more nearly met the significant criteria of effective change. And, incidentally, it would have been dramatically less costly in time and money.

A good test: If the change or the change effort requires persuasion, something's wrong! Sound process produces effective change.

3. *The process of the change-effort must be appropriate to the hoped-for EQ level.*

This principle applies to whatever change is under consideration, from changing a production method to changing the basic nature of a social system.

The Russian revolution, in using EQ I and II processes to accomplish what were to be EQ V social conditions, created at least a half-century of resistance. The American free-enterprise system, in using EQ II and III processes to accomplish what it perceives as EQ IV and V ends, continually creates incongruities and encounters resistance. The scientific community often uses EQ III and IV processes to accomplish EQ V ends. Aware that research shows the importance of participative (EQ V) modes of living, science-based programs often use experts to decide on the data to be gathered and the methods of collecting and interpreting the data, and only then solicit involvement in getting programs activated.

Some growth centers use EQ III, IV, and V methods in the attempt to create EQ VIII and IX states of being. The resulting states are often temporary, partial, and unrelated to the everyday life of the participants. Such centers often operate under EQ II, III, IV, V management systems, trying to coordinate activities directed toward providing experiences appropriate to EQ VI-X aims.

Until some churches can discover methods that rise higher than EQ III in managing the worship system, they are likely to be unsuccessful in creating the spirituality that they hope for. The spiritual episodes that are created on a Sunday morning are not likely to spill over into the everyday lives of the participants.

Since the process is the message, what is learned from an educational effort or a change-induction effort is also the process. The challenge to the modern school is to develop something other than an EQ level III-IV environment to communicate ideals, values, and content in the EQ V-X range. Substantive or content learning in a school is not likely to rise above the EQ-management level. Promising new developments in some churches and schools are being managed by teachers and administrators who are in EQ V through VII levels.

It should be no surprise that psychoanalytic training programs have had little impact on the behavior of the participants in organizational settings relative to effort expended. This is due largely, in my view, to their being managed in an EQ level II-III style. At the same time, they are attempting to impart a message that is appropriate to an EQ VIII level, in which the unconscious lives of the participants are to be integrated into the social and institutional relationships of everyday life. Neo-Freudians are happily developing educational and therapeutic styles more appropriate to the aims of their programs. As a result, they are having commensurately more significant effects on their patients.

4. *The effort is most effective if it includes a significant pilot study at an early stage.*

No matter how brilliant ideas and theories may be, they require implementation in the heat and complexity of the "real" world of practical affairs. Many plans can go askew between the drawing board and the schoolroom or factory floor. The idea or theory may be misunderstood. Some actions will be fortuitous; other actions may have unforeseen effects. The intent and perceptions of those carrying out the change plan may be very different from those of the persons who did the planning. New and underperceived factors may enter into the situation that outweigh the predicted effects of the idea- or theory-based plan.

Useful information can be provided by a series of pilot studies on the effects of plans for change. Such pilot studies may be pre-planned and well-defined efforts especially designed to test out an idea or a theory in a business, a school, a neighborhood, or a nation; or they may be natural events that serve the purpose of the theorist.

For instance, the League of Nations was, in a sense, a pilot run for the United Nations, which may be in turn a pilot run for a more effective attempt yet to be made in the future. Our present political, economic, and societal theories are not yet adequate to form the basis for a truly functional world order. Social experimentation on such a grand scale is very difficult to perform. The application of trust-level theory to international and global living will be the topic of a later book in this series. Fear level among nations is so high, relative to international trust, that we need more differentiated theory and more adequate social tests of theory to determine how *in practice* trust levels may be significantly changed on a global basis. I believe that we are on the right track and have one possible theory base.

Douglas McGregor's Theory Y may be viewed as a powerful,

SOCIAL CHANGE 269

trust-focused, general theory of social change. As is the case with all theory, its wide applicability requires testing in the hot and complex reality of diverse organizational settings.

Such testing is difficult but necessary. While McGregor was president of Antioch College, he made a number of courageous innovations that, in one sense, constituted a test of Theory Y. Many complexities in the situation made the results ambiguous and difficult to interpret conclusively. Later a large corporation financed a major multi-million-dollar test in a large geographical sector of the company, but the executive board of the company placed a powerful Theory-X executive in charge of the Theory-Y operation in order to "guarantee its success"!

After many such discouragements, Doug, Peter Drucker, and I consulted with a corporation that was interested in experimenting with Theory Y on a large scale. Doug and I spent about nine months interviewing key company people in depth at all levels, nationwide, on key questions. We were trying to set up a pilot plant or relatively autonomous operation that could be a pilot run for the usefulness of Theory Y. We tried several mini-tests of the theory, but the total climate was such that we were never able to implement more than a partial test of McGregor's major theories. We believe that our efforts were effective, but they were necessarily inconclusive. Good pilot tests of even powerful theories are hard to come by.

Beginning in 1977, the members of the TORI Professional Intern program are making a three-year series of tests of trust-level theory in a wide variety of family, therapy, training, educational, business, and governmental situations. All of the efforts are TORI-theory related and all are being tried in the member's organization or in client organizations. This program, I believe, holds great promise.

In the sense in which I am using the term here, historical innovative social experiments can be seen as informal pilot studies in the continuous process of building an adequate theory of organizational design. In a broad sense, what the world needs is an adequate "theory" of how we can live together, work together, and be together in more fulfilling ways, at progressively higher levels of environmental quality, however this may be defined.

Think of the wide range of "pilot studies" — good and evil — that provide data for us in our search for discovering better ways to live together: alternative schools, the utopian communities, legal assistance groups, drug information centers, birth control clinics, nudist colonies, ashrams, sexual freedom clubs, the women's liberation movement, the Alberta social credit plan, the Mormon's United Order, the kibbutz, Prohibition, polygamy and bundling, prisons and concentration camps, Teapot Dome and Watergate, no-fault divorce laws, the bombing of Hiroshima, consumer co-ops, and a legion of mini-tests of "theories" of social living.

Consideration of this wide diversity of experience leads me to the next criterion of effective social action.

5. *The effort is most effective if it nurtures diversity and emergence.*

God or the cosmic process apparently designed some undeterminable number of social-discovery experiments, one of which is happening on the planet earth. The experiment is apparently leaderless, unstructured, emergent, blind (from the participant standpoint), and apparently has high diversity on several dimensions. From the standpoint of the participants in the pilot study, the purpose, experimental design, hypotheses being tested, and hoped-for-outcomes are all indeterminable. From the participant's viewpoint, what we see produced is both massive fear and massive trust. The fear produced is certainly awesome and pervasive. But this high-emergence pilot study also makes possible the experience of awesome trust. Presumably, without the experience of fear and perceived risk, we would have no experience of trust.

Perhaps one solution to the collective dilemma is that this massive fear (massive from the participant's viewpoint; perhaps miniscule from the cosmic viewpoint of the experimenter) makes possible the discovery/creation of an even more awesome and transcendent trust state. As one participant in the experiment, my guess is that the I-X EQ scale discussed here contains only one tiny end of a cosmic scale in which my levels I through IX are minute gradations on range I of another scale. Perhaps my EQ level X contains a presently unperceived richness and range of trust experiences (beings — or some state different in quality from what we call experience or being) on a presently unimaginable scale, which is most certainly not likely to be linear or linear-like.

It may be that transcendent trust (at levels we cannot now experience or even conceptualize) is *the* significant outcome of this earth experiment. Perhaps the only way such transcendent trust can be acquired is through *discovery and emergence* in diversity.

To move from this fanciful and cosmic level of speculation to more immediate perspective, I believe that diversity and emergence are enhancing conditions for all social change. We need the range of experiences, models, pilot studies, and data provided by the rich diversity of life as we know it. In fact, we need more diversity, more richness, and less control of the range of experience and models. At this point, people try anything that they have the energy, imagination, courage, and resources to try. Can it be argued that we needed the Ku Klux Klan, the concentration camps, Watergate, and the Vietnamese war to show us convincingly what fear can do to us and our social models? As we learn to trust the human processes of diversity and emergence, we will move toward more and more trusting models of social living. I firmly believe this. We are now in a state of rapid transition, moving into escalating states of fear and trust, and we are probably going at the pace we can handle.

Greater diversity, particularly on the high-trust side, of social models, innovative ideas, and pilot studies can take us to the frontiers of social change: provision of adequate health care for all, conservation of our people and their natural environment, learning ways of living together cooperatively, liberation of all minorities, discovering humanistic and holistic ways of producing goods and services, and ultimately, achievement of transcendence and ecstasy.

The application of this principle of diversity to everyday life means that change in the schoolroom, factory, church, and clinic is best accomplished when we range widely in the tests, methods, and theories we use and when we encourage variation and innovation. In consulting with school, church, business, and governmental systems, I have been impressed by the occasional innovation, but dismayed even more by the standardization, lack of imagination, discouragement of innovation, routine continuance of methods and procedures that have been found time and again to be ineffective and inhuman, and the lack of an atmosphere of spontaneity and emergence.

In a free society, in an emergent workplace, in a free school, optimal diversity of social-change efforts is functional. Alternative models succeed or fail in practice — in the classroom, clinic, or home — not on the drawing board, in the theorist's mind, or in the administrator's office. It is difficult and perhaps impossible in practice to derive adequate change models directly from pure theory. At the present stage of our theory, the process of developing new models of society, work, or living seems to require some give and take, some trial and error.

6. *All change is implemented by persons and probably starts with a change in the person.*

Every person is significant in the change process. Each person who gets in touch with a deep level of trust can say something like the following: "I create my own environment and can change it in any way I wish. I am limited only by my fear, and need not be limited by that. I can change my immediate environment on the job, in my home, in my classroom, in my friendships, in my recreation, in all of my life relationships. I can join with others to change the organizations I belong to and the world around me. I do not need to try to change other people at all, but can accomplish the changes I wish in my environment by making changes in myself. Usually I change myself by letting me go free, allowing myself to be who I am and to discover and create what I want. The more free I allow myself to be, the more I become what I aspire to be.

"I can choose to live and be in my immediate world around me, or I can choose to live and be in larger and larger areas of the world. I can have as much effect upon the larger world, upon societal processes, as I wish to have.

"As I increase in my vision and courage, my choices become simpler and easier because they are clear cut:

"(1) I can choose to be personal or to be in role in as much of my life as I wish.

"(2) I can choose to live an open and direct life, or to live my life in strategy, behind a facade, and by manipulation.

"(3) I can choose to do what I want or I can live my life as I think that I ought.

"(4) I can try to be *with* others in all of my living relationships with persons and with nature; or I can attempt to dominate and control others, or submit to them."

To me, this series of statements defines a way of life that can change any person and that can ultimately change all aspects of our world.

As part of my attempt to understand trust and fear, I have been interested in historical figures who, through their trust and through the processes that I call TORI theory, have contributed significantly to changing the world by moving it in the direction of higher trust levels and have also lived rich personal lives.

Whom would I choose to illustrate this point for me? Wouldn't you agree that Jesus Christ, Abraham Lincoln, Eugene Debs, Jane

Addams, Mahatma Gandhi, and Martin Luther King, Jr., qualify? Each of these lived what I would call a TORI life. Each of them had a profound and positive effect upon the world. Each had a deep sense of being which each showed openly to others. Each had an intensely self-created mission that integrated his or her life around what each deeply wanted to do. Each worked *with* the world, sharing the life process in an interdependent way. It would be difficult to categorize any of them by role. None pursued a covert strategy. None tried to coerce or dominate.

For me, the significant point is that each of these persons had a sense of personhood. Each makes it easy for me to feel that my relationship to each of them is a personal one. The gentle simplicity of Jesus is a living image of trust and openness. The widespread response to the life-being of Jesus seems to be a testament to the inner core of trust in each of us that resonates to His being. It is impossible for me to stand in front of the statue of Abraham Lincoln at the Memorial in Washington without having an intense experience of trust. I have been there many times and have noticed others, particularly children, who seem to respond as I do. The life of every working man and woman is different today because of the intense personhood of Eugene Debs, and the vision, trust, and authenticity of his life. Visiting Hull House in 1937, two years after the death of Jane Addams, I had a similar *feeling* of the intensity of her presence and being. Gandhi *lived* his belief in and trust of the simple process of being and his creed of non-intrusion and non-violence. Martin Luther King taking that final courageous walk on the balcony, immediately after being warned by his friends of danger, testified to the transcending nature of his trust.

When persons relate to each other in a state of high defense at lower EQ levels, self-caring may be an exclusive or excessive concern for one's own well-being without regard for others. It may even have a narcissistic quality. But with growth, reduction of defensiveness, and movement into higher EQ levels, self-caring seems to co-exist with and even intensify one's love for others. At these levels, love of self and love of others seem to come from the same store of well-being. The people I have mentioned above seem to illustrate this coexistence in trusting people of self-caring and of altruistic feelings and motivations. It may be that in order to be fully whole, a person must integrate these needs to be uniquely one's self and to be fully altruistic. Neither self-caring nor altruism need exist at the expense of the other. They are thus not alternatives but mutually supportive processes.

The mixture of self-caring and other-nurturing probably differs with every person, but all growing persons have humanitarian and altruistic motivations. These may be submerged into partially conscious or unconscious levels by traumatizing fear and defense, but they are retrieved by experiences that restore trust.

This means that, to be effective, experimental community and organizational ventures must offer the opportunity for members to discover activities that are personally enriching in an immediate way, as well as activities that have holistic, altruistic, and societal significance *meaningful to the persons involved.* Hopefully both self-caring and societal motivations can be rewarded by the same activities, communal and organizational activities that integrate these aspects of each person.

The defensive change-agent, consultant, manager, parent, or minister looks first to change the people or the situation that is threatening. The trusting parent, consultant, manager, or minister looks first to himself or herself, knowing that enduring change or growth in environmental quality starts with self-caring.

7. *The effective change effort is grounded in some way in an increasing trust level.*

The effective change effort is personal, open, self-determining, and interdependent. That is, the processes are expressive of trust and induce trust. Effective change (growth) is movement along the environmental-quality scale.

When efforts to produce change meet increased resistance, they do so because they have a process that is defense-arousing. Resistance is *not* to the change itself. Change is exciting, fulfilling, enriching, and indigenous to all life. It is the toxic process used by some "change agents" that is frightening and that reduces trust. Any process that is depersonalizing, closed and covertly strategic, persuasive, manipulative, and controlling will produce fear, resistance, defense, and their variants. The commonness of such methods of creating change is the factor which is responsible for the myth that change is resisted.

Trust is the key to societal change. Trust is the inherent capacity of the individual and the institution to be whatever they are to become. The growth process in all forms of energy and being is an inner-outer process — it proceeds from within the being, from the center, moving outward toward interdependence. The outer-inner, intrusive, coercive, manipulative, and attack process is a violation of the nature of being. The external agent can be a force which intrudes upon and violates these intrinsic processes or one that nurtures them.

This principle is true with children in a nursery, with students in a school, with teams in a league, with divisions in a company, with states in a federation, and with nations in a world. Effective change is trust formation. The parent gets along with the child when the parent trusts the child. It is that simple. The manager gets along with the worker when the manager trusts the worker. We will get along with the Soviet Union when we trust the Soviet Union. There seems to be no other solution to the continuing dilemmas that confront our cosmic pilot study.

IMAGES

To trust the future is to know
that I can make my images happen.

Chapter 12

Images of the Future

Trust brings the vision and the courage to shape the future. Vision gives us the clarity to focus our images and the perspective to see the future whole. Courage gives us the will to continue the quest although the fears and barriers — the blocks to growth and change — may loom large.

One way to anticipate the future of humankind is to view it from the perspective of expected changes in environmental-quality level. Because environmental quality is a function of the level of trust, *the* significant trend in history has been the formation of trust — the gradually increasing tendency of humans to trust themselves, to trust other people, to trust the social institutions we create, to trust the processes of nature.

Let's look again at the description of the development of environmental quality in Tables V and VI. In one book in the series I expect to present an analysis of our past history and our fantasied future in terms of changes in the environmental-quality scale. Even a cursory psycho-historical examination shows wide swings in trust level and fear level, but with a gradual increase in overall level of trust over the centuries.

In some ways, we have seen an accompanying increase in fear levels, and certainly changes in the quality and nature of our fears. As our knowledge and experience increase, we become more globally *aware* of frightening possibilities in our environment: destructive explosions in population, global atomic and catastrophic war, a dehumanizing and machine-oriented super-technology, the excreta of our technology gradually destroying our life-giving natural environment. But happily our trust level increases at an even greater pace than our fears of apparent dangers.

The Cultural Movement Toward Higher Trust

The developments of recent years have for the first time in the history of humanity revealed the possibilities of a world-wide consciousness and concern, and of world-community actions that can emerge from global trust and at the same time increase it. As the many forms of communication increase at almost geometric rates at all levels, as our awareness of our economic and materialistic interdependence increases, as inter-governmental collaboration on projects such as population control, monetary stabilization, and space travel seems more feasible, it becomes possible, and perhaps even *necessary,* to move toward EQ-V levels of international interdependence and higher levels of world trust. It now appears at least possible that we may make world-wide, participatory decisions on such global issues as the emancipation of women, international trade, pollution of the atmosphere, reduction of arms, control of disease, and sharing of scientific data.

The basis for such international cooperation and trust will be possible only with widespread development of the four trust-mediating discovering processes. How realistic is it that such development will occur?

1. *Personalization.* The women's liberation movement is a powerful force in freeing women from the role prescriptions they have given themselves and that male-dominated institutions have assigned them. The general issue here is one of role freedom, emancipation from the process of treating oneself as a member of a class, an object, a role-taker. The learning for each of us is how to treat ourselves and others as unique individuals.

Not all current trends are in the direction of role freedom. For instance, to a certain extent the rise of professionalism is a force toward de-personalization. To be "professional" as a physician, athlete, teacher, or manager is to become objective (not to let feelings get in the way of getting the job done), to fulfill the role (to do the job with competence as other professionals do it), to focus on the job and its functions rather than on the persons. Being professional in this sense is the opposite of being personal, which means to own and express non-objective feelings, to become free of the role, and to give priority to persons rather than to functions. The thrust toward professionalization is in part a search for dignity, meaning, power, and respect through the role one takes, and in part a defense against being perceived as inadequate. As a person becomes less fearful and defensive, he or she has less need for status, deference, and other role-derived states.

A continuing tension is the struggle to create a world society in which persons can find fulfilling work paying living and dignified wages. It is difficult to be fully a person when a man or woman is discriminated against, is hungry, lacks adequate medical care, is unemployed, is on welfare, or is on a job which is "managed" by a "superior" and where there is little self-determination or control over the worker's own destiny. Certainly the basic realms of fulfillment are spiritual and psychological and are a matter of inner trust. They are internal; but the basic inequities are external, in our economic, political, and social systems, and these create strong constraints against movement toward higher-quality environments.

2. *Opening.* Great gains are continually being made both in *awareness* of the importance of openness as a key dimension of organic living, and also in the *practice* of openness in most areas of our lives. Openness in our society is obviously on the increase, and this openness is a key index of trust level.

An open society permits the free flow of data of all kinds. Openness requires not only a free flow of feelings, perceptions, and opinions in personal, organizational, and governmental life, but also the open availability of government records, interest rates, test data, criminal charges, salary levels, credit ratings, information on food content, and a variety of other sets of data that importantly affect our lives.

There is a growing awareness that openness is associated with mental health, interpersonal trust, group strength, community well-being, and the effectiveness of parenting, teaching, and managing.

3. *Self-determination.* We are witnessing significant advances in self-determination. We are discovering the depth and validity of mindbody wisdom, and we are beginning to accept more responsibility for our own health, sex preferences, sanity, job satisfaction, environment, feelings, joys, hurts, and salvation. In the fields of medicine, psychiatry, law, government, education, and religion there are deep-seated institutionalized norms encouraging personal responsibility for all aspects of life.

Studies of biofeedback and popularization of its concepts and techniques provide us with a new appreciation of how deeply the principles of self-management apply to even the supposedly "involuntary" processes of the body. The movement toward self-management is a key revolution in our society, and its effects are only beginning to be felt.

The new theories and methods relating to transcendence and altered states promise an even more revolutionary movement in the culture. We now know that it is possible for us to "manage" our own spirituality, our cosmic and nirvanic states, and our unconscious bases of creativity.

There is no need to pit the needs of the individual against the needs of society in a conflict viewed by many social theorists as inevitable and, in fact, basic to the social development of the race. We now realize that we *can* achieve a society in which such conflict is minimized, if not eliminated. We *can* create institutions in which members meet all of their needs fully without self-sacrifice, compromise, or self-denial. Individuals and institutions *can* move up the EQ scale toward higher levels of fulfillment. Surely, the higher we move on the EQ scale, the less conflict there is between personal and societal needs.

4 *Interdependence.* The discovery that necessary interdependence doesn't mean compromise, self-denial, or surrender of basic values, but that it does mean cooperation, enrichment of personal lives, and transcendence, takes away much of the fear of groups, of society, and of *dependence* on others. Inter-*dependence* is a poor term, but I have been unable to find an acceptable term for what I mean by the process. Perhaps "interbeing" is a better expression.

Interbeing in the home, the factory, the school, or the neighborhood means that people can be resources for each other. They can contribute to and enrich each other's lives and can provide stimulation, excitement, and creative energy for each other.

When the EQ level is I, II, or III in high-density populations, we find bureaucracy, tight controls, concentrations of ownership and power, centralization of key functions, hierarchization, competition — and low levels of trust and high levels of fear. As our society is developing the capacity to move into new EQ levels, we are learning to create and discover new forms of creative interdependence: new experiences of community, new forms of cooperation and transcendence, and new levels of interbeing.

Significant Trends that Will Impact the Future

I believe that we are in the beginning phases of a social revolution in which the significant trends in our present culture which will have the greatest impact on the future course of civilization are the following:

1. *The Environment of Emergence.*

The emergent form will be a practical and attainable model of group and institutional life, supplanting the participative model. The current model toward which practitioners, organizational-development consultants, theorists, and social engineers have been aiming is a "skilled-leader-with-active-participants" form, EQ level V. The growing recognition that the participative model is but a transitional step, together with the increasing success of leaderless, emergent groups, is creating a cultural readiness for new practical images of social life. Once the impasse between EQ levels V and VI is broken, practical experiments with EQ levels VI through X will be legitimized. They will then occur more frequently, and the many obvious advantages of these models will become more widely apparent. This breakthrough will make possible a new age of creativity, productivity, ecstasy, and fulfillment. The belief that leadership is the primary determiner of social progress is perhaps the single greatest barrier to institutional and cultural growth and fulfillment.

2. *The New Spirituality.*

A new and emergent spirituality will be an integrative and centering force in all of human life. There is a growing dissatisfaction with naive realism, operationalism, behaviorism, 19th-century science, economic thinking, materialism, determinism, and power as the organizing and central processes of human living. A new and many-faceted new kind of spirituality is growing out of this dissatisfaction and out of the new awareness of transcendent and altered states of being and consciousness. The person is seen to be more than an economic, physical, and mental being. This new consciousness has origins in the mysticism, magic, and spirituality of the past, but is actually *a new force* in the world. Spirituality has always been grounded in awe and wonder, mixed with fear and faith. The new spirituality, it seems to me, is born not so much out of fear and ignorance, but of a venture into new faith and trust. This new trust arises *after* science and materialism and naive realism have been tested — and have been found to produce near-miracles, but also to have real and recognizable limitations. Trust based on knowledge, following disillusionment and worldly experience, may indeed be more enduring and nourishing than a more tender trust based on faith that pre-existed the experience of evil and the dark sides of human history.

For me, spirituality is simply the *expression* of trust. It is trust and faith in myself and in others, and in the natural processes of life. These are deeply and enduringly embedded in the nature of the person. I have no interest in a precise or limiting definition of this state. I am simply referring to the awakening of processes and awarenesses that are *something more* than what is usually called bodily and mental.

3. *Cooperative Living Styles.*

New forms of cooperativeness and awareness of interdependence in social institutions will engender a new valuing of cooperation as an integrating force in all forms of living. Competitiveness seems to be necessary in the contest for survival when we live at lower EQ levels. It becomes less and less relevant, necessary, or even useful as the EQ level rises. Competition simply drops out as civilization advances, certainly as persons begin to transcend the ego needs at levels VIII and IX. Research suggests that all children have latent capacities for both competition and cooperation. As fear declines, as trust evolves, as higher-quality environments are created, cooperation becomes an inevitable and definitive aspect of fulfilling life.

In a fear/distrust society, competition is inevitable, perhaps necessary, and children, students, and workers are more often rewarded for being good competitors than for being cooperative. However, the destructive costs of competitiveness far outweigh the advantages. As trust levels in the society increase, competitiveness is reduced, and children, students, and workers are more frequently rewarded for being cooperative.

4. *Viability of Trust Models*

New theories, images, and models of being will center on trust as the catalytic force in group, organizational, and societal living. Most of our theories, our images, and our models are created out of experiences in fear/distrust societies and organizations. The resultant process creates energies which maintain and even nourish fear and distrust. As we become increasingly aware of the significance of trust in all aspects of our lives and as we come to prize trust-related values and styles of life, viable new theory, images, and models will arise.

5. *Decentralization of Form and Function.*

A decentralization of government, organizations, and all forms of

living will give rise to smaller organizations and smaller govern-
mental units, with a growing sense of community and neighborhood.
Some centralization will persist, of course, largely for reasons of
efficiency and economy. But efficiency and economy are of little
enduring value, except in scarcity and survival environments, where
fear is high and trust is low. Just as many people have discovered that
the large, centralized city is a poor environment for living, so we will
be likely to discover that the large conglomerate and the large
governmental unit are poor environments for living or for supplying
products and services. We will discover what range of size of
production and service units is likely to enhance enriched living.
Smaller businesses and smaller states, provinces, or nations will
evolve. Quality of life will come to have greater value than the
efficiency of government or production.

   6. *The Caring Community.*

   A re-discovery of the meaning and attainability of community
will make possible new caring, intimacy, and depth in all forms of
living. We will discover and create communities for work and life that
enhance the person, the open life, self-determination, and creative
interdependence. People will create new forms of living that will give a
feeling of community, of contact and connection, of freedom in intimacy, and of being valued by neighbors with whom they live and work.
Just as the "discovery" of the small group in the 50's and 60's changed
the flavor and tone of behavioral science, the discovery of community
may well be the energy-releasing mode of the 80's and 90's.

   7. *De-specialization of Groups and Organizations.*

   New multi-purpose, non-specialized, wholized organizational
communities will gradually replace the specialized, highly-different-
iated, specific-purpose, and class-membered organizations of the
present. As role functions have become more clearly differentiated,
groups and organizations have become equally differentiated, such
that, particularly in the managerial and professional classes, a group or
organization tends to emerge for each role and for each function. This
process further reenforces the segmentation, fragmentation, and class
structuring of our society, with a concomitant lack of inter-class and
inter-role understanding and empathy. My prediction is that this trend
will be reversed and that groups, communities, and organizations will
come to have greater intra-unit diversity across lines of race, sex,
occupation, and even interest. Social life will then be more wholized,
with people relating to people in all their richness and diversity.

Ultimately this trend will give rise to the emergence of groups, communities, and organizations in which people learn, work, love, and worship. Thus we will have less need for separate institutions for learning, recreation, work, and worship. Distinctions among work and play and worship will be reduced. Life will be more wholized and rich in all its forms. These developments will accompany the re-discovery of community and will happen at a greater rate than now seems possible.

8. *De-structuring of Life.*

A decrease in all institutions of discipline, control, "law and order", obedience, authority, rewards and punishment, and arbitrary structure, will de-institutionalize fear as a primary organizing and managing principle. As trust grows and as trust-related values increase, people will discover more creative ways of living and working together. With trust, people will learn to allow diversity, freedom, trial and error, and great individual differences in expressing humanness. Willingness to allow freedom for others comes in cycles and waves, intermittent periods of doubt and fear, followed by periods of trust and freedom. As trust grows, in the long course of history, willingness to permit others to have freedom increases more rapidly than do needs to discipline and control others.

9. *De-professionalization of the Culture.*

A decrease in the number of people involved in staff functions of organizations and government, and a decrease in the helping professions in organizational and in private life will accompany dramatic increases in norms of self-responsibility. The presently increasing trend toward more staff and helping functions is motivated by a growing awareness of multiple social needs, a movement into EQ-Level III benevolence, strong needs of people to help and to have professional status, disenchantment with "work" as it is currently "managed", and the over-abundance of money to afford such staff services in an affluent society.

We will discover and create new forms of community living and working — new environments that nurture self-responsibility, self-management, self-caring, proactive and holistic living, and people *who nurture themselves.* With increased trust, executives and workers will learn to communicate with each other rather than hire communications experts to do it for them; people will create their own healthy attitudes and bodies; they will treat each other with respect rather than hire security guards to protect their lives, property, and company secrets; and they will seek and create simpler solutions to people problems than the increasingly complex "personnel" functions that now exist.

The Future of TORI Process as I See It

"TORI" has become, for several thousand of us, a term describing a cooperative lifelong search for a better life for ourselves, a quest for a more wholizing life-view theory, and a framework for joining others in interdependent social action.

What of its future? Energies are being directed in several promising directions:

1. *The Continuing Evolution of the Theory.*

The theory in its continually-emerging state might be viewed as a folk-expression, co-authored through the interaction and processes of about 10,000 persons who have been participating for many years in the TORI community activities.

The writing of this book is but one expression of a quickening of theory-related forces in the TORI communities — focusing of energies, accelerated dialogue, clarification of differences, some visible breakthroughs in applying the theory, sharpening of empirically-testable substantive issues, some interest in hard research, an expansion in the number of university courses in TORI theory, the formation of teams planning publications in the Astron series —many signs that the theory itself is becoming more useful and central to the communities.

2. *Research on the Theory and Its Applications.*

The theory is stimulating a variety of formal and informal research studies.* This research is to be summarized in a later volume in the Astron series.

Studies have been directed toward an understanding of some of the key dynamics related to trust level: persuasion, strategy orientation, role freedom, openness, defensive communication, and interdependence. A few of the studies have been planned to make explicit tests of assumptions from the main body of the theory. Several have attempted to measure the correlaries of trust level, operationally

---

*No attempt will be made here to summarize the body of research findings. Those interested will find a partial list of studies in Appendix D, and may obtain, without cost, an annotated list of research studies, an annotated list of publications on TORI theory and applications, and other descriptions of TORI activities by writing to: TORI United States, P.O. Box 8482, Toledo, Ohio 43623; or TORI Canada, 68 South Drive, Toronto, Ontario, Canada M4W 1R5.

defined in a variety of ways. We have used a universal definition in this book; operationally, it is difficult to define trust. The concept of trust has interested a variety of researchers, for whom it is becoming a useful construct in theory construction and experimental research.

Other studies have assessed the effects of programs and experiences planned as applications of TORI theory: training and development activities, leaderless groups, TORI community experiences, human relations courses, holistic health programs, industrial applications, and educational efforts. The TORI community experience, for instance, has been found to be effective in producing significant changes in such outcomes as interdependence, perceived openness, self-described proactiveness, self-acceptance, and interpersonal effectiveness.

Much of the research is inconclusive or of a preliminary nature. Some shows conflicting results or uses inappropriate methodology. But some, particularly a few doctoral dissertations that have been completed, are highly suggestive and indicate the potential predictive power as well as the practical applicability of the theory.

3. *Invention and Preparation of Resource Processes.*

Members are experimenting with various processes that are resources for community development, communication and dialogue, evolution of theory, new forms of interbeing, team building, and trust formation. We are trying out environmental designs, decorative and functional clothing, dance, music, poetry, photography, organic writing, dream analysis, nonverbal "conferences", the use of cassettes to record and exchange verbal expression, community diaries, movies, open-phone systems, guidebooks, self-development materials, housing design, organic farming, books — whatever forms and processes that can be used in the nourishment of trust.

Community members place a high priority on direct interpersonal communication but are also experimenting with conventional written forms. Individual communities publish frequent newsletters; an international newsletter is issued on special occasions; a new journal will appear during the winter of 1978-79; and several experimental books are in various stages of preparation. Books or multimedia presentations are being prepared focusing upon applications of TORI theory to such activities as parenting and family building, counseling and psychotherapy, group development, managing and administration, organizational development, high trust communications, creating learning climates, psychohistory, and the design of trust-nurturing environments. The community membership includes persons working on resource-processes from a number of professional and vocational backgrounds including psychiatry, organizational development, occupational therapy, medicine, government, labor, law, social work, carpentry, farming, manufacturing, marketing, engineering, journalism, public relations, nursing, marriage counseling, dentistry, and various holistic health fields.

What is needed is the re-examination and very probably discarding of old assumptions about learning, growth, and the nature of "learning aids and resources". In spite of promising developments in the multi-media fields, the whole concept of the relationship between the learner and the resource processes is often based upon low-trust, persuasional, "teaching", and influence models. What is occurring is a new look at processes rather than at "materials". As I am writing this book I am becoming more and more aware of the dissonance between what I see as my own process and the medium I am using, and the difficulties that present themselves in trying to build a co-discovering relationship between you as the person experiencing the book and me as the person wishing a relationship between us. Part of my disquiet comes from my limitations as a communicator, but a significant part comes from limitations possibly inherent in the medium itself. My discomfort is somewhat reduced by my knowledge that you as a reader will create your own experience.

4. *Growth and Development of Persons and Organizations.*

Many of the most active people in the TORI communities are professionals in personal, managerial, and organizational development, fields for which Trust Level theory is particularly relevant.

The four pilot groups in the TORI Professional Development program mentioned in Chapter IV are part of a continuing experimental program aimed at discovering how TORI theory can be applied to the following aims:

a. The improvement of individual effectiveness in all professional fields, particularly in organizational development, therapy and counseling, education, government, management, and the ministry.

b. Acceleration of change in EQ level of an intentional community, group, or organization. Each group of 32, for instance, will use its own community as a pilot experiment in changing EQ levels.

c. The intentional development of alternative community and organizational forms, either working with a client institution, or pioneering a new one.

Many of the programs being planned by the participants are in the fields of personal or organizational development. Factors seen, in preliminary analysis, to be especially powerful in such development are:

a. Trust levels in the individual persons and in the organization.

b. Self-initiated participation in an intensive five-day TORI community experience.

c. Continuing living in a supportive community, such as the TORI local communities, one of the three-year intern groups, or one of the trust-centered Astron companies.

d. Internalization of TORI theory, or a similar *self-created* theory.

e. The *full autogenic experience* of creating one's own idiosyncratic theory, lifestyle, and holistic environment. Preliminary impressions are that this factor is even more powerful than we originally thought.

f. One or more transcendental experiences that emerge from one's own self-centered lifestyle.

5. *Discovery of New Organizational Forms.*

Much of the excitement among TORI theorists and practitioners comes through the processes of creating new forms of community and organization. This discovery occurs in many different ways. Our institutional invention efforts have had some mixture of the following ingredients:

a. The gradual evolution of the emerging form through interaction in the TORI communities.

b. A derivation of the institutional form from the principles in the theory.

c. Fantasy about what higher forms of trust might be like. For example, Robert Heinlein presumably created *Stranger in a Strange Land* in some such manner, and it appears that his fantasy has had a powerful effect upon contemporary social processes.

d. The intentional planning and creation of a pilot organizational prototype. TORI Associates and Astron Corporation were each formed with this intent.

We are in some agreement on the major criteria that we use in selecting among our invented forms, and putting energy into making the "organization" happen:

a. It is fulfilling and exciting for the people who will join in the activities of organization.

b. It is a form that through its intrinsic nature is likely to move up on the EQ scale.

c. It nourishes interbeing relationships.

d. It optimizes trust levels.

e. It is likely to have impact on other organizations and groups (*e.g.,* it is visible, has support, solves a major technical problem in some dramatic way, and has face validity).

TORI Associates and the TORI International Community.

TORI Associates, Inc., is discussed in Chapters VIII and IX as an organizational prototype. The organization meets the five criteria listed above very well. The future of this experiment in multi-national community-in-depth is uncertain. Some see the community as of significance due to its having a spiritual and wholizing effect upon the lives of a few hundred dedicated people. Some speculate that the community will have several million members in various parts of the world in a few years. Others see it as a temporary, albeit exciting, aspect of the current scene that will pass in a few years into something wholly different. My belief is that a few thousand people are working out a radical organizational model and process that will have a powerful effect upon the shape of the future. The factors that seem to be *positive strengths* include the following:

a. A highly dedicated, growing core of active people.

b. The diversity of persons involved.

c. The sense of freedom and lack of constraint.

d. Freedom from financial cost, dues, or expense of professional staffing.

e. Inclusion of all members of the family in the community.

f. The spirit of pioneering and adventure.

g. The sense of pursuing an ideal and engaging in a spiritual quest.

h. A timely meeting of a cultural need for community.

i. The nature of the model itself, which is ideally suited for rapid upward movement on the EQ scale.

The communities naturally meet with occasional frustrations and disappointments. Not unexpectedly, some members get bored, impatient with inactivity, angry at other members, disenchanted with the whole theory, distrusting of others and of the "process" itself, resentful of others who don't do "their share", embarrassed by what some see as other's inelegant or vulgar behavior, or jealous of other's ability to make friends or meet their wants. The factors that are seen by some as negative or hindering include the following:

a. Being ahead of or out-of-step with a culture that has more conventional values.

b. The lack of a leadership structure.

c. The lack of normal constraints and "appropriate" behavior of some members.

d. Fear of censure and social disapproval.

e. Lack of organizing skills for doing things that would normally be done by a formal staff or management.

f. The discomfort of taking responsibility for creating experience and meeting wants.

g. Lack of a structured program of activities.

h. Great geographic spread of membership and expense of travel.

i. Lack of sufficient numbers for some activities.

j. The attractiveness of alternate activities and programs.

Astron Corporation and Other Spin-Off Companies and Organizations.

The basic Astron experiment is described in Chapter VIII. The beginning experiments with profit-making businesses are in very preliminary stages, so it is difficult to predict what the future holds for this program. For many, this is the most exciting and potentially rewarding of the many TORI activities. The possibility of integrating a person's life around intrinsic wants and then making an adequate income while doing this is an exciting and wholizing prospect.

From my own experience and from seeing the experiences of many others, I know that business life need not be dehumanizing, need not lead to a life of compromise and sacrifice of personhood, need not be incongruent with the non-work life of a person, and need not produce the unproductive tension often observed.

I believe that we can do anything we can image. We need dramatic and *readily-available* images and models of humanizing work-environments, of the successful blending of spirituality and work, of *profitable* ventures at EQ levels VI, VII, and VIII, and of organizations which live successfully and realistically in the world *as it is* but composed of persons who believe in what it *can* become. This is a tall order. Many of us who are now engaged in the Astron experiment feel sure that we can make this work *here and now,* even given what seems to be a most uncongenial overall environment for such a radical, trust-oriented theory.

The factors working to the advantage of the program include the following:

a. Participants, many of whom have successful business and professional experience, with marketable skills.

b. A group of about 90 highly-dedicated persons who have internalized the theory and who trust that the experiment will work.

c. The involvement of many of the 128 mature professionals in the four TORI Professional Intern groups, guaranteeing intense contact over a period of at least three years.

d. The earlier success of the TORI Associates model which tested certain key principles of organization.

e. Several years of "drawing board" talk, planning, and testing of ideas.

f. Readiness of the business community to experiment, as compared with the lesser readiness of some other organizational and societal groups.

g. About an equal number of men and women in the group, with the resulting strength and diversity.

We anticipate difficulties, challenges, and barriers, and see these as exciting and stimulating. Anticipated areas of difficulty include the following:

a. The clear priority in TORI theory of personal values over clout, profit, and competitive edge, factors traditionally thought to be critical to business effectiveness.

b. The fact that the large majority of the persons in the Astron group are trained in non-business fields and, by attitude, prefer non-business activities.

c. The lack of venture capital.

d. The uncharted water: trying what has not been done before, with no models to follow.

e. The inability or unwillingness of members to risk full-time involvement and the prospect of a long period of part-time participation by most people.

f. Extreme diversity of concrete images of what members see as the ideal working model of a high-trust business enterprise.

g. Ambiguity of the plan, which creates some fears of what might happen and some distrusts of the process and of each other.

h. Great range of activities that persons prefer doing, as indicated in preliminary discussions, and the difficulty of finding common foci on the kind of product or service around which the corporation or corporations might be organized.

While each of these factors is likely to create a problem area, each will also provide a challenge and an opportunity. The challenges may marshall new and transcendent energy. We think they will.

6. *Discovery of Collaborative Relationships with Other Organizations.*

Many members of the TORI International Community are interested in working in some interdependent way with others toward greater trust, peace, and human betterment. They rightfully feel that efforts that are made in a trust-producing way will have positive effects upon the world we live in.

We are now at a place both in the evolution of the theory and in the growth of the TORI organizations that readies us to work collaboratively with other organizations. We are interested in taking interdependent action and to begin by studying the nature of such action. We will take initiative in proposing this with organizations that meet some of the following criteria, which we believe will increase the likelihood of successful collaboration:

a. The collaborative venture is fulfilling and exciting for members of both of our organizations.

b. The collaborative organization shows probability of moving up the EQ scale and is willing to venture at higher EQ levels.

c. The organization is likely to foster interbeing relationships across organizational lines.

d. It is already in some way attempting to optimize trust levels.

e. It is likely to have an impact on other institutions.

f. It seems to be in a fluid and changing state, looking both inward and outward.

g. There is a reciprocal attraction between the organization and TORI Associates, and both partners see themselves as benefiting from the creative interchange.

h. The opportunity "happens". For many of us, "opportunistic" is a positive word. We believe that opportunities are not accidental — we create them.

i. The relationship between the organizations "feels good". Many of us believe in following impulses, hunches, and intuitions about relationships. This criterion may take priority over any of the other eight.

Many of our members belong to other organizations that meet most of these criteria and that have purposes similar to ours. They are aiming in some way at an increase in trust level or at improving trust-related conditions: better communication among professional members; greater availability of holistic health treatment; improvement in organizational-development practitioner skills; improvement in all levels of education; or improvement of the standards of behavioral-science practice.

The following six organizations are examples of institutions that meet many of our nine criteria. Each organization attempts to create a synergistic interweaving among the three interdependent processes of research, training, and social change. Each provides an environment for creative interchange among the most liberal, humanistic, and innovative members of a particular field — those who are most willing to trust, to risk, to be vulnerable, and to explore the more venturesome areas of inquiry. Each of the organizations has members who also are active in TORI Associates.

Association for Humanistic Psychology. This organization provides a meeting ground for humanistically-oriented psychologists and other social scientists. Originally founded as an attempt to mobilize the Third Force in psychology, as Abraham Maslow's viewpoint was called, AHP provides for cross-fertilization among the most innovative, humanistic, and socially-aware people in the field of personal and organizational development and the human potential movement; for the intermixing of the mysticism of the East with the empiricism of the West; and for the wave of innovation in the fields of psychology, therapy, education, personal growth, organizational development, and human learning. AHP is international, action-oriented, futuristic, and a powerful force in moving toward a more trusting world.

National Training Laboratories Institute of Applied Behavioral Science. Originally founded to integrate the research and theory of Kurt Lewin and his associates in applications of group dynamics and human-relations training, this organization is responsible for many pioneering efforts: sensitivity training; "T-groups", later popularized under the name "encounter groups"; team training; "group dynamics" approaches to therapy, education, and training; and the organization-development professional field. It would be difficult to overemphasize the contributions of NTL to all phases of life, here and abroad.

Energized by the founders, Leland Bradford, Ronald Lippitt, and Kenneth Benne, NTL provides an environment for many thousands of key people throughout the world to participate in NTL training "laboratories", and to capture and translate a new vision of what a trusting world might be like. TORI theory grew, in large part, from experiences Lorraine and I co-created in many years of NTL training groups and from the insights we gained there. NTL has a rich tradition of tri-partite integration of research, training, and social action.

Association for Holistic Health. Brought into being through the creative energies of David J. Harris and his colleagues, this organization centers on the integrating concept of "holistic health" for a wide variety of pioneering and innovative people in the medical and social sciences. Out of the work of pioneers in this field will come new images and models that will help move the culture toward what we have called EQ VIII and IX, holistic and transcendental environments, and new levels of trust. AHH is interested in research and action, and in collaboration with other organizations. It is especially encouraging to see so many physicians active in this organization, coming from a field that has been historically so conservative and resistant to social change.

Association for Creative Change. This organization is the liberal wing of groups interested in change in religious systems. It has grown out of experiences in group dynamics and organizational development, and it is one of the many organizations that have grown up in response to the pioneering work of NTL. Both religious theory and religious organizations are changing rapidly in North America. The "new spirituality" referred to in the preceding chapter is due in part to the work of members of ACC. They are creating a new synergy between the spiritual values and concepts of the traditional church and the rich contributions of holistic medicine, humanistic psychology, the human potential movement, NTL's laboratory method, and the new transcendentalism.

Society for the Psychological Study of Social Issues. SPSSI is the liberal and activist wing of the American Psychological Association. Blending research and social action, the organization is courageous, progressive, and responsive. SPSSI is a useful bridge between conservative bodies like APA and more radical groups like AHP. SPSSI has sponsored distinguished work that is on the frontiers of social psychology.

International College. International College is creating, through its tutor-student educational programs, its Guild of Tutors Press, and a variety of unique conferences and programs, an experimental approach to education and a supportive environment for innovation. For example, Byron Lane and I, as tutors for a TORI- and high-EQ-oriented doctoral program in organizational development and behavioral science, are making it possible for a small group of selected professionals to get a solid scientific and experiential grounding in TORI theory that will enable them to apply it in a variety of professional settings. Along with several other colleges and universities, International College is pioneering ways of bridging the restrictive formal constraints which characterize more traditional educational settings and the active professional and practitioner world.

Members of TORI Associates are at present actively involved in action programs with members of each of the above organizations. We would like to do whatever we can, as an organization, to increase the effectiveness of such collaboration. It is likely to be most effective when:

a. *Relationships are personal* and contacts are made by *persons* talking with other *persons*, exploring interests and relationships, rather than contacts through formal role structures.

b. *Efforts are open and direct;* personal wants, hidden agenda, project aims, and agreements are all examined and made public; covert strategy is either avoided or examined openly.

c. *Efforts are planned by the people who are to undergo change or growth.* Self-determination means that youth plan for youth; the disadvantaged plan for the disadvantaged; consultants plan for consultants; change agents plan for change agents; clients plan for clients. Mass participation in planning is extremely difficult, but somehow the people for whom plans are made must be represented directly in the planning.

d. *The process is a co-discovering one.* If the program is inter-organizational, it must be a *joint* process of inquiry, goal-setting, decision-making, and action-planning. I remember being on the board of one international organization when some members at the meeting tried to get a motion passed. They wanted one of our organizational aims to be to influence business and medicine in such a way as to make these institutions more participative, humanistic, and person-centered. I found myself a vigorous minority of one maintaining that it was business and medicine that needed to decide how person-centered and participative they wanted to be. At the very least, I suggested, we should invite representatives of business and medicine to join us in determining if *we and they* wanted to be more participative. If so, we should then jointly determine how we could improve *both* our organization and their organizations.

I feel uncomfortable when some other organization sets out to change an organization of which I am a member. I become even more uncomfortable when an organization that I'm in sets out to try to change someone else's organization. It is perhaps even more important that the *real* motivations be to improve *both* groups. Sometimes helping groups set out to "involve" others in co-planning when the underlying intent is to plan *for* the group being helped. Particularly with organizations that are formed by members of the helping professions, there is often a collaborative effort between two organizations which set out to change a third or target organization, group, or population.

We want to experiment with ways of increasing inter-organizational trust. Some members of TORI Associates are very much interested in working on international trust, world peace, and international collaboration. We have active members in several countries who are initiating efforts in these directions.

Can People Be Trusted?

Can we make *significant* changes in trust level in ourselves, in our families, in our work places, schools, and organizations? Can we do it globally? Are the changes we make in the occasional classroom, training group, or government program any more than miniscule drops in the oceanic ebb and flow of essentially unchanging nature and being? Is reality perceptual and projective?. Can I *really* create me? Or my environment? Are our hopes of creating a holistic environment and a lasting peace practical or illusory?

I don't know, but I choose to trust that it *can happen.* I choose to live with hope of a better world. I *do* believe we can change it.

The time to begin is now. The future is in us, and it is bright. We are in a critical age in history — the crack in the cosmic egg. The world and the people in it *are* trustworthy. If we believe this, we are on the brink of a new era of creativity and peace. Whatever the level we attain, whatever the time it takes, the future is in the *discovering* — in the process. The pain and dread are real. The trust and love are real. I create it all. Heaven *is* the process.

APPENDIX A

TORI SELF-DIAGNOSIS SCALE

Instructions: In front of each of the following items, place the letter that corresponds to your degree of agreement or disagreement with that statement.

SD = strongly disagree **D** = disagree **A** = agree **SA** = strongly agree

—— 1. I feel that no matter what I might do, people generally would accept and understand me.

—— 2. I feel that there are large areas of me that I don't share with other people.

—— 3. I usually assert myself in most situations in life.

—— 4. I seldom seek help from others.

—— 5. Most people tend to trust each other.

—— 6. People are usually not interested in what others have to say.

—— 7. Most people exert little pressure on other people to try to get them to do what they should be doing.

—— 8. Most people do their own thing with little thought for others.

—— 9. I feel that I am usually a very cautious person.

—— 10. I feel little need to cover up the things I do and keep them from others.

—— 11. I usually try to do what I'm supposed to be doing.

—— 12. I find that people are usually willing to help me when I want help or ask for it.

—— 13. Most people in life are more interested in getting things done than in caring for each other as individuals.

—— 14. Most people usually tell it like it is.

—— 15. Most people do what they ought to do in life, out of a sense of responsibility to others.

—— 16. Most people that I meet "have it together" at a fairly deep level.

—— 17. I usually trust the people I meet.

—— 18. I am afraid that if I showed my real innermost thoughts to most people, they would be shocked.

—— 19. In most life situations I feel free to do what I want to do.

—— 20. I often feel that I am a minority in the groups I belong to.

Reproduced from John E. Jones and J. William Pfeiffer (Eds.), The 1977 Annual Handbook for Group Facilitators. La Jolla, California: University Associates, 1977. Used with permission.

_____ 21. People that I meet usually seem to know who they are; they have a real sense of being individuals.

_____ 22. Most people I know and work with are very careful to express only relevant and appropriate ideas when we do things together.

_____ 23. Most people's goals are very clear to them and they know what they are doing in life.

_____ 24. Most groups I work with or live in have a hard time getting together and doing something they have decided to do.

_____ 25. If I left most groups I belong to, they would miss me very little.

_____ 26. I can trust most people I know with my most private and significant feelings and opinions.

_____ 27. I find that my goals are different from the goals of most people I work with.

_____ 28. I look forward to getting together with the people in the groups I belong to.

_____ 29. Most persons I meet are playing roles and not being themselves.

_____ 30. Most of the people I know communicate with each other very well.

_____ 31. In most of the groups I belong to members put pressure on each other toward group goals.

_____ 32. In an emergency most people act in caring and effective ways.

_____ 33. I almost always feel very good about myself as a person.

_____ 34. If I have negative feelings I do not express them easily.

_____ 35. It is easy for me to take risks in my life.

_____ 36. I often go along with others simply because I feel a sense of obligation to do what is expected.

_____ 37. People in the groups I belong to seem to care very much for each other as individuals.

_____ 38. Most people tend to be dishonest.

_____ 39. Most people I know let others be where they are and how they are.

_____ 40. Most people like either to lead or to be led, rather than to work together with others as equals.

_____ 41. My relationships with most people are impersonal.

_____ 42. Whenever I feel strongly about something I feel comfortable expressing myself to others.

_____ 43. I feel that I have to keep myself under wraps in most life situations.

____ 44. I usually enjoy working with people.

____ 45. Most people I know seem to play definite and clear roles and to be respected on the basis of how well they perform the roles.

____ 46. When the people I know have negative feelings they usually express them at some point.

____ 47. A large portion of the people in groups I belong to are very apathetic and passive.

____ 48. Most of the people I am usually with are well integrated at many levels.

____ 49. I feel like a unique person and I like being unique.

____ 50. I would feel very vulnerable if I told most people I know my most secret and private feelings and opinions.

____ 51. Most of the people I know feel that my personal growth is important.

____ 52. I often don't feel like cooperating with others.

____ 53. People usually have a high opinion of my contributions to the groups I'm in and the conversations I have.

____ 54. Most people are afraid to be open and honest with others.

____ 55. The people that I know usually express what they want pretty well.

____ 56. Most people are pretty individualistic and do not work together well as members of a team.

____ 57. I often don't feel very good about myself.

____ 58. I usually feel free to be exactly who I am and not to pretend I am something else.

____ 59. I feel that it is important in life to make a reasonable attempt to meet others' expectations of me.

____ 60. I feel a sense of interconnectedness with the people I associate with and would miss anyone who left my circle of friends and associates.

____ 61. It is easy to tell who the "in" people are in the groups I associate with.

____ 62. Most people listen to others with understanding and empathy.

____ 63. It seems to me that a great many people spend energy trying to get others to do things they don't really want to do.

____ 64. I think that most people I know enjoy being with people.

____ 65. The groups that I associate with see me as an important group member.

____ 66. My ideas and opinions are often distorted by others.

_____ 67. My basic goals in life are similar to the basic goals of other people.

_____ 68. People are seldom willing to give me help on the things that really matter to me.

_____ 69. People usually listen to the things that I say.

_____ 70. It seems to me that when they feel negative most people keep it to themselves.

_____ 71. The groups that I'm associated with usually have a lot of energy that gets directed into whatever the group does.

_____ 72. You really have to have some power if you want to get anything done in this life.

_____ 73. I often don't feel very genuine and real when I'm with people.

_____ 74. There is very little I don't know about the friends that I associate closely with.

_____ 75. If I did what I really wanted to do in life, I would be doing different things from what I am now doing.

_____ 76. I am often aware of how other people help me in what I am trying to do in life.

_____ 77. It seems to me that most people live in fear.

_____ 78. The people I know are usually very spontaneous and uninhibited with each other.

_____ 79. Most people are very unclear about what they want out of life.

_____ 80. Most of the groups I work with or live in have good team or cooperative relationships.

_____ 81. I care very much for the people I associate with.

_____ 82. People often misunderstand me and how I feel.

_____ 83. When I am with others and we reach a decision about something we want to do I am usually in complete agreement with what we have decided.

_____ 84. I have no real sense of belonging to the groups I associate with.

_____ 85. In the groups I belong to, people treat others as important and significant people.

_____ 86. It is easy for me to express positive feelings, but very difficult for me to express negative feelings to others.

_____ 87. Most of the people I know are growing and changing all the time.

_____ 88. It seems to me that most people need a lot of controls to keep them on the right track.

_____ 89. I often feel defensive.

_____ 90. I keep very few secrets from my associates.

_____ 91. It is often not OK for me to be myself in the groups I'm in.

_____ 92. I feel a strong sense of belonging to several groups in my life.

_____ 93. In the groups I belong to it is easy to see who is important and who is unimportant.

_____ 94. Most people don't keep a lot of secrets from others.

_____ 95. In the groups I belong to a lot of our energy goes into irrelevant and unimportant things.

_____ 96. It seems to me that there is very little destructive competition among the people I know and associate with.

TORI SELF-DIAGNOSIS SCALE SCORE SHEET

Instructions: The TORI Self-Diagnosis Scale yields eight scores: four depicting how you see yourself in your life in terms of the four core growth processes (Trusting-being; Opening; Realizing-becoming; and Interdepending), and four capturing your sense of what the people and world around you are like. Look back at the items for one of the eight scales on the instrument to see how you responded. On the Score Sheet, circle your response for each item according to whether you marked "Strongly Disagree", "Disagree", etc. Then sum the item scores for the scale. Do the same for each scale.

TRUSTING-BEING

Item	SD	D	A	SA
1.	0	1	2	3
9.	3	2	1	0
17.	0	1	2	3
25.	3	2	1	0
33.	0	1	2	3
41.	3	2	1	0
49.	0	1	2	3
57.	3	2	1	0
65.	0	1	2	3
73.	3	2	1	0
81.	0	1	2	3
89.	3	2	1	0

OPENING-SHOWING

Item	SD	D	A	SA
2.	3	2	1	0
10.	0	1	2	3
18.	3	2	1	0
26.	0	1	2	3
34.	3	2	1	0
42.	0	1	2	3
50.	3	2	1	0
58.	0	1	2	3
66.	3	2	1	0
74.	0	1	2	3
82.	3	2	1	0
90.	0	1	2	3

REALIZING-BECOMING

Item	SD	D	A	SA
3.	0	1	2	3
11.	3	2	1	0
19.	0	1	2	3
27.	3	2	1	0
35.	0	1	2	3
43.	3	2	1	0
51.	0	1	2	3
59.	3	2	1	0
67.	0	1	2	3
75.	3	2	1	0
83.	0	1	2	3
91.	3	2	1	0

INTERDEPENDING-INTERBEING

Item	SD	D	A	SA
4.	3	2	1	0
12.	0	1	2	3
20.	3	2	1	0
28.	0	1	2	3
36.	3	2	1	0
44.	0	1	2	3
52.	3	2	1	0
60.	0	1	2	3
68.	3	2	1	0
76.	0	1	2	3
84.	3	2	1	0
92.	0	1	2	3

How I see *Myself* in life

T □   O □   R □   I □

TRUSTING-BEING

Item Score

Item	SD	D	A	SA
5.	0	1	2	3
13.	3	2	1	0
21.	0	1	2	3
29.	3	2	1	0
37.	0	1	2	3
45.	3	2	1	0
53.	0	1	2	3
61.	3	2`	1	0
69.	0	1	2	3
77.	3	2	1	0
85.	0	1	2	3
93.	3	2	1	0

OPENING-SHOWING

Item Score

Item	SD	D	A	SA
6.	3	2	1	0
14.	0	1	2	3
22.	3	2	1	0
30.	0	1	2	3
38.	3	2	1	0
46.	0	1	2	3
54.	3	2	1	0
62.	0	1	2	3
70.	3	2	1	0
78.	0	1	2	3
86.	3	2	1	0
94.	0	1	2	3

REALIZING-BECOMING

Item Score

Item	SD	D	A	SA
7.	0	1	2	3
15.	3	2	1	0
23.	0	1	2	3
31.	3	2	1	0
39.	0	1	2	3
47.	3	2	1	0
55.	0	1	2	3
63.	3	2	1	0
71.	0	1	2	3
79.	3	2	1	0
87.	0	1	2	3
95.	3	2	1	0

INTERDEPENDING-INTERBEING

Item Score

Item	SD	D	A	SA
8.	3	2	1	0
16.	0	1	2	3
24.	3	2	1	0
32.	0	1	2	3
40.	3	2	1	0
48.	0	1	2	3
56.	3	2	1	0
64.	0	1	2	3
72.	3	2	1	0
80.	0	1	2	3
88.	3	2	1	0
96.	0	1	2	3

How I see the *People* World

T ☐   O ☐   R ☐   I ☐

INTERPRETATION SHEET
TORI SELF-DIAGNOSIS SCALE

TRUSTING-BEING:

A person who scores *high* on this set of items is saying:
View of Myself: "I trust myself, have a fairly well-formed sense of my own being and uniqueness, and feel good about myself as a person."
View of People: "I tend to see people as trusting, and as providing a good environment for me to live and be in."

A person who scores *low* on this set of items is saying:
View of Myself: "I feel less trusting of myself, have a less well-formed sense of my own being and uniqueness, and feel less well about myself as a person."
View of People: "I tend to see people as un-trusting, as impersonal and in role, and as providing a somewhat threatening and defense-producing environment for me and for others.

OPENING-SHOWING:

A person who scores *high* on this set of items is saying:
View of Myself: "I feel free to show myself to others, show who I am, and express my feelings and attitudes with little pretense or cover-up."
View of People: "I tend to see people as open and spontaneous and as willing to show themselves to each other."

A person who scores *low* on this set of items is saying:
View of Myself: "I feel un-free to be open, feel vulnerable and unsafe, and I think it is necessary to keep large areas of myself private and unshared."
View of People: "I tend to see people as fearful, cautious, and unwilling to show feelings and opinions, particularly those feelings and opinions that are negative or non-supportive."

REALIZING-BECOMING:

A person who scores *high* on this set of items is saying:
View of Myself: "I feel free to take risks, assert myself, do anything that I really want to do, and follow my intrinsic motivations. I have a sense of self-realization."

View of People: "I tend to see people as allowing other's their freedom, and as providing an environment for me and others that nourishes our striving for intrinsic goals. People allow others to be who they are."

A person who scores *low* on this set of items is saying:
View of Myself: "I am aware of the pressure of extrinsic motivations. I feel that I must try to do what I am supposed to do and that I must attempt to meet the expectations of others."

View of People: "I tend to see other people as exerting pressures on me and others to conform, to do things that we may not want to do, and to work towards goals that are not significant to me as a person."

INTERDEPENDING-INTERBEING:

A person who scores *high* on this set of items is saying:
View of Myself: "I have a strong sense of belonging to the groups that are important to me, and I enjoy working with, helping, or meeting with other people."

View of People: "I tend to see other people as cooperative, working effectively, and relatively well integrated into the life around them and the groups they belong to."

A person who scores *low* on this set of items is saying:
View of Myself: "I do not have a strong sense of belonging to the groups of which I am a member, and do not especially enjoy working with others in a team way. I have competitive, dependent, or other feelings that get in the way of my teaming with others."

View of People: "I tend to see other people as not being cooperative and not working well with others. I see people in general as not easy to work with or team with and as having feelings that get in their way."

APPENDIX B

DIAGNOSING YOUR TEAM
A TORI SCALE

Instructions: In front of each of the following items, place the letter that corresponds to your degree of agreement or disagreement with that statement.

SD = strongly disagree **D** = disagree **A** = agree **SA** = strongly agree

____ 1. I think this team will accept me as a full member no matter what unusual thing I might do.

____ 2. There are lots of things I don't tell the team, and they are just as well left private.

____ 3. I assert myself on this team.

____ 4. I seldom seek help from other members on tasks.

____ 5. Members of this team trust each other very much.

____ 6. Members are not really interested in what other members have to say.

____ 7. The team exerts little pressure on members to do what they should be doing.

____ 8. Everyone on this team does his or her own thing with little thought for other members.

____ 9. I see myself as a very cautious member of this team.

____ 10. I don't think that I have to cover up things with this group.

____ 11. On this team I do only the things that I am supposed to do.

____ 12. I think that everyone on this team is willing to help me when I ask for help.

____ 13. The team is more interested in accomplishing tasks than in helping members on personal problems.

____ 14. Members tell it like it is.

____ 15. Members do what they ought to do, out of a strong sense of responsibility to the team.

____ 16. This team really "has it together" in many ways.

____ 17. I trust members of this team.

____ 18. I am afraid that if I told this team my innermost thoughts they would be shocked and have negative feelings about me.

____ 19. When I am with this team I think I am free to do what I want.

____ 20. I often think that I am in a minority on this team.
____ 21. Members of this team know who they are; they have a real sense of being individuals.
____ 22. When at work, members are very careful to express only relevant ideas about the task.
____ 23. The goals of this team are clear.
____ 24. The team finds it difficult to go ahead and do something it has decided to do.
____ 25. If I left this team they would miss me very much.
____ 26. I can trust this team with my most private and significant ideas and opinions.
____ 27. I often find that my goals are different from those of the team and of other members.
____ 28. I look forward to getting together with this team.
____ 29. Members of this team are often not being themselves and are playing roles.
____ 30. We know each other very well.
____ 31. This team puts work pressure on each member.
____ 32. This team will be able to handle an emergency very well.
____ 33. When I am with this team I feel very good about myself.
____ 34. If I have negative feelings when I am with this team, I don't express them very easily.
____ 35. It is easy for me to take risks when I am working with this team.
____ 36. I often go along with the others simply because I have a sense of obligation.
____ 37. Members seem to care very much for each other.
____ 38. Members often express different feelings and opinions outside meetings than they do when members are present.
____ 39. We really let members be who they are as individuals.
____ 40. Members of this team like to either lead or be led, rather than to work together as equals.
____ 41. My relationship to this team is a very impersonal one.
____ 42. Whenever I feel something strongly I feel easy about expressing it to the team members.
____ 43. I think that I have to keep myself under wraps in here.
____ 44. I enjoy working with members of this team.
____ 45. Each member has a definite and clear role to play and is respected on the basis of how well he or she performs it.
____ 46. Whenever there are negative feelings they are likely to be expressed at some point.
____ 47. At times members seem very apathetic and passive.

_____ 48. We are well integrated and coordinated at many levels.

_____ 49. I feel like a unique person when I am on this team.

_____ 50. I would feel very vulnerable if I told members my most secret and private feelings and opinions.

_____ 51. The team thinks that my personal growth and learnings are very important.

_____ 52. I don't feel like cooperating with others on this team.

_____ 53. Team members have a high opinion of my contributions.

_____ 54. Members are afraid to be open and honest with each other.

_____ 55. When decisions are being made, members quickly express what they want.

_____ 56. Members are very much individuals and do not work together as members of a team.

_____ 57. When with this team I don't feel very good about myself.

_____ 58. When with this team I am free to be exactly who I am and never have to pretend I am something else.

_____ 59. It is very important to me to meet the expectations of other members.

_____ 60. I would miss anyone who left because each of the members is important in what the team is trying to do.

_____ 61. It is easy to tell who the "in" members are.

_____ 62. Members listen to others with understanding and empathy.

_____ 63. The team spends a lot of energy trying to get members to do things they don't really want to do.

_____ 64. Members enjoy being with each other.

_____ 65. I am an important member of the team.

_____ 66. My ideas and opinions are often distorted by the team.

_____ 67. My goals are similar to the goals of the total team.

_____ 68. Members seldom give me help on things that really matter to me.

_____ 69. Members listen to the things I have to say.

_____ 70. On this team, if members feel negative they keep it to themselves.

_____ 71. We have a lot of energy that gets directed into whatever we do as a team.

_____ 72. You really have to have some power if you want to get anything done on this team.

_____ 73. I sometimes don't feel very genuine when I'm with this team.

_____ 74. There is hardly anything I don't know about the other members.

_____ 75. If I did what I wanted to do on this team, I'd be doing different things.

_____ 76. Members often help me in things I am trying to do.

_____ 77. Some members are afraid of the team and of its members.

_____ 78. Members are very spontaneous and uninhibited when they are around each other.

_____ 79. The goals are often not really clear.

_____ 80. We really work together as a smoothly functioning unit.

_____ 81. I care very much for the members of this team.

_____ 82. Members misunderstand me and how I feel and think.

_____ 83. When we reach a decision I am usually in agreement.

_____ 84. I have no real sense of belonging to this team.

_____ 85. We treat each person as an important member.

_____ 86. It is easy to express feelings and opinions in here if they are positive, but not if they are negative.

_____ 87. Members of this team are growing and changing all the time.

_____ 88. We need a lot of controls in order to keep on the track.

_____ 89. I often feel defensive when I'm with this team.

_____ 90. I keep very few secrets from other members.

_____ 91. It is not OK for me to be myself with this team.

_____ 92. I feel a strong sense of belonging.

_____ 93. It is easy to tell who the important members are.

_____ 94. Members don't keep secrets from each other.

_____ 95. A lot of our team energy goes into irrelevant and unimportant things.

_____ 96. We have little destructive competition with each other.

TORI DIAGNOSING YOUR TEAM SCORE SHEET

Instructions: The TORI Diagnosing Your Team scale yields eight scores: four depicting how you see yourself on this team in terms of the four core team processes (Trusting-being; Opening; Realizing-growing; and Interdependence-teaming), and four capturing your sense of what your team is like. Look back at the items for one of the eight scales on the instrument to see how you responded. On the Score Sheet, circle your response for each item according to whether you marked "Strongly Disagree", "Disagree", etc. Then sum the item scores for the scale. Do the same for each scale.

TRUSTING-BEING

Item	SD	D	A	SA
1.	0	1	2	3
9.	3	2	1	0
17.	0	1	2	3
25.	3	2	1	0
33.	0	1	2	3
41.	3	2	1	0
49.	0	1	2	3
57.	3	2	1	0
65.	0	1	2	3
73.	3	2	1	0
81.	0	1	2	3
89.	3	2	1	0

OPENING-SHOWING

Item	SD	D	A	SA
2.	3	2	1	0
10.	0	1	2	3
18.	3	2	1	0
26.	0	1	2	3
34.	3	2	1	0
42.	0	1	2	3
50.	3	2	1	0
58.	0	1	2	3
66.	3	2	1	0
74.	0	1	2	3
82.	3	2	1	0
90.	0	1	2	3

REALIZING-GROWING

Item	SD	D	A	SA
3.	0	1	2	3
11.	3	2	1	0
19.	0	1	2	3
27.	3	2	1	0
35.	0	1	2	3
43.	3	2	1	0
51.	0	1	2	3
59.	3	2	1	0
67.	0	1	2	3
75.	3	2	1	0
83.	0	1	2	3
91.	3	2	1	0

INTERDEPENDING-TEAMING

Item	SD	D	A	SA
4.	3	2	1	0
12.	0	1	2	3
20.	3	2	1	0
28.	0	1	2	3
36.	3	2	1	0
44.	0	1	2	3
52.	3	2	1	0
60.	0	1	2	3
68.	3	2	1	0
76.	0	1	2	3
84.	3	2	1	0
92.	0	1	2	3

How I see *Myself* on the team:

T □   O □   R □   I □

TRUSTING-BEING

Item Score

Item	SD	D	A	SA
5.	0	1	2	3
13.	3	2	1	0
21.	0	1	2	3
29.	3	2	1	0
37.	0	1	2	3
45.	3	2	1	0
53.	0	1	2	3
61.	3	2	1	0
69.	0	1	2	3
77.	3	2	1	0
85.	0	1	2	3
93.	3	2	1	0

OPENING-SHOWING

Item Score

Item	SD	D	A	SA
6.	3	2	1	0
14.	0	1	2	3
22.	3	2	1	0
30.	0	1	2	3
38.	3	2	1	0
46.	0	1	2	3
54.	3	2	1	0
62.	0	1	2	3
70.	3	2	1	0
78.	0	1	2	3
86.	3	2	1	0
94.	0	1	2	3

REALIZING-GROWING

Item Score

Item	SD	D	A	SA
7.	0	1	2	3
15.	3	2	1	0
23.	0	1	2	3
31.	3	2	1	0
39.	0	1	2	3
47.	3	2	1	0
55.	0	1	2	3
63.	3	2	1	0
71.	0	1	2	3
79.	3	2	1	0
87.	0	1	2	3
95.	3	2	1	0

INTERDEPENDING-TEAMING

Item Score

Item	SD	D	A	SA
8.	3	2	1	0
16.	0	1	2	3
24.	3	2	1	0
32.	0	1	2	3
40.	3	2	1	0
48.	0	1	2	3
56.	3	2	1	0
64.	0	1	2	3
72.	3	2	1	0
80.	0	1	2	3
88.	3	2	1	0
96.	0	1	2	3

How I see the *Team:*

T □   O □   R □   I □

INTERPRETATION SHEET
DIAGNOSING YOUR TEAM SCALE

TRUSTING-BEING:

A team member who scores *high* on this set of items is saying:
View of Myself: "I trust myself, have a fairly well-formed sense of my own being and uniqueness, and feel good about myself as a person and team member".

View of the Team: "I tend to see team members as trusting, and as providing a good environment for me to work in".

A team member who scores *low* on this set of items is saying:
View of Myself: "I feel less trusting of myself, have a less well-formed sense of my own being and uniqueness, and feel less well about myself as a person and team member."

View of the Team: "I tend to see team members as un-trusting, as impersonal and in role, and as providing a somewhat negative and defensive environment for me and for other team members."

OPENING-SHOWING:

A team member who scores *high* on this set of items is saying:
View of Myself: "I feel free to show myself to others on the team, show who I am, and express my feelings and attitudes with little pretense to cover-up."

View of the Team: "I tend to see people as open and spontaneous and as willing to show themselves to other team members."

A team member who scores *low* on this set of items is saying:
View of Myself: "I feel un-free to be open, feel vulnerable and not safe, and I think it is necessary to keep large areas of myself private and unshared with the team."

View of the Team: "I tend to see team members as fearful, cautious, and unwilling to show feelings and opinions, particularly those feelings and opinions that are negative or non-supportive of other team members."

REALIZING-GROWING:

A team member who scores *high* on this set of items is saying:
View of Myself: "I feel free to take risks, assert myself, do anything that I really want to do, and follow my own motivations. I have a sense of self-realization".

View of The Team: "I tend to see team members as allowing others their freedom, and as providing an environment for me and other team members that makes it possible for us to reach our goals. Team members allow others to be who they are."

A person who scores *low* on this set of items is saying:
View of Myself: "I am aware of the pressure of extrinsic motivations. I feel that I must try to do what I am supposed to do and that I must attempt to meet the expectations of other team members."

View of Team: "I tend to see other team members as exerting pressures on me and others to conform, to do things that we may not want to do, and to work toward team goals that are not significant to me as a person or team member."

INTERDEPENDING-TEAMING:

A team member who scores *high* on this set of items is saying:
View of Myself: "I have a strong sense of belonging to the groups that are important to me, and I enjoy working with, helping, or meeting with other team members."

View of The Team: "I tend to see other team members as cooperative, working effectively, and relatively well integrated into the life around them and to the teams they belong to."

A person who scores *low* on this set of items is saying:
View of Myself: "I do not have a strong sense of belonging to the groups of which I am a member and do not especially enjoy working with this team or with others in a team way. I have competitive, dependent, or other feelings that get in the way of my working with other members of the team."

View of The Team: "I tend to see other team members as not being cooperative and not working well with others. I see team members in general as not easy to work with or team with, and as having feelings that get in their way."

APPENDIX C

A selected list of readings on TORI theory and its applications.

I. STATEMENTS ABOUT THE GENERAL THEORY.

Gibb, J.R., "Defense Level and Influence Potential in Small Groups." In L. Petrullo & B.M. Bass (Eds.), *Leadership and Interpersonal Behavior*. New York: Holt, Rinehart and Winston, 1961.

Gibb, J.R., *Factors Producing Defensive Behavior Within Groups*. Final Technical Report, Group Psychology Branch, Office of Naval Research, Contract Nonr-3088(00), 1962.

Gibb, J.R., "TORI Community." In G. Egan (Ed.), *Encounter Groups: Basic Readings*. Belmont, California: Brooks/Cole, 1971.

Gibb, J.R., "TORI Theory and Practice." In J.W. Pfeiffer and J.E. Jones (Eds.), *The 1972 Annual Handbook for Group Facilitators*. Iowa City, Iowa: University Associates.

Jones, J.E., "Interviews with TORI Conveners Jack and Lorraine Gibb." *Group and Organizational Studies*, 1976, 1, 398-414.

II. TORI THEORY AS APPLIED TO ORGANIZATIONAL DEVELOPMENT, BUSINESS SYSTEMS, AND OTHER INSTITUTIONS.

Gibb, J.R., "Communication and Productivity." *Personnel Administration*, 1964, 27, 8-13.

Gibb, J.R., "Fear and Facade: Defensive Management." In R.E. Farson (Ed.), *Science and Human Affairs*. Palo Alto: Science and Behavior Books, 1965.

Gibb, J.R., "Building a Teamwork Climate." *Weyerhaeuser Management Viewpoint*, 1969, 1, 10-12.

Gibb, J.R., "Management Tunes In." *Weyerhaeuser World*, 1969, 1, 3.

Gibb, J.R., "Managing for Creativity in the Organization." In C.W. Taylor (Ed.), *Climate for Creativity*. New York: Pergamon Co., 1971.

Gibb, J.R., "The TORI Community Experience as an Organizational Change Intervention." In W.W. Burke (Ed.), *Contemporary Organizational Development*. Washington, D.C.: NTL Institute for Applied Behavioral Science, 1972.

Gibb, J.R., "TORI Theory: Consultantless Team Building." *Journal of Contemporary Business*, 1972, 1(3), 33-42.

Gibb, J.R., "A Case for Nonstructure." *Group and Organizational Studies*, 1976, 1, 135-139.

Gibb, J.R., "Organizational Options: Emergent versus Defensive Management." In B. McWaters (Ed.), *Human Perspectives: Current Trends in Psychology*. Monterey, California: Brooks/Cole, 1977.

Gibb, J.R., "To Structure or Not to Structure." *Contemporary Psychology*, 1977, 22(12), 916-917.

III. TORI THEORY AS APPLIED TO TRAINING AND GROUP DEVELOPMENT.

Gibb, J.R., "Climate for Trust Formation." In L.P. Bradford, J.R. Gibb, and K.D. Benne (Eds.), *T-Group Theory and Laboratory Method*. New York: Wiley, 1964.

Gibb, J.R., "The Search for With-ness: A New Look at Interdependence." In G.W. Dyer (Ed.), *Modern Theory and Method in Group Training*. New York: Van Nostrand, 1972.

Gibb, J.R., "TORI Theory: Nonverbal Behavior and the Experience of Community." *Comparative Group Studies*, 1972, 3, 461-472.

Gibb, J.R., "Meaning of the Small Group Experience." In L.N. Solomon and B. Berzon (Eds.), *New Perspectives on Encounter Groups*. San Francisco: Jossey-Bass, 1972.

Gibb, J.R., "The Training Group." In K.D. Benne, L.P. Bradford, J.R. Gibb, and R.O. Lippitt (Eds.), *The Laboratory Method of Changing and Learning*. Palo Alto, California: Science and Behavior Books, 1975.

Gibb, J.R., "TORI Group Self-Diagnosis Scale." In J.E. Jones and J.W. Pfeiffer (Eds.), *The 1977 Annual Handbook for Group Facilitators*. La Jolla, California: University Associates.

Gibb, J.R., and Gibb, Lorraine M., "Humanistic Elements in Group Growth." In J.F.T. Bugental (Ed.), *Challenges of Humanistic Psychology*. New York: McGraw-Hill, 1967.

Gibb, J.R., and Gibb, Lorraine M., "Leaderless Groups: Growth-Centered Values and Potentials." In H.A. Otto and J. Mann (Eds.), *Ways of Growth*. New York: Grossman, 1968.

Gibb, J.R., and Gibb, Lorraine M., "Group Experiences and Human Possibilities." In H.A. Otto (Ed.), *Human Potentialities*. St. Louis: W.H. Green, 1968.

Gibb, J.R., and Gibb, Lorraine M., "Role Freedom in a TORI Group." In A. Burton (Ed.), *Encounter: The Theory and Practice of Encounter Groups*. San Francisco: Jossey-Bass, 1969.

Gibb, J.R., and Gibb, Lorraine M., "The Process of Group Actualization." In J. Akin, *et al* (Eds.), *Language Behavior*. The Hague, The Netherlands: Mouton, 1971.

IV. TORI THEORY AS APPLIED TO THERAPY, COUNSELING, AND MENTAL HEALTH.

Gibb, J.R., "Defensive Communication." *The Journal of Communication*, 1961, 11(3), 141-148.

Gibb, J.R., "Is Help Helpful?" *YMCA Association Forum and Section Journal*, February, 1964, 25-27.

Gibb, J.R., and Gibb, Lorraine, "Emergence Therapy: The TORI Process in an Emergent Group." In G.M. Gazda (Ed.), *Innovations to Group Psychotherapy*. Springfield, Illinois: Thomas, 1968.

Gibb, J.R., "The Counselor as a Role-free Person." In C.A. Parker (Ed.), *Counseling Theories and Counselor Education*. Boston: Houghton Mifflin, 1968.

Gibb, J.R., "Psycho-sociological Aspects of Holistic Health." *The Journal of Holistic Health*, 1977, 1, 43-46.

V. TORI THEORY AS APPLIED TO EDUCATION AND LEARNING.

Gibb, J.R., "Climate for Growth." *National Education Association Journal*, 1956, 55, 97-103.

Gibb, J.R., "Sociopsychological Processes of Group Instruction." In N.B. Henry (Ed.), "The Dynamics of Instructional Groups." *Yearbook of the National Society for the Study of Education*, Part II. Chicago: University of Chicago Press, 1960.

Gibb, J.R., "Learning Theory in Adult Education." In M.S. Knowles (Ed.), *Handbook of Adult Education in the United States*. Chicago: Adult Education Association of the U.S.A, 1960. Pp. 54-64.

Gibb, J.R., "Achieving Group Membership in the Classroom." *The High School Journal*, 1961, 45, 2-6.

Gibb, J.R., "Learning as a Quest." *Second Yearbook of the National Association of Public Education*, 1962. Pp. 102-107.

Gibb, J.R., "Dynamics of Leadership." In *Current Issues in Higher Education*, Washington, D.C.: American Association for Higher Education, 1967. Pp. 55-66.

Gibb, J.R., "Expanding Role of the Administrator." *The Bulletin of the National Association of Secondary-School Principals*, 1967, 50, 46-40.

Gibb, J.R., "Trust and Freedom: A TORI Innovation in Educational Community." *Journal of Research and Development in Education*, Spring, 1972, 5(3), 76-85.

APPENDIX D

A selected list of research studies related to aspects of TORI theory.

I. STUDIES TESTING ASSUMPTIONS AND PRINCIPLES.

Coppersmith, Evan, "A Study of the Development of Role-Freedom in the TORI Community Experience." Unpublished Master's thesis, California State University, Hayward, 1974.

Draeger, C., "Level of Trust in Intensive Small Groups." Unpublished doctoral dissertation, University of Texas, Austin, 1968.

Friedlander, Frank., "The Primacy of Trust as a Facilitator of Further Group Accomplishment." *Journal of Applied Behavioral Science,* 1970, 6, 387-400.

Garner, H.G., "Effects of Human Relations Training on the Personal, Social and Classroom Adjustment of Elementary School Children with Behavior Problems." Unpublished doctoral dissertation, University of Florida, 1970.

Gibb, J.R., "Defense Level and Influence Potential in Small Groups." In L. Petrullo and B.M. Bass (Eds.), *Leadership and Interpersonal Behavior.* New York: Holt, Rinehart and Winston, 1961.

Gibb, J.R., "Defensive Communication." *The Journal of Communication,* 1961, 2(3), 141-148.

Gibb, J.R., *Factors Producing Defensive Behavior Within Groups.* Final Technical Report, Group Psychology Branch, Office of Naval Research, Contract Nonr-3088(00), 1962.

Gibb, J.R., "Climate for Trust Formation." In L.P. Bradford, J.R. Gibb, and K. Benne (Eds.), *T-group Theory and Laboratory Method.* New York: Wiley, 1964.

Leon, J.E., "Attitude Change, as a Result of T-group Sessions, in a Pre-teaching Population." Unpublished doctoral dissertation, Case Western Reserve University, 1972.

Rutan, J.C., "Self-Acceptance Change as a Function of a Short Term Small Group Experience." Unpublished doctoral dissertation, Boston University, 1971.

II. STUDIES REPORTING RESEARCH ON THE EFFECTS OF THE TORI COMMUNITY EXPERIENCE.

Dahl, Rick F., "The Relationship of the TORI Community Experience to the Perceived-ideal Self Discrepancy." Unpublished doctoral dissertation, United States International University, 1973.

LaBoon, Sandra, "TORI: A Theory of Community Growth." Unpublished Master's thesis, United States International University, 1971.

Lynch, JoAn, "A Study of Interdependence in a TORI Community." Unpublished Master's thesis, United States International University, 1974.

Pressman, Marcia L., "A Study of an Intensive TORI Weekend Group Experience and its Effects on Interpersonal Skills." Unpublished Master's thesis, University of Utah, 1970.

Rossman, Sue A., "A Comparative Study of Self-disclosure in a TORI Community Experience." Unpublished Master's thesis, United States International University, 1974.

III. STUDIES REPORTING RESEARCH ON THE EFFECTS OF APPLICATIONS OF TORI THEORY IN OTHER SETTINGS.

Byrd, Richard E., "Self-actualization Through Creative Risk Taking: A New Laboratory Model." Unpublished doctoral dissertation, New York University, 1970.

Clarke, Jack F., "Some Effects of Nonverbal Activities and Group Discussion on Interpersonal Trust Development in Small Groups." Unpublished doctoral dissertation, Arizona State University, 1971.

Gibb, Lorraine M., and Gibb, J.R., "The Effects of the Use of 'Participative Action' Groups in a Course in General Psychology." *American Psychologist*, 1952, 7, 247.

Himber, Charlotte, "Evaluating Sensitivity Training for Teen-agers." *Journal of Applied Behavioral Science*, 1970, 6, 307-322.

Ralph, Sara J., "The Effects of Positive Value Statements on Self-esteem." Unpublished doctoral dissertation, United States International University, 1972.

Robertson, V.M., & Wallace, S., "Self-perceived Gains by Adolescents from a Sensitivity Lab: A Study of Participants in the 12th National Hi-Y Assembly." Unpublished manuscript, October, 1968, 45 pp.

IV. DISCUSSIONS OF METHODOLOGICAL ASPECTS OF RESEARCH ON TORI VARIABLES.

Gibb, J.R., "The Present Status of T-group Theory." In L.P. Bradford, J.R. Gibb, and K. Benne (Eds.), *T-Group Theory and Laboratory Method.* New York: Wiley, 1964.

Gibb, J.R., "Comments on Longitudinal Methodology." In J.L. Fearing and G. T. Kowitz (Eds.), *Some Views on Longitudinal Inquiry.* Houston, Texas: Bureau of Education Research and Services, University of Houston, 1967, Pp. 28-32.

Gibb, J.R., "Sensitivity Training as a Medium for Personal Growth and Improved Interpersonal Relationships." *Interpersonal Development*, 1970, 1, 6-31.

Gibb, J.R., "Effects of Human Relations Training." In A.E. Bergin and S.L. Garfield (Eds.), *Handbook of Psychotherapy and Behavior Change.* New York: Wiley, 1971.

Gibb, J.R., "The Message from Research." In J.W. Pfeiffer and J.E. Jones (Eds.). *The 1974 Annual Handbook for Group Facilitators.* La Jolla, California: University Associates.

Gibb, J.R., "A Research Perspective on the Laboratory Method." In K.D. Benne, L.P. Bradford, J.R. Gibb, and R.O. Lippitt (Eds.), *The Laboratory Method of Changing and Learning.* Palo Alto, California: Science and Behavior Books, 1975.

Kegan, D.L., "Measures of Trust and Openness" *Comparative Group Studies*, 1972, 3(2), 179-201.

APPENDIX E

A selected list of readings about trust and fear, their effects upon living, and their use as constructs in building theory.

Anderson, Walter, *Politics and the New Humanism.* Pacific Palisades, California: Goodyear, 1973.

Argyris, Chris, *Interpersonal Competence and Organizational Effectiveness.* Homewood, Illinois: Dorsey, 1962.

Benne, Kenneth D., *Education for Tragedy.* Lexington: University of Kentucky Press, 1967.

Bennis, Warren G., *American Bureaucracy.* Chicago: Aldine, 1971.

Bennis, Warren G., *The Leaning Ivory Tower.* San Francisco: Jossey-Bass, 1973.

Bennis, Warren, and Philip Slater, *The Temporary Society.* New York: Harper and Row, 1968.

Bridgman, P.W., *The Nature of Physical Theory.* New York: Wiley, 1964.

Bugental, J.F.T., *The Search for Authenticity.* New York: Holt, Reinhart and Winston, 1965.

Castaneda, Carlos, *Tales of Power.* New York: Simon and Schuster, 1975.

Egan, Gerard, *Interpersonal Living.* Monterey, California: Brooks-Cole, 1976.

Friedman, Maurice, *Touchstones of Reality.* New York: Dutton, 1972.

Hampdon-Turner, Charles, *Radical Man.* Cambridge, Massachusetts: Schenkman, 1970.

Hanna, Thomas, *The End of Tyranny.* Novato, California: Freeperson Press, 1975.

Kaplan, Abraham, *Conduct of Inquiry*. San Francisco: Chandler, 1964.
Keen, Sam, *Apology for Wonder*. New York: Harper and Row, 1969.
Kopp, Sheldon, *If You Meet the Buddha on the Road, Kill Him*. Palo Alto: Science and Behavior Books, 1972.
Krippner, Stanley, *Song of the Siren*. New York: Harper and Row, 1976.
Laing, Ronald D., *The Self and Others*. New York: Pantheon, 1972.
Leonard, George, *The Transformation*. New York: Delacorte, 1972.
Likert, Rensis, *The Human Organization*. New York: McGraw-Hill, 1967.
Marrow, Alfred J., *The Practical Theorist; the Life and Work of Kurt Lewin*. New York: Basic Books, 1969.
Maslow, Abraham, *Psychology of Science*. New York: Harper and Row, 1966.
Matson, Floyd, *Broken Image*. New York: Braziller, 1967.
May, Rollo, *Love and Will*. New York: Norton, 1969.
McGregor, Douglas, *The Human Side of Enterprise*. New York: McGraw-Hill, 1960.
McWaters, B., *Humanistic Perspectives: Current Trends in Psychology*. Monterey, California: Brooks/Cole, 1977.
Murphy, Michael, *Golf in the Kingdom*. New York: Viking, 1972.
Naranjo, Claudio, *The One Quest*. New York: Viking, 1972.
Pearce, Joseph Chilton, *The Crack in the Cosmic Egg*. New York: Julian Press, 1971.
Polanyi, Michael, *Personal Knowledge*. Chicago: University of Chicago Press, 1958.
Satir, Virginia, *Peoplemaking*. Palo Alto, California: Science and Behavior Books, 1972.
Schneider, Kenneth R., *Autokind vs. Mankind*. New York: Norton, 1971.
Schutz, William C., *Joy*. New York: Grove, 1967.
Teilhard de Chardin, Pierre, *The Phenomenon of Man*. New York: Harper, 1959.
Wertheimer, Max, *Productive Thinking*. New York: Harper, 1971.

The end of every maker is himself.

St. Thomas Aquinas